BEER AND FOOD

MARK DREDGE

BRINGING TOGETHER THE FINEST FOOD AND THE BEST CRAFT BEERS

Published in 2014 by Dog 'n' Bone Books
An imprint of Ryland Peters & Small Ltd

20–21 Jockey's Fields   519 Broadway, 5th Floor
London WC1R 4BW   New York, NY 10012

www.rylandpeters.com

10 9 8 7 6 5 4 3 2

A CIP catalog record for this book is available from the Library
of Congress and the British Library.

ISBN: 978 1 909313 23 1

Printed in China

Editor: Caroline West
Designer: Mark Latter
Illustrator: Nicholas John Frith
Food photographer: William Lingwood
Food styling: Luis Peral
Home economist: Lucy Mackelvie
Picture credits: p50 © Brasserie Cantillon, p77 and 83 © Sierra
Nevada Brewing Company

For digital editions, visit www.cicobooks.com/apps.php

CONTENTS

INTRODUCTION

It was the day I was eating dinner and had four glasses of beer in front of me that I realized I was really getting into this beer and food thing. It had come from somewhere, but I'm not exactly certain where. I'd always loved cooking different dishes and was thirsty to try lots of different beers, but I'd never purposefully tried to pair what I was drinking to what I was eating. It seemed a curious thing...

Sure, I loved bar snacks with my pint, pizza with Pale Ale, or cold lager with a hot curry, but it was never anything more than that. Then, one day, I tried a semi-sweet (dark) chocolate mousse with a sour cherry beer, and everything changed. Beer and food became something different, something better, something fun and interesting and challenging. I wanted to learn more.

Learning more meant reading Garrett Oliver's *The Brewmaster's Table*. It's a must-read book for beer lovers and the first dedicated to the combined joys of drinking beer and eating great food. It

succeeded in inspiring me to try the things the Brooklyn Brewmaster was talking about, as well as to try a few pairings of my own. For a couple of years I planned my weekend meals in advance, always knowing the beers I'd put with them and typically choosing a couple of different bottles to see how they worked or didn't work. It became natural to open beers with dinner.

I discovered that beer can do brilliant things with food. There are so many different beer styles, each one with different qualities, strengths, and tastes, which means that there's a beer for every dish and a dish for every beer. I don't think any other drink has as much flavor variety and versatility as beer: dry, snappy Pilsners; spicy Saisons; sweet-and-sour Belgian Reds; bitter IPAs; creamy Milk Stouts; and fruitcake-like Dubbels. There's an extraordinary choice of beers and I loved seeing what each of them did with food.

My ambition with *Beer and Food* is to try to make you both thirsty and hungry by suggesting ideas for pairing different drinks with different dishes. It isn't intended as an indelible list of rules; instead, I hope it inspires you to try combinations of your own and to attempt to find something perfect to go with your favorite beer or food. Taste is subjective, and the things I like could be things you hate, so the best I can do is recommend pairings that I enjoy. You may hate them, but, if you don't like them, then hopefully you'll be able to think of something that will work better. And you'll try it.

The beers I've chosen for this book are deliberately picked because they are available in mainstream markets around the world. Where my previous book *Craft Beer World* was about some of the rarer and harder-to-find beers, I felt it was silly selecting those for *Beer and Food*. I want you to

be able to try these matches and a once-a-year, super-limited-release beer isn't very achievable. And I've tried to keep everything simple and, hopefully, unpretentious—I've included a Big Mac; Budweiser is in here; there's a match for a pint of shandy; and a plate of seasoned fries also features because sometimes the best match for a beer really is something as simple as a plate of fried potatoes. *Beer and Food* isn't about finding unusual and complicated matches (although sometimes it's nice to work a little harder to discover something spectacular). It's about choosing the very best thing to eat with a beer, even if that is just a sandwich, a slice of cheese, or a piece of cake. Simplicity is often the best approach.

There are no secrets to pairing beer and food; all you need is the confidence or curiosity to try different beers with different foods. Sometimes, it just won't work and other matches will be fairly neutral, but then you'll get a match that tastes so good you'll want to have it again and again and again. And I hope that you'll share it with others, because beer is a social drink to enjoy with friends while relaxing and talking. But, since it's a laidback drink, closely linked to the pub, bar, or sports event, it hasn't had a place on the (formal) dinner table, which is a real shame. Now is the time to discover how brilliant beer and food can be together.

Love beer and food. Embrace how they sometimes just don't work, celebrate how other times they are amazing, love how the possibilities are limitless, love how sometimes a beer you don't enjoy can be made delicious by a good dish, and love how beer and food are surprising and interesting and fun.

I love beer and I love food, and I love them together. Hopefully, you'll soon understand why.

1 BASIC INGREDIENTS

WHY BEER AND FOOD?

Whether beer likes it or not, wine is the default drink at most dinner tables. But that's changing. I've heard beer-lovers arguing with an esteemed wine writer about each side's success (or not) with food. The wine guy took the view that the great Old World wine nations—France, Italy, and Spain—have great food cultures and so their joining at the table is a natural fit, whereas the great traditional brewing nations—Britain, Belgium, Germany—are not known for their cuisine. The beer guys disagreed.

While I understand the wine guy's point-of-view, it's definitely a dated mentality that overlooks the way in which food and drink now transcend nations. Beer is great for that: of the world's 200 or so countries, the vast majority make their own beer, with small-scale craft brewing consistently growing worldwide to produce an ever-increasing number of beers.

The early American craft brewing pioneers of the 1970s and 1980s took inspiration from old British brewing and did their own thing with it, using local ingredients to develop recipes. They then looked to Belgium and Germany. Now, brewers around the world are looking at what others are making, or looking back at old recipes, and applying their own influences: British brewers are taking the big hops of American IPA and combining them with the low-ABV, session-strength ales; Italian brewers are using their countrymen's wine barrels to produce Sour Beers, as in Belgium; and New Zealand brewers are making wonderful Pale Lagers in the German style and using local hops to give a glorious fruitiness to their beers.

Brewing is a worldwide industry, but the ingredients in beer tend to come from a small number of countries. For this reason, many breweries have to order their ingredients from around the world. This means the provenance of a beer is often tied to who made it and where, rather than the ingredients used or the inspiration behind it. It also means that any brewer, from anywhere in the world, can create any beer style and compare it with anyone else's. Think of it like French fries or a cheeseburger. Every chef can, or does, make fries and a cheeseburger, but they vary enormously, depending on what ingredients and processes are used. The better versions are always well regarded and the best are worth traveling around the world for. American Pale Ale is the beer equivalent: surely the most-brewed craft-beer style, inspired by American breweries, and made within relatively narrow parameters (straw to amber in color, 4.0–6.0% ABV, hop-forward). Although a huge variety exists in terms of quality and taste, American Pale Ale still manages to be a "local" beer, thanks to where it's made.

BEER DRINKERS: AN INCREASING SOPHISTICATION

As brewing continues to grow and spread, so drinkers want better beers and are gaining more knowledge about what is great and what is not so good. That knowledge is important and is linked to food. Within a few generations we've gone from eating mainly local and traditional recipes to enjoying world cuisine in our daily diets, while a general intellectualization of food and drink has combined with a general search for better-tasting things. Now, if we're going to go out for a coffee, we don't want to pay for instant; we want fresh beans ground while we wait. If we want a sandwich in a café, we don't want pre-sliced white bread; we want something fresh from the bakery. We know more than red, white, rosé, or sparkling. We're becoming more aware of seasonality and where ingredients come from. And we're generally learning more about beer: where it's brewed, how it tastes, and why it tastes the way it does.

We don't go to a pub or bar because we know we can get a great pint of Carling, Castlemaine, or Coors. But we do go to a bar if we know there's a choice of five, ten, 20, or even 50 different craft beers. And we're promiscuous and curious about what we drink, choosing different beers when we go to the bar, searching for something tastier than the last one, or something to suit our particular thirst, mood, or a meal. It's taken a long time—and there's still a long way to go—but drinkers are gradually learning more about beer and expecting more than a plain pint of Pale Lager.

TIME FOR FOOD TO STEP UP

And that's where food can help. We tend to know more about food than we know about beer. If someone offers you a guava, Thai basil, or chorizo, you probably know roughly what to expect, whereas being offered a Berliner Weisse, Saison, or ESB can be more daunting. But, if you are pushed in the right direction with beer and food, you can use this as an opportunity to try the two together with confidence, using your knowledge of the food as a kind of stepping stone toward the drink.

Beer is a worldwide drink. We can now order a Japanese-brewed IPA with BBQ ribs in a diner in London; we can have an American-brewed Saison with Chinese food in Auckland; and Brazilian-brewed Hefeweizen with Banh Mi in San Francisco. We can also order Dubbel in Belgium to go with carbonnade, Golden Ale with fish and chips in Britain, Dunkel with bratwurst in Munich... There is absolutely a romance to drinking local beer styles with local food, but the world of beer can go way beyond that and yet still somehow retain some provenance.

That wine writer's view of beer, wine, and food was outdated. Beer has developed and so has food. And this isn't about beer being better than wine or vice versa. It's about understanding and appreciating the wide variety of beers and seeing their potential with a meal; it's about having the freedom to choose different food and drink, and knowing a little bit about them both to make them better together. It's simply about enjoying good food and good drink.

BEER AND FOOD: TOGETHER FOR 10,000 YEARS

Around 10,000 years ago, in the Near East, a shift in human civilization saw our ancestors change from nomadic peoples who migrated seasonally to find the best food and means of survival to settled groups who began to grow their own produce. Among the first crops to be cultivated were grains such as wheat and barley. As a versatile food-stuff, grain could be ground and mixed with varying amounts of water and turned into bread, porridge, or beer.

Some scientists have argued that brewing was a catalyst for the beginnings of agriculture, while others believe bread and porridge are of greater importance. Either way, beer and bread are key points on the timeline of human evolution. However, exactly why, when, and how the first beer was brewed are questions to which we'll probably never know the answers, so we can only speculate.

What we do know is this: grain contains starch and these starches are converted into fermentable sugars when they are soaked in water. A grain-and-water mix would naturally have attracted airborne wild yeasts and these would've started the fermentation process. So, after a few hours or days, the porridge would start to bubble and fizz. When an intrepid farmer took a sip, he would have felt the pleasing warmth of intoxication and surely set about recreating it and making it even better. One development we are sure of is that grain was baked into dry breads or biscuits, which were then crumbled into water, thus starting off the brewing process.

10,000 years ago beer was a liquid form of bread and bread was a baked form of beer. In other words, beer was food, and the two have been together since the first days of settled human civilization.

CURRENCY, CALORIES, AND CEREMONY

As time passed, grain remained important to human civilization. For example, beer and bread were staples of the Ancient Egyptian diet. The workers who built the Great Pyramids of Egypt were paid a daily ration of beer and bread (about 1 US gallon/4 liters and four loaves), and over 15 different types of beer have been identified from this period, with names such as The Beautiful and the Good, The Joy Bringer, and The Addition to the Meal.

We know that beer also became a sociable drink from depictions of people drinking from large pots with long straws. These straws also helped to remove the sediment that accumulated as a result of the brewing process. This sediment had other benefits in its turn. Since the beer was unfiltered (and so still contained yeast), it was high in vitamins, minerals, and protein, as well as extra calories. For this reason, beer combined the refreshment of a drink with the sustenance of food. On top of all that, once boiling the liquid became a part of the brewing process, beer was safer to drink than water.

There's more: beer also had a religious role and links to the gods. The Egyptians believed that Osiris, who was the god of agriculture, discovered beer—one day, he made some gruel and forgot about it, returning later to a fermented bowl of beer. Osiris told

the world about this magical drink and so confirmed his godly status. Ninkasi was the Sumerian goddess of alcohol and the brewster for the other gods. The Hymn to Ninkasi is a recipe for beer and one of the earliest written mentions of the drink. Beer also played a part in religious ceremonies for birth and death.

FROM HOME-BREWED...

Jumping forward in time and across to Northern Europe, we find that brewing was something predominantly done in the home before it became established in the monasteries (from the 9th to 12th centuries). As something small-scale and local, beer was inextricably linked to the kitchen and would inevitably have been used in cooking. Beer was also a part of people's daily diet and was consumed as both a nutritious drink and liquid bread. Next came a more commercial approach to beer. Home-brewing alewives started to sell their beer (we're in the 14th century now, by the way) before a demand for greater volumes saw a move toward larger, commercial-scale production (now the 16th century)—and so brewing became a proper profession. With the Industrial Revolution (the 18th century), beer was produced on vast scales and then it got smarter with scientific and technical developments in brewing (the 19th century).

TO MASS-BREWED...

By the start of the 20th century, brewing had become a large-scale commercial industry in many parts of the world, with new developments—such as advanced railway networks, pasteurization, and so on—allowing beer to travel. Then came a few decades of worldwide change with the First and Second World Wars, rationing, depressions, and prohibition in America, followed by a rebuilding and return to peacetime. These events all combined to affect food and drink in one major way: flavor disappeared.

The 1950s won't be held up as our greatest culinary decade, as they were blighted by canned food, convenience food, the knock-on effect of rationing, and food shortages... And, where once 50 years earlier there were over 1,700 small local breweries in America, the big ones started getting bigger and dominating the market or buying out smaller breweries. Britain saw lager overtake classic cask ales in popularity. In the 1970s, the number of American breweries fell below 100. The 1970s was also the decade when light beer was introduced...

TO MICRO-BREWED...

The fight-back against the monopolized markets of mainstream lager came with new small breweries all looking to make the most delicious beers possible. They focused on local ingredients and local drinkers, and looked back into beer's long history, as well as toward new tastes and styles. Food changed, too. We became more aware of freshness, provenance, and how to cook things. We looked at different cuisines and became interested in them, and we discovered beers from farther away. We simply got more knowledgeable about the things we consumed. Today, we're more aware than ever about great food and drink from around the world.

THE RECIPE FOR BEER

Water, grain, hops, and yeast are the four main ingredients in beer. Just like creating a recipe in the kitchen, it's a specific combination of different ingredients that defines each beer style and how it tastes. I like to explain the creation of a beer or beer style with an analogy to making a statue (bear with me, this will make sense).

Water and malt create the base of the beer—its color and strength. It's the equivalent of deciding what your statue will be made of and what its approximate size will be. The addition of hops and yeast creates the definition, and determines the type of beer it will become—this is like deciding on all the finer details of the statue: its facial expression, its clothing. What I love is how the exact same base brew can be turned into very different beers by the addition of different hop and yeast combos. For example, say we've brewed a 5.0% black beer: add English hops and English ale yeast, and you've brewed a Stout; add American hops and American ale yeast, and it's a Black Ale; add German hops and lager yeast, and you've got a Schwarzbier. It's like ringing in the changes with a meat-and-tomato-based sauce—into one goes some chili and it's served with rice, another gets basil and is mixed with spaghetti, and a third takes cinnamon and dried herbs to become the base of many Greek dishes. So, different combinations of similar ingredients can create different recipes.

WATER

This isn't simply something that comes from the tap or an underground well. The specific composition of the water—whether it's hard, soft, or high or low in sulfites, calcium, magnesium, and other minerals—affects the final drink in many complicated ways. Brewers have to know what their water is like and all of them will add something to their tanks to balance its composition so that it's the best water for whatever they're brewing. Water is like a chef's plate or artist's palette: it's something in the background that's very important, but shouldn't be noticeable unless the drinker is actively and acutely looking for it.

GRAIN

Malted barley is the most common brewing grain, but wheat, oats, and rye are also frequently used. What we need from the grain is starch because that converts into sugar during the brewing process, and it's those sugars that the yeast consumes to create alcohol. From the grain we also get the color, sweetness, and flavor of the beer and, in combination with the yeast, it also contributes much of the beer's body.

A huge range of potential flavors and colors can be produced from the grain. This comes from how the grain is roasted when in production: the longer it's roasted, the darker it gets. The closest analogy is with bread: it starts off sweet and bready as you begin to apply heat, then it caramelizes and becomes sweeter in the middle, gradually getting darker before it becomes black and bitter with no remaining sweetness. Brewers add different mixes of malt to make up the base of the beer.

DIFFERENT TYPES OF GRAIN

PILSNER MALT: VERY PALE, BISCUITY

PALE MALT: LIGHTLY TOASTY, CEREAL-LIKE

MUNICH MALT: AMBER, TOASTY, NUTTY

CRYSTAL MALT: CARAMEL, TOFFEE

CHOCOLATE MALT: DARK, BITTER, ROASTY

ROASTED BARLEY: BLACK, ACRID, BITTER COFFEE

WHEAT: NUTTY, ADDS SUBTLE ACIDITY

OATS: SMOOTH, CREAMY

RYE: SPICY, HERBAL

HOPS

Hops are the seasoning and spice in beer, providing bitterness, flavor, and aroma. They are varietal and each variety has different qualities. The place where the hop variety grows also has a big impact on the flavor of a beer. Indeed, the same variety grown in England, America, Germany, and New Zealand will give different qualities to a beer.

It's possible to describe hops broadly, depending on where they are grown: English hops are earthy, spicy, and woody (with new varieties giving some orchard fruit and citrus); Central European hops (from Germany, the Czech Republic, Slovenia, and Belgium) are peppery, floral, and grassy, with some stone fruit and lemon; American hops are resinous and citrusy like bitter oranges, pine, and grapefruit; New Zealand hops have tropical fruit with mango, pineapple, and lychee, plus a spiciness; while new hop varieties are being specifically developed around the world for their big citrus and spicy flavor and aroma.

Hop flowers are harvested once a year in each hemisphere. Once picked, they are dried immediately so that they can last until the next harvest. Hops have a high water content when picked and will deteriorate as soon as they leave the bine. Hence the need to dry them—although it's possible to brew with the "green" hops straight from the field, it must be done on the day the hops are picked. Brewers can use hops as dried flowers or, more commonly, they are processed and packed together into pellets. It's also possible to buy extracted hop oil.

Hops vary in flavor and intensity; some can be very delicate, while others can be incredibly pungent. European hops tend to be more subtle than American and Australasian hops, although it all ultimately depends on how many hops are used. It's typical to combine different hop varieties in a beer in the same way that you combine different spices and seasoning when cooking.

GRAIN MIXES FOR POPULAR BEER STYLES

PALE ALE: 80% PALE MALT, 10% MUNICH MALT, 10% CRYSTAL MALT

DARK LAGER: 85% PILSNER MALT, 10% MUNICH MALT, 5% CHOCOLATE MALT

WIT BIER: 50% WHEAT, 50% PILSNER MALT

BROWN ALE: 85% PALE MALT, 5% CRYSTAL MALT, 5% BROWN MALT, 5% CHOCOLATE MALT

STOUT: 85% PALE MALT, 5% CRYSTAL MALT, 8% CHOCOLATE MALT, 2% ROASTED BARLEY

POPULAR HOP VARIETIES—AND THEIR FLAVORS

UNITED STATES

AMARILLO: PEACHES, APRICOTS, ORANGES

CASCADE: GRAPEFRUIT, MANDARIN, FLORAL

CENTENNIAL: ORANGE PITH, BLOSSOM, PINE

CITRA: MANGO, TANGERINE, PASSION FRUIT

SIMCOE: RESINOUS PINE, BITTER ORANGE

CENTRAL EUROPE

SAAZ (CZ): GRASSY, FLORAL, CITRUS BOTANICALS

HALLERTAUER (GER): FLORAL, WOODY HERBS, PITHY

SAPHIR (GER): TANGERINE, LEMON PITH, PEPPER

STYRIAN GOLDINGS (SL): EARTHY, PEPPER, LEMON

MAGNUM (GER AND US): HERBAL, PINE, CITRUS

ENGLAND

BRAMLING CROSS: BERRIES, ORCHARD FRUIT, WOOD

FUGGLES: EARTHY, WOODY, FLORAL

GOLDINGS: TANGY, FLORAL, PEPPERY

TARGET: PINE, WOOD, ROAST FRUIT

AUSTRALIA AND NEW ZEALAND

GALAXY (AUS): MANGO, PINEAPPLE, CITRUS

SUMMER (AUS): APRICOT, PINEAPPLE, CITRUS PITH

MOTUEKA (NZ): TROPICAL FRUIT, SWEET BERRIES

NELSON SAUVIN (NZ): GRAPE, GOOSEBERRY, MANGO

YEAST

Yeast creates the alcohol in beer and the qualities that come with that alcohol—a beer's body, warmth, and depth. The yeast also determines the beer's residual sweetness, which, in turn, contributes to the body and perception of the beer: for example, 50 units of bitterness, which is fairly standard for a Stout or Pale Ale, will seem moderate in a sweet beer but taste very bitter in a dry beer.

There are many different yeast strains and each brings different qualities to beer: some are delicate, some fruity, some peppery, and some will make the beer sour. In many beers, the yeast is in the background and only evident in the effects of the alcohol it's created. However, some beers—typically Wheat Beers and Sour Beers—are dominated by their yeast flavor.

Yeast also produces aroma compounds called esters. These are typically fruity (banana, strawberry, bubble gum), nutty (almond), or spicy (clove). Sometimes, they are supposed to be there; at other times, they are not. (See pages 20–21 for more on beer's off-flavors and their appropriateness.)

It's also worth considering the difference between filtered and unfiltered beer. Filtration removes the residual yeast, while an unfiltered beer still contains that yeast, so giving extra texture, depth, and flavor to the beer. A filtered beer is typically sharper and cleaner to the taste than the soft roundness of an unfiltered beer.

OTHER INGREDIENTS AND PROCESSES

Name something edible. Anything. And it's very likely that someone, somewhere, has brewed with it. Bacon, oysters, chili peppers, garden herbs and flowers, candy, tomatoes. Seriously. Brewers can, and have, made beer with most things. The most common beer ingredients are fruit, chocolate, coffee, vanilla, nuts, and spices. These all add their own qualities to the beer, some subtly so, others in a more dominant way.

You will also find beers aged in wooden barrels, most of which have previously held something else, such as bourbon, whisky, wine, rum, tequila, or other spirit. The wood gives texture and depth, perhaps some vanilla and spice, while the spirit gives its own qualities.

HOW IS BEER MADE?

As with any recipe, brewing beer involves combining a few simple ingredients in different proportions and variations to make new brews. Adding citrusy American hops is very different from adding earthy English hops in the same way as adding parsley and lemon to a dish differs from adding cilantro (coriander) and lime. Similarly, using a clean ale yeast, as opposed to a spicy Belgian yeast, is the equivalent of adding white pepper rather than dried chili.

What I find most interesting about the creation of different beers is that, with so many potential decisions to be made,the brewing process has limitless possibilities.

STAGE 1: Having chosen the grain bill, which will determine the color and alcohol content of a beer, brewers add malt to warm water in a mash tun where it's churned around for an hour or two like a big, bubbling stockpot. Brewers are looking to convert the starch in the grains into fermentable sugars, which happens when the liquid reaches around 154°F (68°C).

STAGE 2: Next, brewers need to separate the grain from the sweet liquid (now called wort). This sometimes happens in a lauter tun or sometimes the wort is just run out of the mash tun. Either way, the grain is no longer of any use and is removed from the process. The wort is then transferred to the kettle (sometimes known as a copper) where it's boiled.

STAGE 3: This is where the hops go in. It's typical to have three hop additions over an extended boil (usually lasting 60–90 minutes)—the first addition is for bitterness, the second for flavor, and the third for aroma. Hops contain acids (which give beer its bitterness) and volatile oils (that provide flavor and aroma). The acids need to be isomerized, making them water soluble, in order to kick out the majority of their bitterness.

For this to happen they need to boil for an extended period of time. To control the level of bitterness, all hops come with an alpha acid content, which is the equivalent of knowing whether the chili peppers you are about to cook with are mild or strong. By knowing the acid content, brewers can calculate the volume of hops to add to get the bitterness they want. Jumping ahead, the third hop addition doesn't allow the acids to isomerize, but it does capture all of the fragrant volatile oils that are boiled away in the first hop addition. The second hop addition gets a bit of everything and rounds out the flavor.

STAGE 4: A quick turn in a whirlpool removes residual hop "trub" before the liquid moves through a heat exchange that cools it down before sending it into the fermentation tank.

STAGE 5: This is where the yeast is added and starts to eat its way through all the delicious sugars, so producing alcohol and carbon dioxide. Every yeast strain works differently, at different temperatures, and takes different amounts of time to do its job. Ales classically ferment at between 61–75°F (16–24°C), while lagers require a temperature of 46–54°F (8–12°C); ales take 2–4 days to ferment, whereas lagers require 6–10 days.

Temperature makes the biggest difference here: the warmer it is, the harder and faster the yeast will work. If the yeast has to work too hard, then it'll give off unusual and unwanted esters and aromas. (These esters are typically desirable in Wheat Beers where the fermentation temperature is higher than for other ales in order to produce these aromas.) If fermentation is too slow, then it'll result in more unwanted qualities, or leave too much residual sweetness in the beer. So, managing temperature is key for good fermentation.

STAGE 6: Once it has fermented, the beer is cooled and left to condition—this is the equivalent of slow-cooking a stew compared with trying to make it in 20 minutes, whereby the long, slow cook tastes immeasurably better because all of the flavors have had a chance to come together. Most ales take around two weeks from brewday to drinking; lagers take four weeks or longer. If a beer is put into a barrel for extended aging, then it could live in there for months or even years before it's ready to drink. After fermentation, more hops can be added to the tank. This is called "dry hopping," and will result in more hop flavor and stronger aroma.

STAGE 7: When the beer is ready, it is packaged in kegs, casks, bottles, or cans. Some beers will be filtered, meaning that the yeast is removed, while others retain the yeast. Real ales often have an isinglass fining agent added to the beer in the barrel, which makes the yeast settle to the bottom of the cask. (Vegetarians might want to check what brewers have added as their finings since isinglass, which comes from the dried swim bladders of fish, is often used.) Real ales and bottle-conditioned beers undergo a secondary fermentation in the cask or bottle. This means that a mix of sugar and yeast is added, and another fermentation occurs that provides the carbonation. Some beers, mostly those produced by the multinational breweries, are pasteurized. This involves heating the beer to a high temperature to kill off any bacteria in the container. Unfortunately, this also effectively "kills" the beer and some of its flavor.

THEN, FINALLY, THE BEER IS READY TO GO— AND WE CAN DRINK.

THE BREWING PROCESS

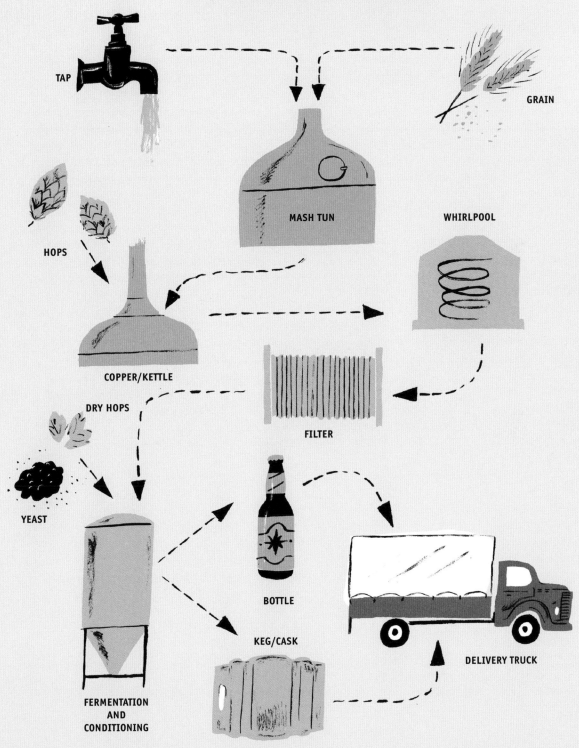

TAP

GRAIN

MASH TUN

WHIRLPOOL

HOPS

COPPER/KETTLE

FILTER

DRY HOPS

YEAST

BOTTLE

DELIVERY TRUCK

KEG/CASK

FERMENTATION
AND
CONDITIONING

THE LANGUAGE OF BEER

When we talk about beer we tend to use some specific phrases or recurring terms. Here's a short beer dictionary of the most frequently used words.

ABV

Alcohol-by-volume. This is the total percentage of your drink that is alcohol

ALE

A broad family of beers brewed with a top-fermenting yeast. Ales typically ferment quickly (taking 2–4 days) at warm temperatures (61–75°F/16–24°C). Styles include Hefeweizen, Kölsch, Best Bitters, Stout, Saison, IPA, Barley Wines, and many others.

ATTENUATION

A way of discussing the percentage of sugars that the yeast converts during the fermentation process. A highly attenuated beer will be dry and have little sweetness; an under-attenuated beer will be sweet.

BEER

An alcoholic drink made from fermented grain. The best drink in the world.

BODY

This is the weight and feeling of the beer in the mouth. It comes from a combination of the grain base, whether it's filtered or not, and is dependent on the attenuation of the beer.

BOTTLE-CONDITIONED BEER

Beer that undergoes a secondary fermentation in the bottle. This means that priming sugar and yeast are added to the bottle, which starts a slow, gradual conditioning process to produce a natural carbonation. Some bottle-conditioned beers will continue to mature for decades. Watch out for yeast when you pour these beers—some drinkers like sediment in the glass, others don't.

BU:GU

This is a way to look at the balance of a beer. Where some people use IBUs (International Bittering Units) to rate a beer's bitterness, others—largely brewers—use BU:GU, which looks at the bitterness (the BU) in relation to the sweetness (the GU) of the beer. (The GU, or gravity, is a way of measuring the fermentable sugars in a brew.) This makes it a more reliable way of telling whether a beer will be sweet, bitter, or balanced.

COLOR

This can be measured on two different scales: the Standard Reference Method (SRM) and the European Brewery Convention (EBC). More usually, the color is simply described as gold, copper, brown, etc. The palest lager will be as low as 1 SRM/2 EBC or straw; American IPA ranges from 6–14 SRM/12–28 EBC or gold to amber; and the darkest Stout will be 70 SRM/138 EBC or black.

CRAFT BEER

This is difficult to define adequately, but craft beer is essentially beer with a story and purpose, produced by a brewer aiming to make the tastiest beer possible. Craft beer is what the majority of small breweries make. Ultimately, it's just beer. We use the word "craft" to show that it's different from macro beers.

DRY-HOPPING

Adding hops to beer after (or during) fermentation. This gives extra hop aroma and flavor to a beer.

ESTERS

Esters come out of beer as aromas, which are created during the higher temperatures of fermentation when alcohol and organic acids react with each other. They are (often) fruity aromas, but can be very harsh and veer toward nail-polish remover. Expect banana, pear, apple, rose, honey, strawberry, almond, bubble gum, and solvent. Sometimes, these are brewing faults, while at other times, they are desirable—it depends on the beer style and the volume at which they are present.

FINISH

This is how the flavor of a beer ends in the mouth and then hangs around. It can be short or long; dry, bitter, sweet, or sharp; or combinations of these.

IBU

International Bittering Unit. Also known as EBU (European Bittering Unit) or just BU. It's the measure of bitterness in a beer and represents the parts-per-million of dissolved iso-alpha acids that the beer contains. Each beer style will have an appropriate IBU level: light lager might be 10 IBUs, Pilsner will be between 20 and 40 IBUs, Stout will be 35–55 IBUs, while Double IPAs and Barley Wines can hit 100 IBUs.

LAGER

Beer made using bottom-fermenting yeast. Lagers typically ferment slowly (taking 6–10 days) at cool temperatures 46–54°F (8–12°C), compared with fast-working, warm-temperature-loving ale yeast. The name comes from the process of lagering (or storing) beer in a cold place for it to mature. The range of lager styles includes Pilsner, Helles, Bock, Doppelbock, Märzen, and more.

MACRO BEER

Beer made by the big, multinational brewing companies. Not all are bad, but not many are great.

MOUTHFEEL

How the beer feels in the mouth. This is another way of describing the body of a beer, although mouthfeel is more about sensation: is the beer prickly, delicate, creamy, sharp, dry, or smooth?

NITROGEN/NITRO

A beer described as "nitro" has been pumped with nitrogen in tank and will pour with a full, creamy mouthfeel. This is often the case with Stouts such as Guinness, but you'll see bars and brewpubs with dedicated "nitro" taps for any kind of beer.

SOUR BEER

Along with ale and lager, this is a broad family of beers. These beers are intentionally sour through the use of wild yeast and different souring bacteria—some are also spontaneously fermented from airborne yeast. Many of the best Sour Beers take years of gradual slow fermentation to develop their complexity, and you should expect funky aromas, sharp acidity, but not a vinegary quality. They will also be clean-tasting—try the Lambics, Gueuzes, and Belgium beers to see how the best taste.

UNFILTERED

This is beer that hasn't had the yeast filtered out of it. Unfiltered beers are generally hazy and have more flavor and texture than a filtered equivalent. The haze may also be cleared by the use of a fining agent, which pulls all the particles left in the beer to the bottom of the container.

WILD YEAST AND BACTERIA

Some brewers deliberately add wild yeast and bacteria to get sourness and funky flavors into their beer. Brettanomyces is a common wild yeast, although it's not always "wild," and can be bought from yeast companies. Common bacteria are pediococcus and lactobacillus. If any of these get into a beer unintentionally, then it's a bad thing.

SERVING BEER

At home, I drink most of my beer from a couple of favorite glasses: a straight glass, a shaker, and a teardrop. If you like to drink your beer out of a wine glass, tea cup, or plastic beaker, that's fine because individual preference is more important than anything. However, there is some science behind using different glasses for different beer styles since the size and shape of the vessel can have an impact on the aroma and taste of the drink. Here are the types of glass that I think cover most beer styles:

STRAIGHT/PILSNER These glasses are tall and thin so the bubbles stream into a tight foam. Ideal for lagers because this style of glass sends the delicate aroma right up your nose, plus the glasses also make the bright, sparkling beers look fantastic.

WEISSBIER These have a vase-like shape for Hefeweizens where the foam is concentrated at the top of the glass like a fragrant pillow. Shaped so that you can see the beautiful haziness in the body and get the full impact of the estery aroma.

SHAKER A chunky all-rounder that is best for American beer styles—American Wheats, Pale Ales, Ambers, Reds, Browns, and IPAs—where you get the hop hit in the aroma without intensifying it too much.

TEARDROP An elegant glass for elegant beers, such as Wit, Saison, Tripel, and Wild Ale, or for styles where you want to swirl, sniff, and focus the aromas in the tapered rim. This is the glass I use most frequently and it works with almost every style of beer.

BOWL/SNIFTER For those big beers that demand more of your attention: Imperial Stouts and Barley Wines. Think of the beers like fine spirits as they roll around your glass, sending their intensified aromas swirling out as you sip.

PINT Nonic, straight-sided, tulip, or a dimpled mug, these are for low-ABV, session-style beers, including Bitter, Stout, Porter, Helles, Pilsner, and Dunkel. Not a swirling and sniffing kind of glass. Just drink it.

CHALICE/GOBLET Squat and round, and used for strong, dark Belgian beers where the high carbonation is softened. There's something rather special about drinking from a chalice or goblet, especially when in a café in Belgium...

OR... JUST USE YOUR WINE GLASSES Large beer glasses can be daunting, plus not everyone has enough cupboard space for a wide range of glassware, so using a large wine glass is a good option for most beers.

SERVING TEMPERATURE

If your beer gets too cold, this will hide some of the flavor and aroma; if it gets too warm, it can seem heavy and overbearing. Each style of beer will have an ideal serving temperature: lagers are usually cold (although in Germany or the Czech Republic, they aren't super-chilled as they are elsewhere around the world); kegged ales come chilled, normally between 37 and 54°F (3–12°C); British cask ales are often described as "warm," which is incorrect—they are cellar temperature, which is between 50 and 57°F (10–14°C); some people (but not me!) like to serve strong beers, such as Imperial Stout, at room temperature.

Personally, when I'm drinking at home I like all my beer, regardless of what it is, served fridge-cold; a beer that starts too cold will warm up, whereas a warm beer isn't going to get cooler. The best advice is simple: drink it at whatever temperature you like best, regardless of whether some people think you should serve it warmer or colder than you prefer.

FRESH VERSUS AGED

Most beers are best drunk fresh, especially those that have a big hop aroma—you should drink these as fresh as possible because hop aroma, flavor, and bitterness all fade. Some beers, especially strong Stouts, Sour Beers, and Barley Wines, benefit from being aged a little, as this can soften the flavors and bring out additional complexity. Just make sure that you don't hoard a special beer hoping that the flavor is gradually getting better and better, only to open it finally and discover that it's stale and tastes terrible. Beer is for drinking, so drink it.

For you to enjoy it, beer has to get from the brewery to your glass. The four most common types of container for beer are the keg, cask, bottle, and can.

KEG is the main draft container around the world. Beer goes into the keg already carbonated and, when the tap is opened on the bar, the beer is pushed out with counter-pressure and gas.

CASK is the other most common draft container, especially in Britain. Beer generally goes into these uncarbonated and a mix of yeast and sugar will start a natural secondary fermentation. A cask beer is not as sparkling as a kegged beer; instead, the beer has a gentle, subtle carbonation. (In Germany and the Czech Republic, you'll find some lagers poured from gravity or direct from the barrel, and these will have a similarly soft carbonation to cask beers.)

BOTTLES AND CANS are generally closer to kegged beers than cask ones, and often have a bright carbonation.

BAD BEER VERSUS GOOD BEER

Here's something that isn't often said in a book championing the best-tasting brews in the world: not every beer is good. In fact, some are just dreadful and undrinkable. This could be personal preference (perhaps they are too bitter or too sweet for you), or it could be down to a brewing or serving fault.

This section is intended to highlight some of the common faults you'll come across, how to identify them, where they come from, and how appropriate they are. (One note of interest: we perceive these things in a very individual way and some people are "taste blind" to certain flavors, while others are super-sensitive.)

BUTTER, BUTTERED POPCORN, BUTTERSCOTCH, FATTY MOUTHFEEL

WHAT? Diacetyl
WHY? A natural by-product of fermentation. If it's in your beer, it could mean the beer was hurried out of the brewery. It can also mean infected yeast.
APPROPRIATE? In very small amounts in some lagers, Porters, and Stouts, but usually unwanted.

APPLE SKIN AND JUICE, CIDER, PAINT IN HIGH VOLUMES

WHAT? Acetaldehyde
WHY? A natural by-product of fermentation. If this is present, it's because the beer is "green" (usually the result of haste on the part of the brewery) or made with poor-quality yeast. If the beer becomes "cidery," it's got to an extreme level.
APPROPRIATE? No.

SWEETCORN, STEWED VEGETABLES, TOMATOES

WHAT? Dimethyl sulfide (DMS)
WHY? Comes from the grain (pale malt) if it hasn't had a vigorous-enough boil in the kettle or fermentation has been slow.
APPROPRIATE? In tiny amounts in some lagers.

PAPER, CARDBOARD, STALE SHERRY

WHAT? Oxidized
WHY? Oxygen is not good for beer. If a beer tastes like this, then you're drinking stale beer.
APPROPRIATE? Never in fresh beer, although it can be an integral part of aged beers and contribute to their character and complexity.

BANANAS, PEAR DROPS, APPLE, ROSE

WHAT? Esters, including Isoamyl acetate (banana and pear drop), Ethyl caprylate and Ethyl caproate (apple and apple/aniseed), Ethyl acetate (solvent), and Phenylethyl acetate (honey, rose)
WHY? Fruity aromas given out by the yeast during fermentation.
APPROPRIATE? Yes, in certain styles and at low volumes—appropriateness is down to the detectable levels. Expect Isoamyl acetate (or banana) in Hefeweizens, but it's often a fault in other styles, too. Can be more evident in strong beers.

SMOKY, ISLAY WHISKY, BAND-AIDS, DISINFECTANT

WHAT? Phenols
WHY? Could be from a reaction between the phenolic acid, which is naturally found in malt, and either the chlorine content in the water or a cleaning solution used by the brewery.
APPROPRIATE? No. And it's not to be confused with the flavors of smoked malt or Belgian yeast that give a phenolic, clove-like spiciness.

"SKUNKY," ROTTING VEGETABLES, GARLIC

WHAT? Light-struck

WHY? Sunlight and beer don't work well together (unless it's a hot day and you're drinking a cold pint). The UV rays break down hop molecules, causing a reaction with the sulfur in the beer and producing some of the same stinky chemicals as a skunk.

APPROPRIATE? Never. Avoid beer in clear or green bottles, and keep all beer out of sunlight—skunking can happen almost immediately.

EGGS OR BURNING MATCHES

WHAT? Sulfur

WHY? Could be from the water (the "Burton Snatch" famously gives Burton-on-Trent's beers a whiff of sulfur) or from the yeast. It could also be a warning sign of infection or of a young beer.

APPROPRIATE? Yes, but only in small amounts in ale and in some styles of lager (especially unfiltered lagers).

SOY SAUCE, BURNT TIRES, MARMITE

WHAT? Autolyzed yeast

WHY? Yeast that has died and ruptured its beer-spoiling guts into your beer.

APPROPRIATE? It's acceptable in small volumes in some aged beers; otherwise, it's not.

SOUR MILK, VINEGAR, LEMON JUICE

WHAT? Sour beer, unless intentional, is bad.

WHY? Souring bacteria or yeast in the beer.

APPROPRIATE? It makes some Wild Ales what they are. Otherwise, it's only good for pouring down the drain.

BABY SICK

WHAT? Butyric acid

WHY? Bacterial spoilage. Not very common, but horrible if you get it.

APPROPRIATE? No. Never. Do you want to drink a beer that smells of vomit?

BOOZY, ALCOHOLIC, NAIL-POLISH REMOVER

WHAT? Fusel, solvent, Ethyl acetate

WHY? From esters in the beer. Low volumes can come across as fruity, but it can sting the eyes in high volumes.

APPROPRIATE? Small amounts are okay. It can be present in strong beers, although it is not always pleasant.

CHEESY, SWEATY SOCKS

WHAT? Isovaleric acid

WHY? Could be a bacterial infection or a sign of using old, oxidized hops.

APPROPRIATE? No. Never is a beer that smells like socks or stinky feet going to be delicious!

MY BEER IS CLOUDY...

WHY? Could be many things: an unfiltered beer with yeast still in it, a "chill haze" from the beer being served cold, a "hop haze" from a very hoppy beer, or an infected beer.

APPROPRIATE? Just because it's cloudy doesn't mean it's bad. If it tastes bad, then it is bad; otherwise, it's fine.

SHARED FLAVORS OF BEER AND FOOD

Beer and food share many qualities and a good approach to getting great matches is to find common flavors between the two elements in order to naturally push them together. This is the basis of a "bridge" pairing, in which we seek those similarities and link them together. Outlined here are some suggestions based on popular ingredients and then, on the following page, we look at how there are flavors in beer which taste similar to flavors in food—by matching them up you build that bridge.

"MY FOOD CONTAINS [INGREDIENT], SO I WANT TO DRINK..."

Certain ingredients are consistent to different cuisines and we can use these to create some general ideas as to which beers will work with which types of food. Often these are ingredients which go on the side of a dish, seasonings, or are added late in the process: a splodge of ketchup, a squeeze of lime, a handful of fresh basil, or a knob of butter. Here are some of those common ingredients and the beer styles which naturally work well with them.

BUTTER:
KÖLSCH, PILSNER, TRIPEL, DUNKEL

BLACK PEPPER:
SAISON, DUBBEL, AMERICAN PALE ALE

LEMON:
PILSNER, HELLES, DUNKEL, SMOKED BEER, WILD ALE, TRIPEL

SOY SAUCE:
STOUT, PORTER, DUNKEL

LIME, BASIL, AND MINT:
PACIFIC PALE ALE, AMERICAN PALE ALE, NEW WORLD LAGER

CILANTRO (FRESH CORIANDER):
SAISON, NEW WORLD LAGER, PILSNER, PACIFIC PALE ALE

CORIANDER (SEEDS):
WITBIER, TRIPEL

BASIL, FENNEL:
SAISON, BELGIAN BLONDES, BELGIAN IPA, STOUT

ROSEMARY, THYME:
SAISON, AMERICAN PALE, IPA AND DOUBLE IPA

ROAST GARLIC, SWEET ONIONS:
AMERICAN PALE, IPA AND DOUBLE IPA

SALSA:
AMERICAN PALE ALE, DUNKEL, SAISON

TOMATO KETCHUP:
AMERICAN PALE ALE, AMERICAN IPA, BLACK ALE

MUSTARD:
SAISON, DUNKEL, AMERICAN PALE ALE

YOGURT:
WHEAT ALE, HEFEWEIZEN

BEER + FOOD = LIQUID DINNER!

Sometimes, you can enjoy a glass of beer with some food, and something miraculous happens: the combination tastes exactly like something else. Take a look at the following examples:

Rauchbier + Cream Cheese on French Bread = Ham and Cheese Sandwich

Porter + Griddled Steak = The Best Barbecue Ever

Sour Cherry Beer + Goats' Cheese and Sweet Biscuits = Cherry Cheesecake

Chocolate Imperial Stout + Chocolate Cake = The Ultimate Chocolate Fondant

Black IPA + Orange Cake = Chocolate Orange

Barrel-Aged Stout + Cream Cheese = Vanilla Cheesecake

Strawberry Beer + Salted Peanuts = Peanut Butter and Jelly

Coffee Stout + Iced Vanilla Cupcake = Tiramisù

Barrel-Aged Cider + Shortbread = Apple Pie

Imperial Oatmeal Stout + Cherry Cake = Black Forest Gateaux

Barrel-Aged Stout + Banana Bread = Banoffee Pie

BEER AND FOOD FLAVOR MATCHING

There are qualities in beer that are found in different foods, such as the shared roasted flavor of Stout and char-grilled steak. This chart presents different beer flavors and aromas, the styles in which you're most likely to find them, and the foods they are in. This knowledge enables us to find commonalities to help bridge the flavor between your drink and your dinner.

BEER QUALITY	PROMINENT IN...	FOODS TO TRY
BREADY AND TOASTY (MALT)	DUNKEL, PALE ALE, BRITISH ALE	GRILLED MEAT, NUTS, CHEESE, BREAD
CARAMEL (MALT)	PALE ALE, IPA	GRILLED MEAT, AGED CHEESE, ROAST VEGETABLES, CAKE, TOFFEE, ROAST ONION AND GARLIC
NUTTY (MALT)	DUNKEL	CHEESE, NUTS, GRILLED MEAT, WHOLE GRAINS, WILD RICE
ROAST (MALT)	STOUT, PORTER	ROASTED AND BARBECUE MEAT, SMOKED FOOD, CHOCOLATE, COFFEE
DRIED FRUIT	DUBBEL, QUADRUPEL, AGED BEERS	DRIED FRUIT, BALSAMIC VINEGAR
SMOKE (MALT, YEAST)	SMOKED BEER, WHEAT BEERS	SMOKED FOOD, PAPRIKA, CLOVES, BRAZIL NUTS
SWEETNESS (MALT)	IMPERIAL STOUT, SWEET STOUT	BREAD, CAKES, PASTRIES, CHOCOLATE, VANILLA CREAM
CREAMY (YEAST, MALT)	SWEET STOUTS, WHEAT BEERS	CREAM CHEESE, SEAFOOD, APRICOTS, CHOCOLATE
SPICY (YEAST)	SAISON, WHEAT BEERS, BELGIAN ALES	PEPPER, CLOVES, CINNAMON, ANISEED, BASIL, DRIED FRUIT
FRUITY (YEAST)	PALE ALE, BRITISH ALE	CHUTNEY, DRIED FRUIT, STONE FRUIT, MATURE CHEESES
ACETIC (YEAST)	SOUR ALES	VINEGAR, TOMATOES, KETCHUP, PICKLES, CHUTNEY
SOURNESS (YEAST)	SOUR ALES	FERMENTED FOODS, SUCH AS SOURDOUGH, YOGURT, KIMCHI
FUNKY (YEAST)	SOUR ALES	FARMHOUSE AND BLUE CHEESES, TRUFFLES, BERRIES
SHARP FRUIT (MALT, YEAST, HOPS)	STOUT, PORTER	COFFEE, SEMI-SWEET (DARK) CHOCOLATE, BERRIES, LIME, MANGO, PASSION FRUIT
BITTERNESS (HOPS, MALT)	ALL BEER	ENDIVE, CHICORY, ARUGULA (ROCKET), WATERCRESS, OLIVES, SEMI-SWEET (DARK) CHOCOLATE, COFFEE, ROASTED MEAT
CITRUS (HOPS)	AMERICAN PALE ALE, IPA	CITRUS FRUIT, GINGER, CILANTRO (FRESH CORIANDER), WHITE WINE VINEGAR
TROPICAL (HOPS)	PACIFIC PALE ALES AND IPAS	MANGO, PASSION FRUIT, PINEAPPLE, AGED CHEESE
HERBAL (HOPS, YEAST)	SAISON, TRIPEL, PILSNER	GREEN HERBS, PEPPER, SAUSAGES
EARTHY (HOPS)	SAISON, BRITISH ALES, STOUTS	AGED CHEESE, DRIED MEAT, MUSHROOMS, TRUFFLES, CUMIN, POTATO, EGGPLANT (AUBERGINE)
OAK (BARREL)	BARREL-AGED BEER	VANILLA, COCONUT, WOODY SPICES, TOFFEE

FLAVOR COMPOUNDS IN BEER AND FOOD

The interaction between aroma, taste, and texture creates our interpretation of flavor. Break aroma down further, and you'll find that it is made up of many different aromatic molecules and compounds, including esters, terpenes, ketones, lactones, organic compounds, and aldehydes. These are found in beer and food, and many of them naturally cross over, which can help us to create bridges of flavor between the drink and the food. Below are some of the most common:

HOPS contain a variety of different oils and each of these has a different flavor. The common oils in all varieties are myrcene, humulene, farnesene, and caryophyllene (see the table below). Others include linalool (floral, orange, aniseed; found in oranges, cilantro/fresh coriander, and basil); limonene (floral and citrus; found in lemons, pepper, fennel, and grapefruit); pinene (resinous, spicy; found in rosemary, curry leaf, and mint); and citral (lemon, orange; found in limes and lemongrass).

HOP OIL	HIGH IN HOP VARIETY	FLAVOR	FOUND IN FOOD
MYRCENE	CITRA, SIMCOE, MANY AUS/NZ HOPS	RESINOUS, HERBAL, SPICY	THYME, BAY, MANGO
HUMULENE	NOBLE HOPS, NORTHDOWN, GOLDINGS	HERBAL, WOODY, SPICY	CILANTRO (FRESH CORIANDER), CLOVES, BASIL
FARNESENE	NOBLE HOPS	SPICY, CITRUS, FLORAL	GRAPEFRUIT, ORANGE, GINGER
CARYOPHYLLENE	GOLDINGS, BRAMLING CROSS, APOLLO	WOODY, PEPPERY	ROSEMARY, BLACK PEPPER, CLOVES

YEAST Through the action of fermentation, a range of different aromas and flavors are produced. Often, we don't want them to be there—flavors such as apple, butter, roses, and nail-polish remover are undesirable—but certain yeast-produced qualities, in certain beer styles, add important flavors. These shared qualities can point toward natural bridges of flavor. The most relevant is a 4-vinyl guaiacol, a phenol that gives a clove-like flavor. It's often found in Hefeweizen and Witbier, plus similar qualities come from barrel-aged beers and smoked food. Isoamyl acetate smells like bananas or pear drops. It is often found in Hefeweizen and gives a natural fruity flavor. You might also find tropical fruit, aniseed, bubble gum, and others; their general fruitiness can be very nice with foods that share a similar fruitiness.

THE MAILLARD REACTION Put a piece of steak on a hot griddle, cook it for two minutes, then turn it over: it'll be brown in color, grill-marked, and a lot tastier than when it was raw. This is known as the Maillard Reaction. It happens when proteins and sugars interact with each other on being heated, changing the color of the food and also giving new aromas and flavors. This reaction takes place on meat, on toast, coffee, French fries, and the production of malt, which means that there are naturally shared flavors between beer and baked foods, grilled foods, fried foods, and coffee, plus many more.

AROMA, TASTE, TEXTURE, AND FLAVOR

By chewing on some food, or rolling some beer across the tongue, we pick up the sensation of touch, we recognize the basic tastes (sweet, bitter, sour, salty, umami), and a load of aromas ping around and find their way to the olfactory bulb. The combination of these factors creates our impression of flavor.

AROMA

Made up of many volatile compounds, aroma is like a jigsaw as it comes together to complete a whole picture. The aromatic compounds are rarely unique to one ingredient and will be found in a large variety of foods, which is why some beers smell like chocolate or lime without those items coming anywhere near the brewing process. We pick out these aromas in beer as the brain flicks through all the scents it remembers and matches them to similar things. For example, the fruity aromas of a Hefeweizen are largely due to the esters from the yeast; these esters are also naturally found in fruit, explaining why we can smell banana or pear.

Aroma is key to flavor. One good experiment that demonstrates its impact is to pinch your nose and then to take a mouthful of beer or food and swallow it, never unpinching your nose (this might make your ears pop); you will get almost no sense of flavor, but you will pick up on sensation and taste (fatty, fizzy; sweet, bitter). Take another mouthful with your nose still pinched, then release your nose before you swallow and you'll get a burst of flavor, particularly as you breathe in—it's the "retro-nasal" inhalation that carries much of the aroma.

The sense of smell, and therefore flavor, also has a hardwired link to the part of the brain that deals with memory and emotion. This explains why some smells are particularly powerful for us: homemade cakes, certain perfumes, Proust's Madeleine, a fragrant Pilsner, which makes you pine for Prague, or an IPA so citrusy that your brain bolts to California.

THE FIVE TASTES

1. BITTER Bitterness is an evolutionary sign of potential poison, which should be rejected, so it's understandably something that takes some getting used to: children will drink lemonade, but not tonic water; they'll eat carrots, but not chicory. We generally acquire a taste for bitterness as we mature (there are also more bitter receptors on the tongue than any other taste, so we're physiologically designed to be sensitive to it).

Beer's bitterness comes primarily from hops (plus some from the roasted bitterness of dark malt). Some beers are extraordinarily bitter, while others are not so. A key consideration with bitterness is that it can be balanced. Think of it like this: make a large pot of strong coffee and pour it into four cups; leave one black, have one black with sugar, add milk to another, and milk and sugar to the fourth. It's the same coffee in the cups but they all taste different as the fat and sweetness balance the bitterness. The same works with sweetness in beer and two brews could taste very different even if they technically have the same levels of bitterness.

Imagine two 5.0% ABV brews, each with 50 bitterness units (a generic mainstream lager is 10–15 international bitterness units, or IBUs; most IPAs are 50–70 IBUs). One of the beers is a dry Pilsner, the other is a malty Scotch Ale; even though they have the same amount of measured bitterness, one tastes much more bitter than the other.

With food, fat, salt, and sweetness can all balance beer's bitterness.

2. SWEET Something sweet means the food or drink contains energy and goodness, which we're innately drawn toward, so, unlike bitter tastes, it's easy to like and crave for sweetness.

Beer's sweetness comes from the grain, as starches in the malt are converted into sugars during the brewing process. The yeast then converts those sugars into alcohol, although some sugars always remain and they contribute to balance, flavor, and mouthfeel. Some beers finish very dry (Pilsners, Wild Ales), whereas others can have more residual sweetness (Imperial Stout, Scotch Ale, Sweet Stout). Sweetness can be either overt or subtle and it often increases with alcohol content.

With food, sweetness can balance spice and richness.

3. SOUR Usually a sign that things aren't quite right: the milk has gone bad, the meat is too old, or the fruit isn't for eating.

In beer, sourness depends on appropriateness: is it meant to be sour or not? If it is, then you can expect anything from a tang of tartness up to an eye-watering and challenging acidity. Some people love it, others hate it, and, like bitter beers, sour beers are an acquired taste. Sourness is typically given to beer by bacteria or wild yeast, which naturally also give some fairly unusual (and sometimes unappealing) aromas. Those wild yeasts will voraciously eat lots of the sugars, meaning that the beers tend to be dry.

With food, we want salt or fat to work with the puckering sharpness. The acidity can be good for the appetite, making us feel hungry.

4. SALTY Not something you'll taste in many beers, although the salt and mineral content of the brewing water will have an impact on flavor. In food, salt has the ability to enhance flavor and also to balance bitterness by bringing out sweetness, which is why it's sometimes added to semi-sweet (dark) chocolate.

Salty food is great with beer; first, the food makes us thirsty, then the salt makes the beer taste less bitter.

5. UMAMI This is a rich, savory, and meaty taste. High-umami foods include soy sauce, aged cheese, cured meat, mushrooms, tomatoes, and oily fish. It works as a booster to other flavors (which is why a cheeseburger with ketchup is tastier than a plain hamburger), plus, it's naturally tasty on its own. Grain and yeast both have an inherent savory depth, albeit subtle and in the background, which tends to become more dominant in darker beers. Caramel sweetness is good with umami, although it generally works as a background flavor-enhancer to everything.

TRIGEMINAL SENSATIONS

The tongue doesn't just experience the five tastes; it also has to deal with different textures and sensations.

TOUCH AND TEMPERATURE Think about a glass of hot water, one of room-temperature sparkling water, and one of cold milk; their textures and temperatures are very different and they combine to have a big impact on flavor. For an interesting experiment, eat some hot chili followed by a mouthful of each of those drinks and the sensation and taste will differ vastly: the warm water becomes unpleasantly hot, the sparkling water is aggravating, and the cold milk is cooling. Beer works in similar ways, with temperature, mouthfeel, and carbonation (plus warm, flat beer just doesn't taste as good as cold, carbonated beer).

HOT HOT HOT! If you've ever chopped up a chili, and then rubbed your eye, you'll know that it feels as if it's burning; when we eat chili, we have the same sensation of burning—it just happens on our lips and tongue. Chili heat is an irritation, which we sense as burning pain. It isn't physically burning us; instead, it's evoking the feeling of a burn, and we can become acclimatized to it as our sensory fibers become numb to this type of pain, meaning that over time we can handle more heat.

KEEP IT COOL! Cucumber, avocado, mint, cilantro (fresh coriander), and yogurt are all ingredients that leave a zing of freshness, which we perceive as coolness. These provide balance of flavor, particularly to chili heat.

ASTRINGENT TANNINS If you've drunk strong tea, some red wines, or eaten unripe bananas, then you'll be familiar with the feeling of tannins. It's a kind of puckering sensation that makes your mouth feel dry.

PUNGENT Mustard, horseradish, ginger, and pepper, plus raw onion and garlic, are all pungent in their aroma and flavor. They are similar to chili in that they can be irritants.

CAPSAICIN VERSUS HOPS VERSUS CARBONATION

It's worth looking more closely at chili heat, particularly because a lot of hop-heads are also chili-freaks.

The burning sensation from a chili comes from capsaicin and its level of potency is measured on the Scoville Scale: a bell (sweet) pepper is 0, Tabasco sauce is around 4,000, a Scotch bonnet can reach 300,000, and some super chilis have passed two million Scovilles. While capsaicin can cause pain, it's a fickle thing, as it's also capable

of releasing endorphins to give us a heightened rush of pleasure to combat that pain.

Capsaicin is insoluble in water, but soluble in fatty, sugary, and alcoholic substances, so a glass of milk is better than a glass of water if you need to cool down a curry. (This is also the reason why yogurt, cheese, coleslaw, coconut, and avocado sometimes come with hot foods.) Capsaicin creates temporary inflammation in whatever it touches, making the area extra sensitive for a few minutes. Some things are gentle against this inflammation (such as dairy products), others will irritate it: carbonation pokes at the burn and increases the hot sensation; bitterness seems to scream and punch at the inflamed and sensitive areas; and high levels of booze can increase the burn, rather like rubbing alcohol into a fresh cut.

Personally, I find that bitter beer, like IPA, is very often terrible and uncomfortable with spicy food; it's like hops and capsaicin are fighting and causing pain, instead of pleasure. A far better approach for feisty, spicy food is beer that is low in carbonation, low in bitterness, moderate in alcohol, and has plenty of residual sweetness, which is why Sweet Stout, Helles, Dunkel, and Hefeweizen tend to work very well with chili heat. Some very hoppy beers can work really well with heat, but they need sweetness.

SIGHT AND SOUND

While taste, smell, and touch are the main contributors to flavor and to our appreciation of something delicious, sight and sound also have an impact.

When looking at a glass of beer, we have certain expectations: a hazy, muddy brown beer doesn't look as tasty as a bright golden pint, while a green or blue beer would challenge our preconceptions of flavor. Plus, imagine you're really thirsty or hungry, and you see a picture of a beautiful-looking beer or sandwich; the picture makes you want to drink or eat it, so increasing anticipation and desire.

You might not hear much when it comes to beer, but the popping of a cap followed by the fizzing sound is always nice (as is the glug of a beer being poured or the gulp of a big mouthful going down). With food, the crunch of a potato chip or the crisp bite of fresh salad leaves are important to show freshness and texture, and those sounds generally make the food more appetizing.

THE PRINCIPLES OF PAIRING BEER AND FOOD

When you want to enjoy beer and food together, and find matches that go beyond simply being "not bad," then you need to take into consideration a few of the qualities of beer to figure out how they'll interact with whatever you're eating.

INTENSITY You don't put a Helles with a semi-sweet (dark) chocolate brownie, just as an Imperial Stout won't work well with a piece of poached white fish. Each dish and drink has its own intensity and weight, and it's good to try to find a balance between them.

TEXTURE Do you want a light, dry beer or one with a full body? A general rule is that a beer with a full or smooth body will work better with food than a thin beer, especially with rich flavors such as cream or cheese, although a dry, crisp beer can provide a counterpoint to fatty or salty food.

CARBONATION Beer has bubbles and, when they burst, they give a pop to flavors and lift richness. Bubbles are refreshing, especially with big, heavy flavors. But watch out for high carbonation if you've got very spicy food, because the bubbles can irritate the chili burn.

BITTERNESS Beer is bitter, we know that, and we should embrace this because bitterness is as refreshing as acidity and carbonation, particularly with salt and fat. Bitterness also tends to work well with other bitter flavors and likes sweetness—a Porter with charred meat, semi-sweet (dark) chocolate with Stout, or IPA with carrot cake.

SWEETNESS All beer has some sweetness. Very sweet beers actually work surprisingly well with most things, but are best with spice, sweetness, or richness.

ACIDITY Wine's one-up over beer is that it has acidity, which is quenching and hunger-inducing. Look to Wild Ales and European Sours for beers with acidity. They are great with fat and salt, plus bitterness.

ALCOHOL CONTENT Generally, the stronger the beer, the stronger the flavors in it. Alcohol can sometimes be too dominant in a pairing, particularly with sweet or spicy food. Beers of around 9.0% ABV are often better paired with rich foods—fatty meats, fried food, cheeses, and desserts—because the two key tools to balance booze are fat and salt.

DON'T WORRY ABOUT...

COLOR Just because a beer is very pale blonde doesn't mean that it'll taste of nothing. In the same way, just because a beer is as black as coal doesn't mean it'll taste that way. There are no soundbyte rules that say "blonde beer with fish, amber beer with chicken, dark beer with steak." Color doesn't dictate a pairing.

TEMPERATURE I serve all my beer, no matter what it is, straight out of a regular refrigerator. That's my preference. If you like beer at room temperature, then pour it at room temperature. The science of taste tells us that temperature does have an impact on appreciation (a very cold beer reveals less flavor than a cool one), but, really, it's more important that you enjoy the experience.

UNSUCCESSFUL PAIRINGS You carefully chose a beer to go with dinner, but it doesn't come together as a great pairing. So what? Forget it because it doesn't matter. Just finish the food and then have the beer, or go and open another bottle. Next time you cook that recipe, try something else. You won't always get it right, but you'll still have a nice meal and a nice beer, just independently.

WINE Beer and wine are not the same thing, so don't try to compare them. You wouldn't compare cheese and chocolate because, even though some share similar flavors (cream, fruit, acidity) in certain types, they are vastly different things made in completely different ways. Beer and wine are both brilliant, but they do different things with food.

A NEW APPROACH TO BEER AND FOOD

Think about the Three B's: Bridge, Balance, and Boost. Now, consider these three combinations: bitter (dark) chocolate with coffee; bitter chocolate with chili; bitter chocolate with sour cherry. The chocolate is the same in each example; it's dark, bitter, and naturally a little bit fruity. With coffee, there's a **bridge** between the bitter cocoa and the roasted bean. With the chili, you get heat, which threatens to overpower, but the fat in the chocolate gives it **balance** and stops either ingredient from dominating, while still tasting great together and letting their individual flavors through. Sour cherry gives a **boost** to all the roasted flavors in bitter chocolate, but also enhances a whole range of fruitiness in the chocolate.

Thinking about Bridge, Balance, and Boost are how I approach beer and food. Sometimes they overlap, other times one particular approach becomes the best one, but you'll always be able to find a few beers that'll work differently with each dish. I use the Three B's throughout *Beer and Food* and they are described in detail on the next page.

THE THREE B'S OF BEER AND FOOD

Bridge, Balance, and Boost; remember these three concepts when trying to match your beer with food and you'll always achieve successful results.

BRIDGE This is chocolate with coffee. It's Belgian Quadrupel with fruit cake. It's Thai curry with the lime-like hops of a New Zealand Pilsner. It's the sweetly caramelized flavor of roasted veg with American Pale Ale. This approach aims to find similarities in both the beer and the food that pulls them together by hoisting a bridge between the two. That bridge naturally helps to bring the flavors together, although we still need to consider intensity and texture—a thin and weak Stout, even though it has a roasty and chocolatey flavor, won't work with a gooey chocolate brownie.

You can focus on something small and specific, such as a shared ingredient or flavor (Witbier with a dish using ground coriander, for example), or it could be a more general bridge, like pouring a Porter with barbecued food, where the roasted malt shares grilled flavors with the meat.

HERE ARE SOME BEER STYLES AND EXAMPLES OF FLAVORS THAT BRIDGE:

PILSNER	LEMON, WOODY HERBS, FRESH OR TOASTED BREAD
DUNKEL	GRILLED MEAT, TOAST, ROAST VEGETABLES
WITBIER	CILANTRO (FRESH CORIANDER), LEMON, LEMONGRASS, GINGER
HEFEWEIZEN	TOASTED NUTS, YOGURT, BEANS
SAISON	PEPPER, FENNEL, ARUGULA (ROCKET), GARLIC, APPLE
BELGIAN DARK/QUAD	DRIED FRUIT, CINNAMON, CHOCOLATE, PEPPER
AMERICAN PALE ALE	CITRUS FRUIT, ROASTED ONION, ROSEMARY, THYME
PACIFIC IPA	LIME, CILANTRO (FRESH CORIANDER), MINT, LEMONGRASS
SMOKED BEER	ROASTED MEAT, BACON, CLOVES, PAPRIKA
IMPERIAL STOUT	CHOCOLATE, COFFEE, VANILLA, BERRIES

BALANCE This is chocolate with chili. It's a smooth Hefeweizen with spicy chicken tacos; a malty Brown Ale with rich mac 'n' cheese; herb-roasted belly pork with the sharp carbonation of a Tripel.

This keeps everything between the beer and food controlled by balancing and softening bold flavors and not letting anything overpower, while still pushing the individual elements forward. And, if you get it right, you'll also get a boost of flavor.

Two strong characters, when put together, can clash. What seems like a great idea at first turns into a loser-takes-all fight, and we want to avoid that. This approach typically starts with the food, as you are aiming to find a beer that can emphasize certain flavors and balance others, as if adding shading and highlights to make everything stand out in the right ways. This lifts the richness of fat, stops salt taking over, lightens deep-fried food, carves through creaminess, and keeps chili in check.

Some ingredients help us by providing balance: avocado, rice, yogurt, coleslaw, bread, ketchup, coconut, cream, apple, fennel, cucumber, and others. These add a cooling quality, give a sensation of freshness, and can calm heat and alcohol—they tend to work alongside the beers, like a superhero's sidekick.

Here are a few examples of balanced beer and food pairings:

SALT *BALANCES* BITTERNESS: Try Pale Ale with fried chicken, Pilsner with pretzels.

SWEETNESS AND FAT *BALANCE* BITTERNESS: Try carrot cake and American IPA, blueberry muffin with coffee Stout.

FAT AND SALT *BALANCE* ALCOHOL (AND BITTERNESS): Try Double IPA with French fries, blue cheese with Imperial Stout.

SWEETNESS AND A FULL BODY *BALANCE* CHILI HEAT: Try Milk Stout with jerk chicken, Hefeweizen with jalfrezi curry.

ACIDITY AND CARBONATION *BALANCE* OILY, FATTY, SMOKY FOODS: Try Gueuze with mackerel, Saison with belly pork.

BITTERNESS AND CARBONATION *BALANCE* RICHNESS: Try Tripel and pâté, Pilsner with fried fish.

SWEETNESS *BALANCES* SWEETNESS: Try Imperial Stout with vanilla cheesecake, Quadrupel with cookies.

SWEETNESS *BALANCES* UMAMI: Try IPA with a cheeseburger, Oatmeal Stout with spaghetti and meatballs.

ROASTED BITTERNESS *BALANCES* ACIDITY: Try Porter with buffalo wings, Imperial Stout with lemon meringue pie.

BOOST This is chocolate with sour cherry. It's Cheddar cheese with American IPA, where a whole basket of fruit bursts forward. It's Saison with Vietnamese food, as the dry spiciness makes everything taste so fresh. It's a crème brûlée with a sour raspberry beer.

In this we want to make the beer like a missing ingredient in the food, which, when put together, gives it a big boost of new flavors that are tastier than their constituent parts. It's not the easiest of things to get right, but it's definitely the most rewarding, and gives some of the most spectacular and surprising matches.

Here are ten great boost pairings:
1. Semi-sweet (dark) chocolate with sweet-and-sour cherry beer
2. Steak, parsnips, and horseradish with Oatmeal Stout
3. Stilton with Barley Wine
4. Black bean sauce with Belgian Dubbel
5. Smoked ham with dry farmhouse Cider
6. Strong Cheddar cheese with American IPA
7. Sausages with Belgian Red
8. Smoked chicken with American Pale Ale
9. Grilled mackerel and lemon with Rauchbier
10. Thai green curry with hoppy American Wheat

Look Beyond the Bs and Stay Local
Another consideration is to match the food to where a beer was brewed or where a style originates. Bridge, Balance, and Boost still apply, but they now work with a local focus. In general, taking this approach is good because freshness is very important with both beer and food.

Some suggestions include Belgian Carbonnade with a Dubbel, moules frites with Witbier, pretzel and Helles, weisswurst and Hefeweizen, schnitzel and Pilsner, Scotch egg and a pint of Bitter, meat pie and Porter, Cal-Mex quesadilla and Pale Ale.

2 BEER STYLES

The main part of this book is split into two chapters: Beer Styles and Matching Food and Beer. This Beer Styles chapter (see pages 36–107) approaches the concept of combining beer and food by looking at the beer first. This means that you know what the drink tastes like and want to choose something that works well with it, whether this is a simple snack or a complete dish. The beers in this section have been chosen because they are excellent examples of the style, as well as beers that taste great and have a great story. Matching Food and Beer (see pages 108–161) looks at the food first, focusing on popular and well-known dishes, and makes suggestions for beers that will work well with them.

The great thing about beer and food is that there are no real rules. These are simply the best matches I know for each entry and you can either use that as a guide (by finding the exact beer or a similar brew in the same style) or as inspiration to find something that will taste even better. For many of these matches I've opened a few beers with each dish, just to see which works best and why, and that's a fun way to approach beer and food combinations, as you can see which qualities are good or bad together.

And here's something important to consider: a beer that you love will taste great with anything. So, I think it's better to have a beer you enjoy, even if it isn't necessarily a brilliant match for the food, than to have a beer that you don't really like just because someone says it works fantastically well with a particular dish. Also, we all taste and experience things differently. If I taste pineapple and tangerine in an IPA, but you taste mango and grapefruit, that doesn't make either of us wrong; we're both right because taste is subjective and individual.

Enjoy beer and food, enjoy how well they can work together, and, if you don't like a match, who cares? Just eat the food and then drink the beer.

Opposite is a useful flavor wheel that I've designed as a way to look at and understand the aromas, flavors, and tastes of different beers, and to help you see where these elements might be coming from.

BEER FLAVOR WHEEL

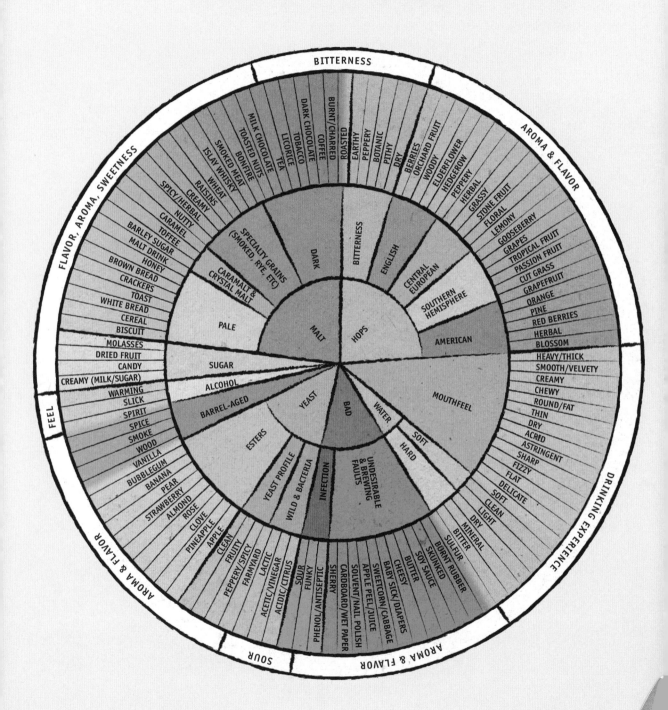

PALE LAGER

AROUND 95% OF BEERS DRUNK AROUND THE WORLD ARE PALE LAGERS. UNFORTUNATELY, MUCH OF THIS IS LIGHT IN FLAVOR AND CHOSEN BECAUSE OF BRAND OR PRICE RATHER THAN DELICIOUSNESS, WHICH UNDERMINES THE FACT THAT THIS IS ONE OF THE GREATEST AND MOST INTERESTING STYLES, WHERE LOOKING BEYOND THE OBVIOUS REVEALS A FANTASTIC, VARIED, AND EXCITING RANGE OF BEERS.

BRIDGE: CAESAR SALAD, JERK SPICES, LEMON AND HERB CHICKEN

BALANCE: FRIED AND OILY FISH, CHILI SPICE, PAD THAI

BOOST: MOZZARELLA WITH TOMATO AND BASIL, FRIED POTATOES, ROAST PORK

LOCAL: PORK SCHNITZEL, BRATWURST, HOT DOG

AVOID: ANY DESSERT

The best Pale Lagers have a subtle richness of malt, intoxicating citrusy, grassy, and floral aromas, a satisfying, quenching finish, and wonderful balance of malt and hop. They aren't big impact beers but they are capable of being utterly unforgettable in their easy-drinking magnificence. The two main styles joined here are Pilsner and Helles—Pilsner provides a dry cut of bitterness and carbonation while Helles has a comfort of malt richness. They are both capable of handling full-on flavors, but are equally agile with delicate dishes. Pale Lagers can be some of the most versatile beers, capable of working with a huge range of foods.

SCHÖNRAMER HELL

TRY WITH: **THAI YELLOW CURRY**

BREWED IN: SCHÖNRAM, GERMANY
ABV: 5.0%

Schönramer's Hell is straw colored and light on malt sweetness, but still comes with the sort of satisfying mouthfeel you expect from a Bavarian beer. The hops are clean and dry with a touch of pithy and herbal bitterness making it a classic quencher that, for me, is more interesting than many of the more famous Pale Lagers brewed in the region. The pairing of Lager and curry may be ubiquitous and clichéd, but they genuinely work well together, so we should embrace it and look for the best matches possible. In this case, I want to bring the Hell together with this fragrant lemongrass and ginger-scented curry where the hops balance the spices and creaminess while the malt body softens the sear of chili.

FIRESTONE WALKER PILS

TRY WITH: **FISH TACOS**

BREWED IN: PASO ROBLES, CALIFORNIA
ABV: 5.3%

Pilsner is one of my favorite beer styles. It's something I'll never ignore if I see it on the bar, if only to try to find the beautiful dance of malt and hops that I know the style is capable of. Firestone Walker's Pils is a brilliant beer that showcases how fantastic German hops (Magnum, Spalter Select, Saphir) can be when added in large quantities, showing off stone fruit, lime, lush tropical fruit, and floral grassiness before a long, dry bitterness. It's great with avocado-topped fish tacos, doused in hot salsa. The hops are fragrant like the herbs and spices, while the avocado (which has a grassiness to match that in the hops) calms everything down and lets the sweetness of the fish come through.

ÚNĚTICKÉ PIVO 12° NEFILTROVANÉ

TRY WITH: PORK SCHNITZEL

BREWED IN: ÚNĚTICE, CZECH REPUBLIC
ABV: 5.0%

In the Czech Republic you get Světlý Ležák, which falls somewhere between Pilsner and Helles in its depth, drinkability, and elegance. The brewery name is pronounced "oon-yeh-tits-keh" and it's worth the trouble to try to say it because they make great beer. The unfiltered 12° is pale gold and slightly hazy. There's an impossible-to-describe freshness—a mix of spring air alongside stone and citrus fruits—and the body is soft and satisfying yet still light and quenching. It's a modern classic unfiltered Lager. The smooth body is what makes this great with food, especially something like pork schnitzel, which is breadcrumbed and fried and has a buttery richness (freshened with a squeeze of lemon), which the fruity hop in the beer balances and boosts. Can't get Únětické? Any unfiltered Lager works almost as well.

SAMUEL ADAMS NOBLE PILS

TRY WITH: LOADED HOT DOGS

BREWED IN: BOSTON, MASSACHUSETTS
ABV: 4.9%

Having watched baseball on TV for a few years while at university, my friend Matt and I are among the minority of British people who love America's national pastime. For the first game we attended, we paid for great seats behind the plate, which were leather-cushioned and came with in-seat service. When asked what we'd like, we simply said, "Two of the best beers you have," and our server brought us a couple of bottles of Noble Pils. Brightly, boldly hoppy, it demonstrated perfectly the characteristics of classic noble varieties: lemon, stone fruit, and resinous herbs. Have it with a loaded hot dog, piled high with soft onions, mustard, and ketchup, because the hops balance the sweet-sour condiments and the sweet-salty onion. It's simple, it's obvious, but it's still a grand slam pairing.

HARVIESTOUN SCHIEHALLION

TRY WITH: SPICY WHITEBAIT

BREWED IN: ALVA, SCOTLAND
ABV: 4.8%

Unusual for a Lager, you can find Schiehallion (pronounced "she-hal-yun") served from cask, keg, and bottle. All share a wonderful hoppiness, which is floral, spicy, and citrusy in the aroma and flavor. The difference comes in the mouthfeel. The cask version is smoother and more delicate whereas the keg and bottle are zippier and sharper. The cask Lager is great with lemon and herb chicken, while the keg and bottle are best with tiny whitebait that are covered in cayenne pepper and flour before being fried. This is one of my favorite beer snacks; the salty-hot crunch of the fried fish is so good with Schiehallion's refreshing bubbles and spicy, citrusy hop flavor. Add a squeeze of fresh lemon to the fish and it brings everything together perfectly. It tastes even better if you're sitting in the sun.

DARK LAGER

SOME BEER STYLES ARE SIMPLY BRILLIANT WITH FOOD; YOU CAN PUT THEM WITH ALMOST ANYTHING AND THEY JUST WORK. DARK LAGER IS ONE OF THOSE STYLES. IT'S GOT MALT DEPTH, BUT NOT SO MUCH THAT IT DOMINATES; IT'S GOT THE TOASTY, NUTTY FLAVOR OF PALE MALT, PLUS A LITTLE ROAST FROM DARK MALT, WHICH MIRRORS THE CARAMELIZATION THAT COMES FROM COOKING; AND IT USUALLY HAS A LIFT OF CARBONATION, A REFRESHING BITTERNESS, AND A QUENCHING DRINKABILITY, ALL OF WHICH KEEP IT LIGHT. IT CAN WORK WITH SUBTLE FOOD, SPICY FOOD, SWEET FOOD, OR SOUR FOOD... IT'S A BEER AND FOOD SUPERSTAR. THE STYLE IS THE ORIGINAL LAGER BEER AND RECALLS A TIME WHEN ALL BEERS WOULD'VE BEEN DARK, BUT NOW THE BEST DON'T HAVE A DARK MALT DOMINANCE IN THE FLAVOR. INSTEAD, THERE'S A SUGGESTION OF FULLNESS, RICHNESS, AND CARAMEL, WHICH DOESN'T OVERPOWER THE CLEAN MALT DEPTH OF A CLASSIC LAGER. YOU MIGHT GET DUNKEL, WHICH ARE RED-BROWN IN COLOR, OR SCHWARZBIER, WHICH ARE A LOT DARKER AND MAY HAVE A LITTLE COFFEE BITTERNESS TO THEM.

BRIDGE: GRILLED STEAK AND SMOKED MEAT, BLACKENED FISH, EGG FRIED RICE

BALANCE: MEXICAN FOOD, TOMATO-BASED CURRIES, ROAST PORK

BOOST: MOST JAPANESE FOOD, MOST SAVORY ITALIAN DISHES, MOST BARBECUE DISHES

LOCAL: ROAST PORK OR DUCK, BRATWURST AND SAUERKRAUT, GOULASH

AVOID: ANYTHING TOO SWEET, BUT OTHERWISE DARK LAGER CAN HANDLE IT

BUDVAR DARK

BEST WITH: ROAST DUCK, DUMPLINGS, AND RED CABBAGE

BREWED IN: ČESKÉ BUDĚJOVICE, CZECH REPUBLIC
ABV: 4.7%

The Czech Republic is rightly known for being one of the best brewing nations in the world. It is not, however, known for its culinary excellence. Instead, you'll get huge hunks of roast meat, dense dumplings, and pickled cabbage. Thankfully, this is exactly what you want to eat when drinking Budvar Dark. It's deep brown in color with a tan foam; there's caramel, chocolate, roasted malt, a strong malt depth and satisfying body, and the teasing loveliness of Czech hops. With a roast duck leg and sharp braised red cabbage, the caramelized flavor in the meat matches that in the beer, while the dark malt can smother and sweeten the sourness in the cabbage. Any kind of roast meat is buddies with Budvar Dark.

ASAHI BLACK

BEST WITH: FRIED GYOZA

BREWED IN: TOKYO, JAPAN
ABV: 5.0%

Japanese food is wonderful with Dark Lager and, as Asahi Black is widely available, it's the beer to look out for—it's what I always order in Japanese restaurants. Pan-fried gyoza (the fried part gives crunch and caramelization) are little dumplings of meat/fish and vegetables with garlic, sesame oil, and ginger as dominant flavors. They are dipped in soy and chili sauce, and Asahi Black's clean body, distant hint of dark savory roast, and nuttiness work to balance and boost all the flavors. It doesn't interfere, doesn't dominate, doesn't stamp all over the place like an angry sumo wrestler; it just quietly does a brilliant job of working with your dinner. It's universally good with savory Japanese food.

UINTA BABA

BEST WITH: FIVE-SPICE RIBS

BREWED IN: SALT LAKE CITY, UTAH
ABV: 4.0%

While researching this book, I got some mates together and we ordered ten different spicy takeaway dishes and poured 16 different beers. The aim was to try different combinations of everything to see what did and didn't work together. It was at this gathering, while drinking Baba, that we realized how much of a hero Dark Lager is with dinner. It wrapped around heat, it balanced sweetness, and it boosted caramel flavors, while the hops bridged spices—and all in a modest ABV. Baba has cocoa, a little caramel, some chocolate milk, and floral hops, plus it's superbly balanced. With five-spice-dusted pork ribs, it was amazing. The fragrant hops made the aniseed spice more vibrant and the pork was boosted by the dark malt.

ESCHENBRÄU DUNKEL

BEST WITH: FLAMMKUCHEN

BREWED IN: BERLIN, GERMANY
ABV: 5.3%

Eschenbräu is a small brewpub hidden away in the basement of a student apartment block in Berlin. It can be tricky to find, but it's worth the search because the beers are excellent. The brewpub's Pils is slightly hazy, it's got a lemon-pith hop aroma, the body has a lush creaminess, and then the bitterness is dry and sharp. The Dunkel is a classic Bavarian-style in that it's deep copper in color and the malt has a hint of toffee apple before the hops finish it with a refreshing lightness. At the brewpub, they serve flammkuchen, which are thin dough bases covered with smoked ham and cream cheese. The char from the oven, plus the bacon smoke, hold hands with the dark malt, while the fruitiness in the hops gets together with the cheese. If you don't fancy flammkuchen, you can take your own food into Eschenbräu and find your perfect match.

MOONLIGHT DEATH & TAXES

BEST WITH: QUESADILLA

BREWED IN: SANTA ROSA, CALIFORNIA
ABV: 5.0%

This is a remarkably good Schwarzbier and sits next to Moonlight's remarkably good Pilsner, Reality Czeck. Both have wonderfully full bodies that make you want to drink more, both have wonderful aromas (cocoa and vanilla in Death & Taxes and floral orange pith in Reality Czeck), and both are excellent with food. The smoothness of Death & Taxes, plus a little toffee sweetness and just a hint of roast, makes it a versatile food beer. Barbecue works brilliantly, but the Latin influence of California gives the best match for this beer. Quesadilla, or toasted tortilla sandwiches of cheese and chili, are what I want. You get the charred outside of the tortilla, which bridges the dark grain, while the rich cheese filling is boosted by the caramel and fragrant hops in the beer. It's a great beer snack combo.

NEW WORLD LAGER

AN ESSENTIAL AND WONDERFUL QUALITY OF A GREAT LAGER IS A SIMPLE AND CLEAN MALT BODY, WHICH IS RICH IN TEXTURE AND YET STILL LIGHT. NEW WORLD LAGERS HAVE A TEASING BALANCE BETWEEN MALT AND HOPS, WHERE THEY TAKE THAT CLASSIC CLARITY OF FLAVOR AND ADD NEW WORLD HOPS, WHICH GIVES CITRUS AND TROPICAL-FRUIT QUALITIES—THEY'RE A SORT OF MID-POINT BETWEEN PILSNER AND PALE ALE. A FURTHER DEVELOPMENT ON THIS INCLUDES IMPERIAL LAGERS, WHICH ARE 6.0% ABV OR ABOVE AND SHOW WHAT HAPPENS WHEN YOU TAKE A LAGER AND BLOW IT UP INTO A BIGGER, BOLDER THING, ALMOST LIKE THE MID-POINT BETWEEN PILSNER AND IPA. NEW WORLD LAGERS ARE FUN AND EASY-GOING, WITH A VIBRANT FRESHNESS THAT POINTS TOWARD THE SORT OF DISHES YOU SHOULD EAT WITH THEM, WHERE FRUITINESS IN THE FOOD CAN BE ENHANCED BY THE HOPS IN THE BEER.

BRIDGE: WHITE FISH WITH MANGO SALSA, ROAST CHICKEN WITH LIME, VIETNAMESE SALAD

BALANCE: NASI LEMAK, SPICY CRAB CAKES, FRIED SEAFOOD

BOOST: PARMESAN (AND OTHER AGED CHEESES), COCONUT-BASED CURRIES, PORK BURGER

LOCAL: FISH TACOS, FRESH SEAFOOD, BAR SNACKS

AVOID: MILK CHOCOLATE

CAMDEN TOWN BREWERY USA HELLS

BEST WITH: FRIED DOUGH, PARMA HAM, AND PARMESAN CHEESE

BREWED IN: LONDON, ENGLAND
ABV: 4.6%

When working at Camden Town, this was the beer I always ordered at the end of the day. It takes the brewery's flagship Hells Lager and uses lots of American hops in place of the German hops with which it's usually brewed, and then it's left unfiltered. It's a hazy pale gold, the aroma is pineapple, tangerine, and peach, and it finishes with juicy fruit and pithy bitterness. There's a bar at the brewery and food trucks stop outside. One of these, Gurmetti, had little pockets of fried Italian dough stuffed with freshly carved Parma ham and a Parmesan cream. They're incredible with USA Hells: the fruity pineapple notes in the Parmesan, ham, and the beer combine in the most perfect of ways. Look out for a stronger version of this beer called Indian Hells—it rocks!

SEPTEM MONDAY'S PILSNER

BEST WITH: FRIED SQUID OR BARBECUED OCTOPUS

BREWED IN: EVIA, GREECE
ABV: 5.0%

While mass-market lagers continue to dominate in Greece, there's been an increase in small craft breweries making a broader range of brews since the calendar passed into the 2010s. Septem is one of the best, and its judicious and clever use of hops shows off the skills of brewer, Sofoklis Panagiotou, who jumped from winemaking to brewing in order to open Septem. Monday's Pilsner is very pale blonde; New Zealand hops give a fresh, grape-like fruitiness and a little lemon, tangerine, and mango; and then you get a clean, dry, and quenching finish. It's very good with fried squid or barbecued octopus, covered in salt and lemon juice, as both celaphods have an inherent sweetness, which the fruity hops draw out. A cold glass of Pilsner and plate of squid or octopus, while sitting by the sea, is my idea of a dream lunch.

NEW BELGIUM SHIFT

BEST WITH: CRAB AND COCONUT CAKES

BREWED IN: FORT COLLINS, COLORADO
ABV: 5.0%

New Belgium Brewery is an impressive place with a brilliant tour and tasting room. It's one of the biggest craft breweries in America, yet still manages to be regarded as one of the best. Plus, it's regularly voted one of the best places to work by *Outside Magazine*: the brewery is entirely employee-owned; it is deeply committed to sustainability; and, when employees hit their one-year working anniversary, they are given a bike, which is pretty cool. Shift is a Pale Lager hopped with Target, Nelson Sauvin, Liberty, and Cascade, giving a great mix of leafy green hops and some soft citrus, backed up with a herbal, dry bitterness. With crab cakes made with dried coconut and chili, Shift is a great match: coconut is wonderful with these hops, while the toasty sweetness in the malt softens the chili kick.

TUATARA PILSNER

BEST WITH: LIME AND CHILI CRAYFISH

BREWED IN: WELLINGTON, NEW ZEALAND
ABV: 5.0%

New Zealand Pilsner, which is the original "New World Lager," has become its own beer category, thanks to a few fantastic examples of Pale Lagers brewed with local Kiwi hops. A lot of these hops have a European parentage, so there's an underlying quality that aligns them to lagers (floral, pepper, delicate citrus), then whacks on the sort of fruity fragrance you'd expect to find in an NZ Sauvignon Blanc wine. Tuatara's Pilsner uses four of the most famous New Zealand hops—Pacific Jade, Motueka, Nelson Sauvin, and Riwaka—to give a lush lime, mango, green bell pepper, and passionfruit aroma. With the zest and zing of lime and chili, the beer gives a glorious fruitiness in the background and a caramel-like sweetness to go with the crayfish. Eat with your fingers and drink from the bottle.

MOON DOG LOVE TAP

BEST WITH: CURRIED RICE AND SEAFOOD SOUP

BREWED IN: ABBOTSFORD, AUSTRALIA
ABV: 5.9%

Love Tap is a cross between a "smashable lager and a hoppy IPA," and it's brewed with Aussie Galaxy, Kiwi Motueka, and German Tettnang hops, which give an almighty burst of citrus, floral, and tropical fruit, backed by the herbal, lemony Tettnang. The malt gives a toasty, toffee depth that wraps around the sweetness and spice in a curried rice and seafood soup—a thick broth of stock and coconut milk, garlic, ginger, classic curry spices, seafood, and rice, with lime and cilantro (fresh coriander) to finish—before the hops work like an extra squeeze of citrus. The brewery says this about Love Tap: "It has a pig on the label, wearing a hat, a monocle, and a bow tie. Very fancy pig indeed. Well suited to a very fancy beer." Only a fool would disagree.

STRONG LAGER

MÄRZEN, BOCK, AND DOPPELBOCK ARE STRONG LAGERS THAT HAVE SPENT MOST OF THEIR LIVES IN BAVARIA. WHEN YOU DRINK IN BAVARIA, YOU'LL FIND THAT MOST OF THE BEERS, FROM LIGHT HELLES TO BIG DOPPELBOCK, SHARE A DEEP, RICH MALT FLAVOR, BUT THEY ARE NEVER CHUBBY OR SWEET—IT'S MORE OF A FULL TEXTURE AND DEPTH OF MALT. THE BEERS RANGE FROM PALE GOLD TO NEARLY BLACK, ALTHOUGH MOST MEET AROUND THE COPPER COLOR. MÄRZEN AND BOCK TEND TO BE 5.5–6.5% ABV, WHILE DOPPELBOCK WILL BE 6.5–8% ABV. AS MALT MONOLOGS, YOU GET A LOT OF BREAD, TOFFEE, CHOCOLATE, AND DRIED-FRUIT FLAVORS, WHICH, ADDED TO THE MALT'S INHERENT SAVORINESS, MAKES THEM WORK WELL WITH A WIDE RANGE OF FOODS. BITTERNESS IS USUALLY LOW IN THESE STYLES, THE BODY IS BIG, AND THE AROMA IS LIKE WALKING INTO A BAKERY. IN FACT, THESE BEERS AREN'T FAR FROM BEING THE LIQUID EQUIVALENT OF A SANDWICH AND, IF YOU PUT MOST THINGS NEAR A SANDWICH, THEY WORK.

BRIDGE: APPLE CAKE, FRUIT CAKE, RAGÙ PASTA, GRILLED MEAT

BALANCE: MEXICAN FOOD, SAUERKRAUT, KOREAN FOOD

BOOST: LAMB TAGINE, BARBECUED RIBS, GRILLED CHEESE

LOCAL: ROAST PORK, BRATWURST, KÄSESPÄTZLE

AVOID: CITRUS, LIGHT DESSERTS

TRÖEGS TROEGENATOR

BEST WITH: BANANA BREAD

BREWED IN: HERSHEY, PENNSYLVANIA
ABV: 8.2%

Chocolate, caramel, toasted nuts, cherries, raisins, bread, peppery spice, and brown sugar... Just the tasting notes make me hungry for this one. Don't expect this to be sweet, however, as it's got a bitter, dry finish. The fact that it tastes like liquid fruit cake points it toward the bakery for the best match, and banana bread is a great choice. It gets the caramelized flavor of cooked banana, which works really well with the caramel, dried fruit, and nuttiness in the beer. An aged steak with blue cheese sauce is the savory option, as Troegenator's suggestion of sweetness can blast aside the blue cheese's powerful flavor and let the meat's caramelized char come through.

FÄSSLA ZWERGLA

BEST WITH: ROAST PORK

BREWED IN: BAMBERG, GERMANY
ABV: 6.0%

There are very few beers that don't work well with roast pork. It's a sweet, juicy meat that's not overpowering. It also has fattiness, and so loves the balancing abilities of carbonation and either hops or acidity. It's with Märzen and Bock that roast pork really belongs. These beers have caramel, toast, apple, spice, and smoke, and work like a sauce on the side of the dish. Fässla's Zwergla is a local pairing and a boost pairing; it's got balance and there's a bridge: it's a full house. If you go to Bamberg, and you really must go, then book one of the rooms at Fässla. They are cosy and affordable, and your morning wake-up call will come from the chimes of the bottling line before you head downstairs for a breakfast beer.

LAMBRATE PORPORA

BEST WITH: GNOCCHI
WITH SAGE BUTTER

BREWED IN: MILAN, ITALY
ABV: 7.8%

A red-amber pour with a full, creamy foam, Porpora is a hoppy Doppelbock that's got caramel, malt, and toasted nuts, and then a herbal freshness. Use the hops in this beer to bridge it to a big bowl of gnocchi cooked with butter, sage, garlic, and lots of Parmesan cheese. The deep resinous savoriness in the sage is softened by the sweetness in the beer, while the hops pick out its pepper—hops and sage share a few woody aromatic compounds, such as pinene and linalool, so they naturally fit together. The butter and cheese combine like a coat of richness, which means that the dish can handle the big body and alcohol. Porpora is also very good with panettone, the classic Milanese Christmas cake, in which the beer adds a herbal depth to the dried-fruit bread.

PAULANER SALVATOR

BEST WITH: SMOKED CHEESE
SANDWICH

BREWED IN: MUNICH, GERMANY
ABV: 7.9%

This is the original beer of the Paulaner brewery from the days when it was a monastery. When Salvator was first brewed, it was drunk by the monks as a substitute for food during Lent—it was their liquid bread. Today, at 71 calories per 3 US fl oz (100ml) of beer, it is still, quite literally, a liquid bread. There's dried fruit, cherries, roast apple, and plum in the aroma, the malt gives bread, toffee, and toast, and the hops have a definite earthy dryness, plus a little festive spiciness. I want to eat something really simple with this classic Doppelbock, a little snack that just makes all the flavors pop—and that's smoked cheese in a grilled sandwich with some sweet onion chutney. All the fruitiness in the lager goes straight for the savory smoke in the cheese and gives it a big boost of flavor.

ANCHOR BOCK

BEST WITH: ENCHILADAS

BREWED IN: SAN FRANCISCO, CALIFORNIA
ABV: 5.5%

Demonstrating the style's versatility, Anchor's Bock is a dark brown brew that's got a light and elegant depth of dark malt, some semi-sweet (dark) chocolate, molasses, a little toast, roasted orchard fruit, and a fresh hoppiness. With Mexican food, you find a fantastic match. Enchiladas are rolled tortillas stuffed with meat, beans, and cheese, and then topped with a spicy tomato sauce. The acidity of the tomato is balanced by the dark malt, the sweetness in the beer matches the meat, the cheese and beans give a creaminess to go with the grain, and the hops act like an extra seasoning—a British Brown Ale does a similar job to the Bock. An alternative match for Anchor Bock is smoked ham, where the smoke and malt combine like a cheeky double act.

AMBER LAGER AND AMBER ALE

AMBER LAGER AND AMBER ALE ARE TWO OF THE TOP FIVE BEST-SELLING CRAFT BEER STYLES IN AMERICAN STORES, TOGETHER ACCOUNTING FOR ALMOST 14 PERCENT OF BEERS SOLD (IPA IS THE NUMBER ONE BEST-SELLER). IT'S PROBABLY A LITTLE UNFAIR TO CALL THEM AN ENTRY-LEVEL CRAFT BEER STYLE, BUT THEY DO TEND TO BE THE KIND OF BREW THAT EASES DRINKERS FROM MAINSTREAM LAGERS ONTO SOMETHING DIFFERENT. THEY ARE UNCHALLENGING, THEY ARE EASY-DRINKING, AND THEY ARE THE KIND OF BEERS YOU BUY IN A SIX-PACK AND LEAVE IN THE REFRIGERATOR FOR WHEN YOU JUST WANT A BEER. ALE AND LAGER CAN COME TOGETHER HERE BECAUSE THEIR FLAVOR PROFILES ARE SIMILAR: TOASTY MALT, PERHAPS A LITTLE TOFFEE, AND THEN CLEAN (AMERICAN) HOPS, WHICH ARE FRAGRANT BUT NOT FULL ON. OUTSIDE OF AMERICA, THEY DON'T HAVE QUITE THE SAME DOMINANCE, ALTHOUGH THERE ARE COMPARABLE STYLES: VIENNA LAGER, GOLDEN ALE, ALTBIER.

TWO BIRDS SUNSET ALE

BEST WITH: EGGPLANT (AUBERGINE) PARMIGIANA

BREWED IN: MELBOURNE, AUSTRALIA
ABV: 4.4%

Eggplant (aubergine) Parmigiana is a summer comfort food—layers of grilled eggplant with tomato, basil, mozzarella, and Parmesan cheese, all baked until bubbling. I can take a big dish of this and sit in the garden with some good bread and a couple of bottles of beer, and I'm happy. The Sunset Ale is exactly the sort of beer I want to drink with it. It's got a bready, toffee sweetness to handle the sweet-salty tomato, and sweetness to go with the cheese, while the hops—American Citra and Aussie-grown Cascade—share a fruitiness with the basil and Parmesan. Two Birds also brew a lush Golden Ale, bursting with a tropical-fruit-salad freshness, which is great with some crostini that have been topped with mozzarella, chili, and fresh lemon.

NEW BELGIUM FAT TIRE

BEST WITH: MUSHROOM CHEESEBURGERS

BREWED IN: FORT COLLINS, COLORADO
ABV: 5.2%

This is one of the best-selling craft brews in America and it's the epitome of balance, consistency, simplicity, and quality. The malt body is assertive enough for you to know that you're drinking it, but still subtle and unimposing. The hops (a mix of American Willamette and English Golding and Target) give a stone-fruit brightness and a little earthiness, but nothing that wobbles the balance of the brew. It's an easy beer to like and a hard beer to hate, and it calls for something that is equally easy-going, where you'll find that pretty much anything savory works with Fat Tire. With a mushroom cheeseburger, loaded with fried onions, you get earthiness and beefiness from the Portobello mushrooms, the cheese and onion provide a caramel flavor for the beer to grip onto, and the hops add a little earthy, citrus refresh. It's also a favorite of Walter White in the TV show *Breaking Bad*.

YUENGLING TRADITIONAL LAGER

BEST WITH: JAMBALAYA

BREWED IN: POTTSVILLE, PENNSYLVANIA
ABV: 4.4%

In 1829, David Yuengling, a 23-year-old from Württemberg, Germany, started the Eagle Brewery in Pottsville, Pennsylvania. In 1873, David's son Frederick joined his father and the brewery's name changed to D.G. Yuengling & Son. The Yuengling family has owned and managed the brewery from the start and Dick Yuengling Jr is currently the fifth generation in charge, with two of his daughters also working in the family business. All of this makes it the oldest brewery still in operation in America, and Traditional Lager is its flagship brew. It's copper-amber in color and has a toasty depth of malt and a rich body, while the hops (Cluster and Cascade) give a subtle citrus dryness and quench. It has an iced-tea quality and that throws up an interesting Southern food pairing: jambalaya. The caramelized depth in the beer is great with the seafood and sausage, while the crisp hops cut past the rice.

BAIRD RED ROSE AMBER ALE

BEST WITH: YAKISOBA FRIED NOODLES

BREWED IN: NUMAZU, JAPAN
ABV: 5.8%

Amber is a great fit for Japanese food. The beer is balanced and delicate, and yet still has enough malt depth to handle bold flavors, while the hops add a bonus freshness. Baird's Red Rose is described as a kind of Altbier in that it's brewed with an ale yeast at cold temperatures, but to me it's more like an American Amber: light citrus, grassy, and floral, but really clean; the malt is toasty with toffee and then there's a pithy bitterness to finish. It's yummy with yakisoba, or fried noodles, because the beer's deep-down sweetness balances the soy saltiness, while the hops hit it off with the fresh vegetables, ginger, and scallions (spring onions). Any Amber is good for fried noodles.

BROOKLYN LAGER

BEST WITH: COLA PORK RIB SLIDERS

BREWED IN: BROOKLYN, NEW YORK
ABV: 5.2%

Bear with me here, but I think Brooklyn Lager tastes like cola. Think about the dominant flavors of cola: caramel, vanilla, and lime. Brooklyn Lager has a bready, caramel depth; I get some cake-shop vanilla way back in the malt; and then I get fresh citrus and lime from the Mittelfrüh, Vanguard, and Cascade hops. Cola is good with hamburgers, where the sweetness and fizz cuts through the fat and the lime keeps everything fresh. So, have a Brooklyn with a burger. Or try this: braise some pork ribs in cola with chili, thyme, garlic, mustard, ketchup, vinegar, Worcestershire sauce, and salt and pepper. Pull the meat off the bones and serve in a bun with some coleslaw and beer-battered onion rings on the side. Ribs in cherry cola, or even Dr Pepper, work better with Brooklyn's Brown Ale.

LAGER/ALE HYBRID

THIS CATEGORY INCLUDES KÖLSCH, ALTBIER, AND STEAM BEER, WHICH ARE GROUPED TOGETHER BECAUSE THEY ARE SOMEWHERE BETWEEN ALE AND LAGER, ALTHOUGH THEIR PARTICULAR BREWING PROCESSES CONTRIBUTE TO THEIR INDIVIDUAL QUALITIES. KÖLSCH AND ALTBIER ARE FROM COLOGNE AND DÜSSELDORF, RESPECTIVELY. THEY DEVELOPED AS A RESULT OF THOSE TOWNS RESISTING THE TAKEOVER OF PALE LAGERS AND STICKING RESOLUTELY TO THEIR TRADITIONAL ALE STYLES, WHILE USING THE COLD-CONDITIONING THAT IS MORE COMMON WITH LAGERS. THIS GIVES BEERS WITH A LIGHT FRUITINESS FROM THE ALE YEAST AND THEN A CLEAN, SUBTLE DEPTH FROM THE LAGERING PROCESS. STEAM BEER, OR CALIFORNIA COMMON, STARTED IN SAN FRANCISCO AND IS BEER FERMENTED WITH A LAGER YEAST AT WARM TEMPERATURES, GIVING FRUITY ESTERS. KÖLSCH HAS A PROTECTED DESIGNATION OF ORIGIN AND ALSO SEVERAL RULES ON WHAT IS AN OFFICIAL COLOGNE KÖLSCH (I.E. IT HAS TO BE MADE IN THE CITY, FILTERED, HOPPY), WHILE ANCHOR STEAM HOLDS THE TRADEMARK ON THE NAME STEAM BEER, HENCE CALIFORNIA COMMON IS ANOTHER NAME FOR IT.

BRIDGE: WHITE FISH WITH BUTTER, SAUSAGES (ALT), CAESAR SALAD (KÖLSCH)

BALANCE: ROTISSERIE CHICKEN, FRESH SEAFOOD, HOT DOGS

BOOST: FRIED RICE, ASPARAGUS AND POACHED EGGS (KÖLSCH), BAR SNACKS

LOCAL: BLACK PUDDING (ALT), HALVE HAHN (CHEESE ROLL), CALIFORNIA ROLLS (A TYPE OF SUSHI ROLL)

AVOID: SEMI-SWEET (DARK) CHOCOLATE

ANCHOR STEAM

BEST WITH: AVOCADO ON TOAST

BREWED IN: SAN FRANCISCO, CALIFORNIA
ABV: 4.9%

This is the original Steam Beer. As brewing moved west across America, it reached San Francisco before the invention of artificial refrigeration, so brewers had to find a way to make beers in their local environment. Opting for the lager yeasts that had become the choice of most breweries by the end of the 19th century, they fermented warmer than usual, meaning that there were more fruity esters than in other lagers. You get a great match with avocado on toast: grill some granary bread and then top with mashed avocado, chili flakes, salt, and lemon juice. The floral and woody Northern Brewer hops mix well with the avocado's fatty earthiness, bringing out sweetness, which is emphasized by the toasty malt.

UERIGE ALT

BEST WITH: HIMMEL UND ERDE

BREWED IN: DÜSSELDORF, GERMANY
ABV: 4.7%

In March 2013, I spent 24 hours in Düsseldorf, in Germany—and I loved it. I went to seven breweries in the city center, having a couple of beers at each, and then moving on to the next. All Altbiers are similar, although each is different in its own way: all are copper-amber in color and have a fresh, earthy, apple, and peppery hop aroma, while the body is toasty, but light, and then finishes dry and bitter. They are served in 7 US fl oz (200ml) glasses and, as you finish one, it's immediately replaced with a fresh glass. Uerige is hoppier than others and I liked it the most (I also loved Kürzer and Schlüssel). A local food specialty, Himmel und Erde (meaning Heaven and Earth), is black pudding, mashed potatoes, fried onions, and apple. Alt's hops balance the blood sausage and they share an earthy, orchard-fruit flavor with the apple, while there's a great symmetry between the caramelized malt and crispy onion.

GAFFEL KÖLSCH

BEST WITH: HALVE HAHN (CHEESE ROLL)

BREWED IN: COLOGNE, GERMANY
ABV: 4.8%

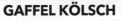

After a day in Düsseldorf, I took a train to Cologne and swapped Altbier for Kölsch. Again, I went to seven breweries or brewery taverns in town, trying all their various Kölsches; again they come in 7 US fl oz (200ml) glasses, only this time they are blonde, have a soft carbonation, a smooth clean body, and a dry, crisp bitterness. More so than in Düsseldorf, there's a variety in how each one tastes: some are really fruity (Malzmühle), some simpler (Früh), and some more bitter (Päffgen), the latter being my favorite and only available in the city. Gaffel sits right between all the others, with a soft body, extra malt depth, and lemony hops. The classic local pairing is halve hahn, a rye bread roll filled with Gouda cheese and mustard—the beer's crisp fruitiness loves the cheese and poke of mustard. Kölsch is equally happy with Southeast Asian dishes and fried food.

SCHLAFLY KÖLSCH

BEST WITH: LOBSTER ROLL

BREWED IN: ST LOUIS, MISSOURI
ABV: 4.8%

Think about the buttery, creamy sweetness of lobster, a soft, sweet, doughy roll, a slick of mayonnaise, plus a squeeze of lemon, and a grinding of pepper on top. Think about that with the clean, easy-going freshness of a Kölsch, with its simple malt sweetness, creamy texture, and hop freshness. They fit together seamlessly. With Schlafly's Kölsch, which gets its lemony-peppery aroma from two German hops (Hallertau Tradition and Perle), you get a damn fine match, especially as the beer's smooth body has a surprising depth of malt before a dry, refreshing finish. Tom Schlafly, the co-founder of the brewery, couldn't ignore Kölsch as one of their year-round brews: his wife is from Cologne.

OH! LA! HO! KÖLSCH

BEST WITH: FRIED RICE

BREWED IN: NAGANO, JAPAN
ABV: 4.5%

A mate returned from Japan with a bunch of beers in his suitcase. As he cracked open this inconspicuous-looking can, it could've been anything—green tea, soda, crap lager—but it surprised us by being an excellent take on a Kölsch. It pours a pale blonde, with a slightly hazy, rosy glow, as if it's blushing. Being unfiltered, it's got a creamy, smooth body; there's some fruity esters, such as strawberry and vanilla, and a pleasing richness of malt. With the nuttiness of fried rice, this is excellent, especially with sweet little shrimp (prawns) and peas, plus the added luxury of egg. There's a creaminess to both the food and the beer, while the drink's bitterness refreshes everything.

WHEAT ALE

These are beers brewed with a significant amount of wheat in the grain bill (30–60 percent), but typically without the dominant yeast aromas and flavors associated with the European classics of Belgian-style Wit and German-style Hefeweizen (although some fruity and spicy esters are still generally expected). Some of these beers use traditional hops for a gentle flavor, but many go for the sort of hop additions that are usually seen in Pale Ales and IPAs, which shows how craft beer's hop-first influence developed this type of beer. With food, they give the full body you'd expect in a Wheat Beer and also have an underlying subtle acidity of wheat. Some contain spices, while others have a hint of yeast fragrance, but it's the fruity, juicy hop flavor and aroma that dominate.

BRIDGE: LOBSTER ROLL OR PO BOY (A TYPE OF SUBMARINE SANDWICH), THAI CURRY, SPICY CRAB CAKES

BALANCE: JERK CHICKEN, COCONUT SHRIMP (PRAWNS), MILD CREAMY CHEESE

BOOST: TURKEY BURGER, CLAM CHOWDER, CHICKEN TENDERS

LOCAL: BREAKFAST BURRITO, GUACAMOLE, GRILLED CHEESE

AVOID: SEMI-SWEET (DARK) CHOCOLATE

HALF ACRE AKARI SHOGUN

BEST WITH: JERK SHRIMP (PRAWNS) AND COCONUT RICE

BREWED IN: CHICAGO, ILLINOIS
ABV: 5.5%

Akari Shogun uses a mix of hops, including Motueka from New Zealand, which together give a lime, tangerine, and tropical-fruit freshness that calls out for coconut's sweetly fragrant nuttiness, while also working to perk up the spices, such as thyme, all spice, cinnamon, ginger, and pepper, in the jerk seasoning. Put those things on some jumbo shrimp (king prawns), barbecue them, and serve with some coconut rice and a squeeze of lime. You'll then discover that the creamy body in the beer bridges the coconut, while the hops and spices lift each other. The hops cut through any fattiness and the rice keeps everything cool. Just make sure you avoid too much chili heat, or that'll overpower everything. The beer is also good with coconut and pineapple cake.

BOULEVARD 80-ACRE HOPPY WHEAT BEER

BEST WITH: SALT AND PEPPER WINGS

BREWED IN: KANSAS CITY, MISSOURI
ABV: 5.5%

This is exactly what I want from this type of beer: a massive fruity hop aroma (from Bravo, Zeus, Summit, Cascade, and Nelson Sauvin hops), a smooth body, and a light, balanced bitterness. It's fresh, it's clean, and, most of all, it's really fun to drink— the equivalent of fireworks at Disneyland. With food, I want something that is equally fun and, to me, fun food is something that's messy to eat (your idea of fun may be different...). With salt and pepper wings, with chili and five spice, you get a bright, bursting combination of spices, heat, salt and pepper, and citrusy hops, where the five spice makes the whole thing explode with exciting flavors.

JANDRAIN-JANDRENOUILLE VI WHEAT

BEST WITH: CAMEMBERT, APRICOTS, AND SHORTBREAD

BREWED IN: JANDRAIN-JANDRENOUILLE, BELGIUM
ABV: 6.5%

This is a remarkable brew and one of my favorites. Wheat through the middle makes the body full and smooth, although it's the hops that you'll notice, as they give an elegant, summery spectrum of floral, tangerine, apricot, pepper, lemon, grass, and earthy spice. This beer is light, while the carbonation makes it pop and gives the body a brightness that belies the booze content. It's the kind of beer that makes me want some small snacks and not a full meal. A creamy, soft cheese, such as Camembert (goats' cheese is also good), which loves orange and lemon flavors, topped with some stewed apricot, plus a couple of thyme leaves, on salty shortbread gives a wonderful mix of texture and flavor to play with the beer.

MURRAY'S WHALE ALE

BEST WITH: BACON AND AVOCADO SANDWICH

BREWED IN: PORT STEPHENS, AUSTRALIA
ABV: 4.5%

Whale Ale is a hazy gold brew with a thick foam; there's fresh floral and tropical fruit in the aroma, as well as some melon, lychee, and fruity esters; the body is smooth and satisfying; and the quenching, lemon-zest finish keeps everything wonderfully light and refreshing. It's best at brunch, especially with this toasted sandwich: grill some smoky bacon and then layer this into a sandwich of thick granary bread with fresh avocado, salt, sweet chili sauce, and mayo. The lemony bittering hops ease through the fattiness of the avocado and bacon; there's a bridge of creaminess between the beer and the avocado; and the fruity aroma hops work like added citrus juice squeezed on top.

DESCHUTES CHAINBREAKER WHITE IPA

BEST WITH: BEEF RENDANG

BREWED IN: BEND, OREGON
ABV: 5.6%

This is the mid-point between a Belgian Wit and an American IPA. It's made with plenty of wheat, a fruity-spicy Belgian yeast, and the classic combo of coriander and orange peel. Then, on top of that, you get juicy, citrusy American hops (Bravo, Citra, Centennial, and Cascade). These hops share many aromatic compounds with the yeast and coriander, so they work well together, especially when other bridging ingredients, such as lemongrass, galangal, garlic, chili, and lime leaves, are used in Indonesian rendang curry. Slow-cooked in coconut milk, this dish is fragrant and rich, and works amazingly well with the creaminess in the beer and its grapefruit and mango hop flavor. Beef also loves all of the cross-over flavors, so is the perfect source of protein to have with beer.

BELGIAN-STYLE WHEAT BEER

FRAGRANT, FULL-BODIED, SUBTLE, AND YET SPIKY, BELGIAN-STYLE WHEAT BEERS DESERVE SUPERSTAR STATUS ON THE DINNER TABLE BECAUSE OF THEIR VERSATILITY WITH FOOD. WIT BEER, OR WHITE BEER, IS UNFILTERED, SO YOU GET A SMOOTH FULLNESS FROM THE YEAST AND A BEER THAT IS BOTH REFRESHING AND SATISFYING TO DRINK. WHEN PAIRED WITH FOOD, THIS BEER GRIPS HOLD OF BOLD FLAVORS AS EFFORTLESSLY AS IT DANCES PAST DELICATE DISHES. SOME WIT BEERS ARE CREAMY, SOME ARE CITRUSY, SOME ARE SPICY, AND SOME ARE ALL THREE. MANY ARE BREWED WITH ORANGE PEEL AND CORIANDER SEED, THE LATTER GIVING AN INHERENT SAVORINESS, WHICH NATURALLY MAKES IT FIT WITH FOOD. THE WIT YEAST ADDS A DEPTH OF CITRUS AND SPICE (THINK LEMON WITH CLOVE AND PEPPER). THERE'S USUALLY A DRYNESS IN THE BEER, WHICH HEADS TOWARD ACIDITY AND ITS ACCOMPANYING QUENCH. CLASSICALLY LOW IN BITTERNESS AND ALCOHOL, IT'S AN EASY-DRINKING AND POPULAR BEER.

BRIDGE: LEMON-ROASTED CHICKEN, SEAFOOD PASTA, LEMON SPONGE CAKE

BALANCE: MOROCCAN TAGINE, FRIED CALAMARI, MILD CHEESES

BOOST: COCONUT AND CITRUS THAI DISHES, ROAST PORK, STEAK WITH THYME

LOCAL: MOULES FRITES, FRITES AND MAYONNAISE, CURED MEAT AND BELGIAN CHEESE

AVOID: MILK CHOCOLATE, RAGÙ SAUCES, GRAVY-BASED DISHES

AVERY WHITE RASCAL

BEST WITH: **LEMONGRASS AND THAI BASIL SALMON**

BREWED IN: BOULDER, COLORADO
ABV: 5.6%

The beer: hazy lemon color, with a bright white foam, it has a creamy, vanilla-custard quality, with some banana and a hint of clove, before earthy coriander spice and orange peel come through; it's lip-smackingly refreshing and one of my favorite Wits.

The food: stir-fry scallions (spring onions), ginger, garlic, ground coriander, lemongrass, and Thai basil, pour in coconut milk, and simmer, and then blitz before pouring over roasted salmon and serving with rice, cilantro (fresh coriander), more Thai basil, and lemon.

The science: Thai basil, which is sweeter and more aniseed-like than regular basil, contains citral (which is also found in lemongrass), eugenol (also in cloves), linalool (found in hops and coriander), and limonene (in oranges, lemons, and hops).

The result: with numerous aromatic and flavor cross-overs between dinner and drink, you get a really natural fit for Witbier with Thai basil and lemongrass.

BLUE MOON BELGIAN WHITE

BEST WITH: CURRIED MUSSELS

BREWED IN: DENVER, COLORADO
ABV: 5.4%

Blue Moon should be one of your go-to food beers, as it's widely available, it tastes good, and it seems to work with everything. It's a brand under the MolsonCoors megalith, but don't be a beer snob and let that put you off. A Wit made with sweet Valencia orange peel and coriander seed, it has a hazy, honey color. You get the coriander first, which is savory and appetizing; the body is creamy, thanks to the addition of oats; there's some nuttiness, a little banana, and a background hint of orange freshness, all subtle and simple. Blue Moon is especially good with spice and citrus, and Wit is a favorite of mussels, so combine the two: cook mussels with scallions (spring onions), ginger, garlic, lemongrass, cilantro (fresh coriander), curry powder, and chili, and then finish with coconut milk and lemon juice. Brilliant with Blue Moon.

ALLAGASH WHITE

BEST WITH: CORIANDER FRIES AND LEMON MAYO

BREWED IN: PORTLAND, MAINE
ABV: 5.0%

Allagash White is brewed with curacao orange peel and coriander seeds, and you get a hazy blonde beer that has a floral, citrusy depth, with some vanilla and cloves, and a dry, earthy finish. It's interesting to look at the coriander more closely: it contains linalool, pinene, myrcene, limonene, and geraniol, which contribute to coriander's floral, citrus, and woody aromas. All of those compounds are also found in hops. The yeast's clove spiciness gives eugenol, a phenolic compound that shares similarities with thyme and anise. This is where science helps us to create an amazing food pairing. With fries seasoned with freshly toasted coriander, fennel seeds, thyme, and salt and pepper, and served with a lemon mayonnaise, you get a wonderful bridge of coriander, which really enhances the potato flavor, before the peppery, spiciness in the yeast and hops find further similarities in the fennel and thyme. The lemon mayo gives a citrus burst for the wheat and orange. It's a dream dish for any Wit (and the recipe is on page 167).

BALADIN ISAAC

BEST WITH: ANTIPASTO

BREWED IN: PIOZZO, ITALY
ABV: 5.0%

A plate of antipasto, with cured meats, cheeses, olives, and more, is designed to go before a meal, which is exactly the right time to drink Isaac. Hazy pale gold in color, with a full and creamy foam, it's got the classic orange and coriander depth, a spicy, orangey aroma, plus apples, bananas, and peaches. The body is dry and refreshing, and heads toward a tartness at the end. With meat and cheese, it's superb. The cured hams share a clove-like spiciness with the beer, the apple-like fruitiness is brilliant with meat, the carbonation lifts the richness of the cheese and the saltiness in the olives, and the anchovies become sweet when the beer gets near. Simple, and yet very good.

BRASSERIE CARACOLE TROUBLETTE

BEST WITH: LEEK AND SMOKED BACON TART

BREWED IN: DINANT, BELGIUM
ABV: 5.5%

A classic Belgian Wit that gives all the yeast-derived fruitiness you'd expect, with lemon, banana, bubble gum, apple, and spice all poking out of the glass. The creamy body is full and has a classy and satisfying depth of flavor before the hops strike a lemony final chord. At 5.5% ABV, it's bigger and fuller-bodied than many other Wits, meaning that it can handle a lot of flavor. With a leek, smoked bacon, mozzarella, and Parmesan cheese tart, you find the yeast spice and smoked bacon pair up, the creamy body chums up with the cheese, and the leeks and hops hit it off. The buttery pastry is then able to bring all the individual parts together into one complete whole. An arugula (rocket) and lemon side salad adds an extra zing of freshness.

GERMAN-STYLE WHEAT BEER

GERMAN-STYLE WHEAT BEERS HAVE A BANANA AND BUBBLE-GUM QUALITY, AND YOU CAN ALSO EXPECT FOOD-FRIENDLY FLAVORS, SUCH AS TOFFEE, ROASTED NUTS, CLOVES (WHICH SUGGEST AN APPETIZING SMOKINESS), PEPPER, VANILLA, AND APPLE, PLUS A CREAMY TEXTURE. TYPICALLY UNFILTERED, SO HAZY IN THE GLASS, THAT FULL TEXTURE MAKES THIS STYLE AN ALL-ROUNDER THAT WILL BE GOOD WITH MOST FOODS. WITH THEIR BANANA AND TOFFEE FLAVOR, PLUS SMOOTH BODY, HEFEWEIZENS CAN PROMISE SWEETNESS AT FIRST SIP, BUT THEY FINISH DRY, PERHAPS EVEN GIVING THE SAME NEAR-ACIDIC QUENCH AND SPICINESS OF THEIR BELGIAN NEIGHBORS. THE CARAMEL BACKGROUND OF MALT MIRRORS CARAMELIZED COOKING FLAVORS, THERE'S AN AFFINITY WITH ROASTED FLAVORS, THEY HANDLE CHILI HEAT, AND THE BITTERNESS IS OFTEN LOW. AS A GROUP, THE BEERS POUR PALE GOLD TO DARK BROWN (WHICH IS A DUNKELWEIZEN BREWED WITH DARK MALT). WEIZENBOCK GIVES ALL THE SAME FLAVORS, BUT IN A STRONGER, BIGGER BEER.

BRIDGE: MASSAMAN CURRY, BANANA BREAD, BARBECUED MEAT AND FISH

BALANCE: CREAMY INDIAN CURRIES, MUSHROOM STROGANOFF, MEXICAN FOOD

BOOST: SMOKED MEAT, ROASTED EGGPLANT (AUBERGINE), ROAST PORK

LOCAL: WEISSWURST, KÄSESPÄTZLE, APPLE STRUDEL

AVOID: BERRIES, GRAVY-BASED DISHES

TWO BROTHERS EBEL'S WEISS

BEST WITH: SPICY BEAN AND AVOCADO TOSTADOS

BREWED IN: WARRENVILLE, ILLINOIS
ABV: 4.9%

A handsome, hazy, gold-orange color, with a creamy, white foam, this one is easy on the spice and citrus, which I like in this type of beer, and this makes it super smooth and easy to drink. It's lighter than other Hefeweizens, and has a fresh floral aroma, making it a perfect summer-day sipper. There are so many foods that this beer works well with, but I love how the creaminess in beans and avocado matches the smooth body of the beer. Together they calm the chili, while a floral flavor crosses the hops and avocado. Ebel's Weiss also mimics a sour-cream quality in the way that it can cool things down and give its own unique tang to the tostados.

BIRRIFICIO ITALIANO
B.I.-WEIZEN

BEST WITH: VEAL MILANESE

BREWED IN: LURAGO MARINONE,
ITALY
ABV: 5.0%

"When summer is at the height of madness and hormones flow from the toes to the brain and back, when the heat vaporizes all coherent thought and only primeval instincts remain—the real ones that count—when thousands of people are taking a dip in the sea and indulging in sweet idleness, then I'd like to take the most marvellous woman by the hand, tap off two half-liters of B.I.-Weizen, walk slowly but surely to the cellar, and, finally, dive into Fermentation Vat number 3, the B.I.-Weizen." Sounds good to me. After the cellar, the woman and I will order veal Milanese with lemon squeezed on top. The fruitiness in the beer—apple, pear, banana, and lemon—balances the veal before a dry, bitter finish. After dinner, we'll grab more beers and indulge in more sweet idleness. (I can't take credit for that quote, by the way: it's from Italiano's website.)

SCHNEIDER WEISSE TAP 6 UNSER AVENTINUS

BEST WITH: HONEY AND APPLE CAKE

BREWED IN: KELHEIM, GERMANY
ABV: 8.2%

Isoamyl acetate is produced by yeast during fermentation, and it's what gives Hefeweizens their distinctive fruity aroma of banana, pear drops, and bubble gum ("mmm, Juicy Fruit"). However, when a bee stings, it also releases isoamyl acetate as an alarm pheromone, which is the equivalent of the bee yelling: "Guys, I need you! Help me attack!" Just watch out for the bees if you're enjoying this combo outside in the Summer. Tap 6 has a deep toffee color and taste. There's roasted banana, dried fruit, bourbon-like spice, roast apples, and a warming background of booze. It's great with belly pork or creamy curries, but with honey and apple cake, it's fantastic.

WEIHENSTEPHANER
HEFEWEISSBIER DUNKEL

BEST WITH: BABA GANOUSH AND FLATBREADS

BREWED IN: WEIHENSTEPHAN, GERMANY
ABV: 5.3%

This is a Dunkelweiss, and it has a similar caramel-banana-vanilla-clove flavor as Hefeweizen, plus you get chocolate on top, thanks to the dark malt used in the brewhouse. This pours the color of an old penny with a big, creamy foam. There's a round richness of malt and some dark cocoa before it dries out, leaving you with a mix of clove and citrus. Look to Lebanese food for some really interesting matches, such as falafel and hummus, or shish taouk, which are marinated and spiced skewers of chicken grilled over an open fire. Baba ganoush is a dip of smoky roasted eggplant (aubergine) blended with garlic, lemon, and tahini (sesame seed paste). Served with flatbreads or pitta, it works amazingly with Dunkelweiss because the beer bridges the smoke, balances the garlic, softens the eggplant's natural bitterness, and boosts the creamy, nutty tahini.

BAMBERG WEIZEN

BEST WITH: VATAPÁ

BREWED IN: SAO PAULO, BRAZIL
ABV: 5.0%

All Bamberg beers have a German influence, and are excellent renditions of classic styles: the Rauchbier, inspired by the city from which the brewery's name originates, is superb; the Dark Lagers are fantastic; the Pale Lagers are superior to any mass-made Brazilian brew. The Weizen is pale gold and cloudy, and it's got everything you'd expect from the style, but it's subtle and not like drinking banana juice. It finishes with a lemony sharpness and that's what really helps with the food match. Try the Brazilian dish vatapá, a seafood stew thickened with bread and made with coconut milk and peanuts, because the beer's spicy acidity balances the stew's richness, but also adds some caramelized nut sweetness.

EUROPEAN "SOUR" BEER

THESE IDIOSYNCRATIC STYLES, WHICH ARE INTENTIONALLY ACIDIC OR ACETIC, ORIGINATED IN BELGIUM AND GERMANY, WHERE A FEW PASSIONATE BREWERS HAVE KEPT THE BEERS GOING IN SPITE OF THE DOMINANCE OF CLEAN, LIGHT-TASTING LAGERS. NOW, THERE'S A SURGE OF BREWERS AROUND THE WORLD EXPERIMENTING WITH TECHNIQUES TO TURN THEIR BEERS SOUR; ALL OF THEM CAN LOOK BACK TO THESE CLASSIC BEERS, WHICH INCLUDE GUEUZE, LAMBIC, FLEMISH BRUIN, AND FLANDERS RED FROM BELGIUM, AND BERLINER WEISSE AND GOSE FROM GERMANY. EACH IS VERY DIFFERENT IN TASTE AND PRODUCTION, FROM THE LIGHTLY TART BERLINER WEISSE, WHICH TAKES A MONTH OR TWO TO MAKE (BACTERIA GIVES THE TARTNESS), TO SWEET-SOUR RED AND ACIDIC, DRY GUEUZE, WHICH CAN TAKE THREE YEARS TO MAKE AND IS AGED IN WOODEN BARRELS (A MIX OF WILD YEAST AND BACTERIA GIVES THE ACIDITY HERE). QUENCHING AND REFRESHING, COMPLEX, OFTEN LIVELY WITH CARBONATION, THEY ARE APPETIZING AND MAKE YOU HUNGRY AS YOU DRINK. LOOK TO SALTY OR FATTY SNACKS FOR SOME EXCELLENT MATCHES.

BRIDGE: CAESAR SALAD, TOMATO SALSA, GOATS' CHEESE

BALANCE: CREAMY CHEESES, VIETNAMESE SUMMER ROLLS, SMOKED FISH

BOOST: FRIED FISH, SAUSAGES AND CURED MEAT (RED/BROWN), OYSTERS

LOCAL: MOULES ET FRITES, PÂTÉ, CROQUE MONSIEUR (RED/BROWN)

AVOID: CHILI HEAT

RODENBACH GRAND CRU

BEST WITH: STEAK AND CHEESE SANDWICH

BREWED IN: ROESELARE, BELGIUM
ABV: 6.0%

Classic Flanders Red is aged in large wooden barrels called foeders for up to two years before beers of different maturity are blended and then bottled. Wild yeast and bacteria inherent in the foeders contribute toward an acetic sourness, giving a lot of depth and complexity around a beer that has a vinous, caramel, vanilla, sherry, and dried-fruit background. You can find Rodenbach and Rodenbach Grand Cru; the Grand Cru is mostly made with aged beer, whereas the regular version is mostly younger beer. Both are good with food and, for me, they have a tomato-like flavor, which is savory (even umami), sweet, and acetic. The Grand Cru loves grilled meats, cheese, fried onions, toasted bread, and tomatoes, so have a steak and cheese sandwich with onions and ketchup. It's also good with meaty seafood, such as lobster and scallops, especially if the seafood is cooked in butter.

BAYERISCHER BAHNHOF LEIPZIGER GOSE

BEST WITH: GRILLED MACKEREL
AND FENNEL 'SLAW

BREWED IN: LEIPZIG, GERMANY
ABV: 4.6%

Gose is a glorious and unusual style
that neared extinction before a couple
of breweries in its adopted home town
of Leipzig brought it back. It's a hazy,
pale blonde Wheat Beer and brewed
with coriander, salt, and lactic bacteria,
making it savory, spicy, and lightly
tart. Bayerischer Bahnhof's Gose is a
wonderful beer. Coriander dominates
the aroma, fragrant and floral; the beer is subtle
in its lemony tartness; there's a seaside salinity
and lively carbonation; and it ends with a pleasing
savory edge, which makes you want to eat. Try
with grilled mackerel seasoned with ground
coriander and curry powder, plus fennel 'slaw on
the side. The salt in the beer boosts the fish's
richness, the tartness balances the oiliness, and
you get the best bridge as the corianders combine.
If you're in the US, Westbrook make a canned Gose
and several other breweries have given Gose a go.

DRIE FONTEINEN OUDE GUEUZE

BEST WITH: ROAST CHICKEN SKIN

BREWED IN: BEERSEL, BELGIUM
ABV: 6.0%

Every Gueuze starts out as a Lambic, which
is a spontaneously fermented beer that is aged
in wooden barrels for up to three years. By
blending young, sweet Lambic with funky,
sour, old Lambic, the brewer creates a balanced
Gueuze, which is effervescent, acidic, and dry.
Gueuze shares characteristics of Champagne
and should be served cold in fluted glasses.
Drie Fonteinen's Oude Gueuze is pale blonde,
with a fluffy, white foam; there's lemon, green
apples, and some funky yeast. The body is dry
and tart, but not puckering, and the balance is
extraordinary, as it leads to an oaky, peppery
bitterness—it's so quenching and refreshing,
yet eternally interesting. Roasted chicken skin
is my ultimate favorite thing to eat with
Gueuze—sprinkled with loads of salt and
pepper and roasted until the skin is crispy.
Together they are simple and unbeatable.

BOGK-BIER BERLINER WEISSE

BEST WITH: SMOKED SAUSAGE

BREWED IN: BERLIN, GERMANY
ABV: 2.5%

Berliner Weisse is a low-ABV tart Wheat Beer.
It's local to Berlin and has been made there for
hundreds of years, but today only one major
brand, Berliner Kindl, remains. Andreas Bogk,
a homebrewer from Berlin, was looking into
the city's beer history when he realized the
lack of a Berliner Weisse, so he crowd-funded
some money to start a brewery dedicated to the
style. He wanted to brew a genuine recreation
of how the beer tasted two decades earlier
(Kindl's version tastes like little more than a
slightly sour Pilsner). He managed to get hold
of a bottle of Berliner Weisse from 1989, which
he drank, but he kept some of the yeast from
the bottle and propagated it so that he could
use the original yeast culture in a new batch.
His version is very light, there's apple and
lemon, a dry body, a Brettanomyces earthiness,
a lactic tartness, and a delicate, Champagne-like
finish, making it super refreshing. With smoked
sausage, the smoke brings out more of the yeast
flavor, while the savory meat balances the
acidity—a simple snack is all you want here.

LIEFMANS OUD BRUIN

BEST WITH: PÂTÉ AND CURED MEATS

BREWED IN: OUDENAARDE, BELGIUM
ABV: 5.0%

Where Flanders Red is aged in wood, Flemish
Bruin is aged in steel tanks. Bruins still
contain bacteria and wild yeast, and still
develop the characteristics and complexity of
aged beers, just without the additional wood
flavor. They are also a mix of sweet young and
sour old beers, just like Red and Gueuze. In
Oud Bruin, you get caramel, berries, and floral
fruitiness, and a little sweetness before a
lightly acetic finish—it's wonderfully balanced.
I like it with pâté, cured meat, and cheese. It's
got sweetness and tartness to balance the
richness, while the aged depth of the beer
enhances the cured-meat flavor. Liefmans
Goudenband (8.0% ABV) is a bigger version of
Oud Bruin and great with stronger liver pâtés.

WILD BEER

INSPIRED BY THE EUROPEAN CLASSICS, THESE BEERS ARE NEW INTERPRETATIONS AND EVOLUTIONS OF SOUR BEERS, WHICH ARE GROUPED UNDER THE TITLE OF "WILD BEER," THANKS TO A COMMON USE OF WILD YEAST. IT MIGHT BE THAT THEY ARE FULLY FERMENTED WITH THE WILD YEAST BRETTANOMYCES, WHICH GIVES AROMATIC QUALITIES LIKE TROPICAL FRUIT, LEMON, EARTHINESS, OR FARMYARD; THEY COULD USE SOURING BACTERIA TO GIVE PUCKERING ACIDITY TO NEW BERLINER-WEISSE-STYLE BEERS; IT COULD BE THAT THEY ARE STRONGER THAN THEIR EUROPEAN EQUIVALENT; THEY MIGHT BE AGED IN WINE OR BOURBON BARRELS; THEY MAY BE BREWED WITH LOTS OF HOPS, AS WELL AS WILD YEAST AND SOURING BACTERIA. IT'S A BROAD AND GROWING RANGE OF BEERS, WHICH IS POPULAR AROUND THE WORLD. NOT MUCH NATURALLY JOINS THEM TO PROVIDE IDEAS FOR FOOD MATCHING. THE SIMPLEST RULE TO FOLLOW IS THAT THEY ALL TEND TO WORK VERY WELL WITH CHEESE.

THERE'S WILD YEAST AND BACTERIA IN MY BEER?

Yep! The classic Belgian Lambic gets its acidity from an inherent mix of wild yeast (Brettanomyces, or Brett) and bacteria (typically pediococcus and lactobacillus). The yeast gives farm-like, earthy, leathery, and fruity aromas as it slowly works through the sugars in beer, while the bacteria give the acidity. Together, they make these Wild Ales complex and sometimes challenging, and yet unique in their shock of quenching sharpness.

CROOKED STAVE SURETTE PROVISION SAISON

BEST WITH: CHEESE SOUFFLÉ

BREWED IN: DENVER, COLORADO
ABV: 6.2%

I love Crooked Stave. The brews are mind-bogglingly, astonishingly complex, yet elegantly subtle, and you could drink a bottle in minutes. All beers are fermented with Brettanomyces, which makes sense when you know that the brewery's owner, Chad Yakobson, studied Brett at brewing school, isolating a number of unique strains of the yeast. Surette is matured in giant wooden foeders and leaves a blonde beer with a wonderful stone-fruit and grape aroma, which mixes with light wood and spice. Almost ethereal, the body is super clean, the carbonation in sharp, and it ends with a slight tartness. The lightness of the beer is outstanding with a cheese soufflé, allowing the tropical fruitiness in the beer really to burst forward.

LOST ABBEY CUVEE DE TOMME

BEST WITH: STEAK WITH BLUE CHEESE

BREWED IN: SAN MARCOS, CALIFORNIA
ABV: 11.0%

This is a great example of how American brewers have taken Belgian inspiration and mixed it with their own supersized sensibilities. Taking Judgement Day, a Quadrupel brewed with raisins and candi sugar, Lost Abbey turn it into something completely new by putting it into old bourbon barrels with sour cherries and wild yeast. What you get is a dark, strong beer that's tart, tannic, layered with oak and vanilla, a fruit sourness, and a dry bitterness which demands food. A hunky piece of beef, especially with rosemary and thyme, works really well, especially with blue cheese. The malt sweetness hits the meat's char, the wine-like acidity cuts right through everything, the hops hit the herbs, and the blue cheese makes it extra rich to go with the beer's big character.

BREW BY NUMBERS 04/01 BERLINER WEISSE

BEST WITH: MUSHROOM PÂTÉ

```
BREWED IN:
LONDON, ENGLAND
ABV: 4.0%
```

BREW BY NUMBERS
— BBNo —
04|01
BERLINER WEISSE
CLASSIC
— 3.7% —
HANDCRAFTED IN LONDON

Each Brew By Numbers beer is given a numbered code (01/02, for example) and then a name. The first number is the style, while the second is the variation on that style. 01 is the range of fragrant Saisons, 02 are hoppy Golden Ales, and 08 are Stouts, which all share a seductive nuttiness. 04 is Berliner Weisse, where 04/02 is a double-strength version of the style, 04/04 is made with lime and tastes like a mojito, and 04/01 is the classic, German-style, sour Wheat Beer. It is delicate, and yet devilishly tart, refreshing, light, acidic, and all kinds of fruity. The guys behind the brewery— Tom and Dave—started brewing in their apartment and selling some bottles before moving into a nearby railway arch within walking distance of London's famous Borough Market. They open the brewery on Saturdays, so stop at the market on the way to BBNo. and grab some oysters, Spanish jamon, or mushroom pâté.

LOVERBEER MADAMIN

BEST WITH: TOMATO AND ANCHOVY BRUSCHETTA

```
BREWED IN: MARENTINO, ITALY
ABV: 6.2%
```

Madamin is an Amber Ale that's fermented and aged in oak barrels with wild yeast. This leaves a beer that's full of fruitiness, with peaches, grapes, berries, and a little farmyard funkiness; the body is rich, but then any hint of sweetness is ripped away as the beer finishes dry, bitter, and gently acidic, almost like a Campari-style herb liqueur. It's a perfect aperitivo before a meal, as it's bitter and tart, and gets the taste buds excited. With any aperitivo, you need a snack. Olives work really well, but some toasted bruschetta with tomato and anchovy is even better. There's a shared acidity, the saltiness of the anchovy brings out the sweetness and loves the dry bitterness, while the bread offers balance.

RUSSIAN RIVER TEMPTATION

BEST WITH: GOATS' CHEESE, APPLE, AND TOASTED BAGUETTE

```
BREWED IN: SONOMA, CALIFORNIA
ABV: 7.5%
```

Brewing in Californian wine country, Russian River uses old wine barrels to age its superlative Sour Ales, which include Supplication (aged in Pinot Noir barrels with sour cherries) and Consecration (aged in Cabernet Sauvignon barrels with currants). Temptation goes into Chardonnay barrels with the typical souring threesome of Brettanomyces yeast and lactobacillus and pediococcus bacteria, which turn this golden ale into a tart, complex, and phenomenal beer. Lemon, white wine, vanilla, apple, and funky fruit in the aroma ensure the first sip shocks with sourness, but, by the second, it's hard not to love the refreshing sharpness, the fruit, the wine character, the wood-barrel toastiness and texture, and the way in which the beer finishes with a dry quench like the world's finest lemonade. The acidity will make you hungry, so have this before dinner with some soft goats' cheese and a thin slice of tart apple on some toasted baguette—the shared sharpness is superb.

SOUR AND FRUITY BEER

MANY OF THE MOST FAMOUS SOUR BEERS ARE MADE AND AGED IN WOODEN BARRELS AND TAKE A LONG TIME TO PRODUCE. DURING THE AGING PROCESS, IT'S POSSIBLE TO ADD FRESH FRUIT TO THE BARRELS WHERE THEIR HIGHLY FERMENTABLE SUGARS GET THE YEAST EXCITED AND POWER THEM BACK TO LIFE. IN THE BEST EXAMPLES, THE FRUIT LEAVES COLOR, A HINT OF FLAVOR, SOME TARTNESS, AND DRY TANNIC QUALITIES. LIKE THE EUROPEAN SOURS, THESE ARE COMPLEX BEERS, INTERESTING AND UNUSUAL, WITH ACIDITY MIXING WITH SUBTLE FRUIT. THERE'S OFTEN A PLEASING CREAMINESS, WHICH COMES FROM LACTIC ACID, AND THIS MAKES THE BEERS WORK VERY WELL WITH CHEESE AND CREAM, WHILE THE DRY ACIDITY AND CARBONATION MAKES THEM REFRESHING, RATHER LIKE A FRUITY CHAMPAGNE. GOOD BEFORE A MEAL WITH A SALTY SNACK, EXCELLENT WITH GAME OR DUCK, OR SAVE IT FOR A CREAMY DESSERT OR CHOCOLATE.

CANTILLON ROSÉ DE GAMBRINUS

BEST WITH: BEETROOT AND MACKEREL; ROAST DUCK; CHOCOLATE BROWNIES

BREWED IN: BRUSSELS, BELGIUM
ABV: 5.0%

Add bucketloads of fresh raspberries to Cantillon's Lambic, leave them inside oak barrels for a year or so, and you get Rosé de Gambrinus. It's a vibrant red color, with a shock of pink foam, and smells like raspberry pips, cherries, and strawberries. The body is bursting with fruit and alive with dancing carbonation, and the beer ends unapologetically tart and dry. Buy a big bottle, serve it in Champagne glasses, and start with mackerel and beetroot. Then, have roast duck tacos (or crispy Peking duck) followed by chocolate brownies for dessert—it's great with all three courses. The Cantillon brewery has records of using raspberries from the beginning of the 20th century, but production stopped during the war and didn't start again until the 1970s. Now, this beer is a favorite and always available.

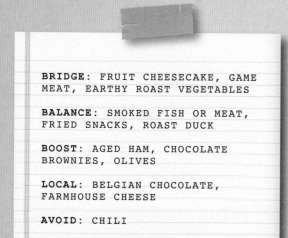

BRIDGE: FRUIT CHEESECAKE, GAME MEAT, EARTHY ROAST VEGETABLES

BALANCE: SMOKED FISH OR MEAT, FRIED SNACKS, ROAST DUCK

BOOST: AGED HAM, CHOCOLATE BROWNIES, OLIVES

LOCAL: BELGIAN CHOCOLATE, FARMHOUSE CHEESE

AVOID: CHILI

CANTILLON

Rosé de Gambrinus

CASCADE BLUEBERRY

BEST WITH: BAKED BLUEBERRY CHEESECAKE

BREWED IN: PORTLAND, OREGON
ABV: 7.33%

This beer blends oak-aged Wheat Ale and Blonde Ale, then adds loads of fresh blueberries and ages it some more. What you get is a blueberry-stained beer with a blush-violet foam. It's really juicily fresh with blueberries, so much so that you expect your lips to be stained blue after drinking it. Never sweet, the fruit gives the beer a floral fragrance, plus blueberry pie, lemon, and vanilla. The body is light and dry, surprisingly so for such a strong beer, and then the tartness of wild yeast comes through with a hint of citrusy acidity and creaminess, followed by berry and oak tannins, which are almost wine-like. It's the sort of beer that tastes different with each sip, so, with a plate of cheese and charcuterie, you can always find something different to go with it. Or a baked blueberry cheesecake gives a boost to all the fruit and makes a damn fine dessert.

GOOSE ISLAND HALIA

BEST WITH: BAKED GOATS CHEESE

BREWED IN: CHICAGO, ILLINOIS
ABV: 7.5%

The Goose Island barrel room is one of the seven wonders of the craft beer world (other contenders: Pilsner Urquell cellars; Cantillon's brewhouse; Schlenkerla's tavern in Bamberg; Munich's Oktoberfest). An astonishing cathedral of wood, it has an intoxicating aroma of fermentation coming from thousands of wooden barrels, some which previously held wine, others bourbon. The wine barrels all also contain fruit and make up the "sisters" of Goose Island: raspberries in Lolita, blackberries in Juliet, strawberry in Gillian, and Halia has peaches which are blitzed into a pale Farmhouse ale before being aged in sauvignon blanc and chardonnay barrels. It's like a peachy sparkling wine; dry with wild yeast, there's vanilla, lemon, woody spices, and grapes. It's superb with goats cheese as they share an earthy acidity which the beer's fruitiness is able to sweeten. Coat the cheese in breadcrumbs, bake it, then serve with salad and cider vinegar dressing.

BOON KRIEK MARIAGE PARFAIT

BEST WITH: GOATS' CHEESE AND CHERRY

BREWED IN: LAMBEEK, BELGIUM
ABV: 8.0%

The by-products of Brettanomyces fermentation include 4-ethylphenol, caproic acid, and isovaleric acid, all of which can be a little goaty or farmyard-like. In most beers this is disgusting, but it is tolerated in small amounts in Sour Beers and it leads us to a very good food pairing with goats' cheese. On its own, this can be a bit too much goat for even the greatest goat fan, so some fresh fruit helps to cut through the goatiness. Kriek Mariage Parfait is aged in oak barrels with 14oz (400g) fresh cherries per 34 US fl oz (1 liter) of beer. They turn the beer pink and give a gorgeous cherry-pip and almond aroma. Then, cinnamon, leather, and a deep, earthy finish combine with a dry tartness. Fruity, fragrant, and fantastic with goats' cheese and cherry jam, this should be your go-to goaty pairing.

LOGSDON PECHE 'N' BRETT

BEST WITH: PEACH AND MASCARPONE

BREWED IN: HOOD RIVER, OREGON
ABV: 10.0%

A traditional farmhouse brewery situated on 10 acres of farmland in Hood River County, Logsdon makes organic beer in a red barn and feeds cattle with its spent grain. The brewery has planted a Schaerbeekse cherry orchard so that the fruit can eventually be used in the beer. It's a rustic place, with elegant, refined, interesting beers. Seizoen Bretta is a Brett-aged, Saison-style beer. Put that beer into oak barrels, add a lot of fresh local peaches, and a few months later you get Peche 'n' Brett. Peachy colored and hazy, there's loads of fresh peach, tangy peach skin, lemon, and earthiness. Rich and soft, fruity yet tart, some background funkiness, oak texture, and you'd never notice that it's 10.0% ABV. Try it with a simple baked puff pastry base, freshly sliced peaches, and some mascarpone or blue cheese on top.

FRUIT BEER

These are beers brewed with fruit, which are not sour. Name almost any fruit and you'll be able to find a beer made with it, including classics such as cherries and raspberries, or more unusual things like grapefruit, banana, and pineapple. The fruit can be added in a variety of different ways, whether as whole fresh fruit, puréed fruit, fresh juice, syrup, or extract, and all can produce great beers—just watch out for the saccharine, fake-tasting, and supersweet versions, which generally taste nothing like beer at all. Any style can have fruit added to it, ranging from subtle Wheat Beers, through bitter IPAs, up to Imperial Stouts, meaning that there aren't any general rules for matching Fruit Beers with food.

SAMUEL SMITH'S ORGANIC STRAWBERRY FRUIT BEER

BEST WITH: PEANUT BUTTER ON BRIOCHE

BREWED IN: STAMFORD, ENGLAND
ABV: 5.2%

Sam Smith's have four Fruit Beers in this range—cherry, raspberry, apricot, and strawberry—which are all brewed with wheat and malt and then blended with organic fruit syrups. They are quite sweet and you might not manage these beers by the six-pack, but they can be excellent with food, as they can handle sweet and savory equally well. I'm going with the strawberry, as it's a slightly less common Fruit Beer, which contradicts the fact that it's the most popular berry in the world. My favorite partner for strawberry jelly (jam), after clotted cream, is peanut butter, so spread that on some toasted brioche and enjoy with the jammy fruitiness of the beer to recreate a PB&J sandwich. Adding some smoked bacon works as well.

MAUI BREWING MANA WHEAT

BEST WITH: HAWAIIAN PIZZA

BREWED IN: MAUI, HAWAII
ABV: 5.5%

Yes, it says Hawaiian pizza. And, yes, I know Hawaiian pizza is not a Hawaiian thing. I also know it's the pizza equivalent of a pink cowboy hat. But it's just a very good match with Maui's Mana Wheat. Sure, there are other great matches, like Thai curries and grilled pork or fish, but I like it best with this pizza. The beer is an American Wheat brewed with Maui Gold Pineapple. It's got a tropical aroma of pineapple skin and juice, plus citrus groves; the body is full, thanks to the beer being unfiltered; and then it ends clean, refreshing, a little fruity, and the pineapple runs right through it. With a mouthful of ham and pineapple pizza, you really bring out the fruit flavor, while the wheat deals with the tomato sauce and salty ham. It's genuinely great.

DOGFISH HEAD SIXTY-ONE

BEST WITH: CHICKEN MOLE TACOS

BREWED IN: MILTON, DELAWARE
ABV: 6.5%

There's always a good story with a Dogfish Head beer. Sixty-One came out of an unusual tradition that brewery owner Sam Calagione had with some drinking buddies in that they'd all meet up, order a 60 Minute IPA, take a big quenching gulp, and then pour a little Pinot Noir wine into their beer. Calagione liked the taste so much that he spent a year developing the drink in the brewhouse and turned it into a year-round beer. It starts out as 60 Minute IPA, the brewery's biggest-selling beer, and then syrah grape must from California is blended in during fermentation (the must is cold-tankered all the way from the West Coast). It leaves a violet beer with the floral and pithy hops of an IPA and the dry, spicy, berry-like complexity of red wine. The label was painted by Calagione and, mixed in with his watercolors, was beer in the green paint, wine in the red paint, and chocolate in the brown. Why chocolate? Because it tastes great with Sixty-One. Fill some soft tacos with shredded chicken and mole sauce, where the chocolate is enhanced and the hops hit the spices.

LINDEMAN'S PECHERESSE

BEST WITH: IBERICO HAM

BREWED IN: VLEZENBEEK, BELGIUM
ABV: 2.5%

Lindeman's started brewing Lambic Beer in 1811 as a side business to the family farm. In 1930, the farming finished and all the focus went into the brewing, which is when the brewery released its first Gueuze and Kriek (Gueuze is a blend of Lambic and Kriek is made with cherries). Today, their classic Cuvée René Gueuze is like a charming collusion of Champagne and Cider, and they also make a range of Fruit Beers using fruit juice: there's a blackcurrant Cassis, classic Kriek, Framboise, and a rarely seen Apple Lambic. Pecheresse is a cute 2.5% ABV peach beer, best served cold in fluted glasses. It's full of juicy sweet peaches, there's almond and lemon, and it ends with a teasing, refreshing tartness. It's excellent with the saltiness of Iberico ham; you could also add mozzarella, peach, and basil for a simple salad.

21ST AMENDMENT HELL OR HIGH WATERMELON WHEAT

BEST WITH: BARBECUE PORK, ROSEMARY, AND WATERMELON

BREWED IN: SAN FRANCISCO, CALIFORNIA
ABV: 4.9%

Watermelon Wheat tastes so much like you've just bitten into a large watermelon that you half expect to have to spit out some little black pips. It's an American Wheat Beer that pours a blush, hazy pink. It's refreshing with a hint of sweetness, some floral aroma, strawberry, and just this unbelievable and unmistakable depth of watermelon (if you drink it at the brewpub in San Francisco, they also add some of the fruit to the side of the glass). You might as well eat watermelon with this and in her book, *The Flavor Thesaurus*, Niki Segnit suggests watermelon, rosemary, and barbecue pork as a good combo. Slide a branch of rosemary through the melon and grill before serving. It'll surprise you just how good this combination tastes.

EDIBLE INGREDIENTS

On top of water, malt, hops, and yeast, beers can be brewed with many other ingredients. The most common are herbs, spices, chocolate, coffee, vanilla, and fruit, but you could also come across oysters, chilis, pumpkin, flowers, tea, and more. The base beer could vary from a Pale Lager to an Imperial Stout, so no common notes fit. One way to match the food and beer in this case is to use the edible ingredient in the beer as a direct bridge to the food: if the beer is brewed with chocolate, then eat chocolate with it. Another approach is to use the edible ingredient as an addition to a dish: put a chocolate beer with banana cake and it's as if you've poured chocolate sauce on the side.

Five Unusual Beers to Try:

1 BALLAST POINT INDRA KUNINDRA IS SPICED LIKE A CURRY WITH CUMIN, CAYENNE, COCONUT, AND KAFFIR LIME LEAVES.

2 LOST ABBEY GIFT OF THE MAGI IS A GOLDEN ALE BREWED WITH MYRRH AND BITTERED WITH THE BARK OF FRANKINCENSE.

3 SHORT'S BREWING KEY LIME PIE USES LIMES, MILK SUGAR (LACTOSE), GRAHAM CRACKERS, AND MARSHMALLOW FLUFF TO RECREATE THE DESSERT IT'S NAMED AFTER.

4 ROGUE THE BEARD BEER WAS MADE FROM A YEAST STRAIN FOUND IN ITS BREWMASTER JOHN MAIER'S BEARD.

5 UNCOMMON BREWERS BACON BROWN ALE IS, AS YOU CAN PROBABLY GUESS, MADE WITH BACON.

CIGAR CITY CUCUMBER SAISON

BEST WITH: LAMB AND MINT SOUVLAKI

BREWED IN: TAMPA, FLORIDA
ABV: 5.0%

This literally smells just like cucumber. It's astonishing. Sure, I kind of expected there to be some cucumber in there, given the name and everything, but I wasn't expecting it to be like a mouthful of cucumber juice followed by a bite of pickled gherkin. Herbal elements suggest dill and mint, hops give lemon and a light tropical aroma, and there's a dry, pickle-like tartness, which makes it wonderfully unusual, uniquely refreshing, and a beer that gets better with food. Have a hamburger and use the beer instead of a gherkin; try key lime pie for a surprising local pair; or go with a lamb and mint souvlaki served in a pitta with a mint, tomato, and onion salad—something like a Greek salad minus the cucumber. The beer reminds you of the ingredient you've left out.

DUCLAW SWEET BABY JESUS!

BEST WITH: PEANUT BUTTER COOKIES

BREWED IN: HANOVER, MARYLAND
ABV: 6.5%

This is a chocolate peanut butter Porter. If I see that on a menu, then there's no way I don't order it. Sweet Baby Jesus! has been phenomenally successful and the dudes at DuClaw can barely keep up with its production. The beer is dark brown and the first mouthful is like opening a Reese's Peanut Butter Cup: chocolate, peanuts, and candy-store sweetness. It's smooth, toasty, and roasty with semi-sweet (dark) chocolate and coffee, and then there's a high hop bitterness, while the savory peanut butter is there throughout. Pair it with peanuts: perhaps beef with satay sauce or a turkey and peanut butter sandwich, or just a tray of peanut butter cookies, where the beer's bitter roast keeps everything balanced.

ELYSIAN NIGHT OWL

BEST WITH: HONEY-GLAZED HAM

BREWED IN: SEATTLE, WASHINGTON
ABV: 5.9%

Halloween to Thanksgiving is when pumpkin beers become the seasonal brew du jour. Very much a US thing, they tend to be love-hate beers and polarize opinion with their additions of pumpkin pie spices. By using pumpkin flesh brewers can get extra sweetness (centuries ago it was used as a starch when barley was scarce), a creamy texture, and it's often spiked with woody, fragrant spices. It can be good with the Thanksgiving turkey, but my personal choice is a whole ham baked with honey and cloves and served with roast pumpkin or sweet potato—there's a lovely shared sweet-spiciness between everything. No one does pumpkin beers like Elysian, who even hold a festival in their honor. Night Owl is softly spicy, a little honey sweetness, then just lots of pumpkin flavor.

SALTAIRE TRIPLE CHOCOHOLIC

BEST WITH: CHOCOLATE STOUT CAKE

BREWED IN: SALTAIRE, ENGLAND
ABV: 4.8%

If this beer is pouring at a British beer festival, then you'd better get to the bar quick, because you can guarantee it'll sell out before anything else. A chocoholic's dream beer, this one is brewed with chocolate malt, cocoa, and chocolate essence. Take one gulp and it'll leave you smiling like a seven-year-old in a sweet shop. Milk chocolate, vanilla, sweet candy, and cocoa all come out immediately, there's a medium body of dark malt, coffee, and sweet chocolate, and then it dries right out at the end to be nicely bitter and balanced. Too chocolatey to go with a main course, this is fun with cheese, but better with a slice of chocolate cake, especially if the cake is made with Stout.

PORTERHOUSE OYSTER STOUT

BEST WITH: SHEPHERD'S PIE

BREWED IN: DUBLIN, IRELAND
ABV: 4.6%

It's called Oyster Stout because it's brewed with the bivalves shucked straight into the conditioning tank. It's a surprisingly popular style seen around the world, even if it seems like a squeamish ingredient to brew with. The Porterhouse's version is luxuriously creamy and full-bodied, rich with chocolate and coffee, an earthy bitterness, some berry fruit, and then, in the background, you get a flavor-boosting saltiness and umami (but no fishiness) from the oysters. The obvious food choice is a plate of fresh oysters, but there are better matches: mussels, anchovy pizza, porterhouse steak, clam chowder… It's a good and versatile food beer. Shepherd's pie works because the dark grain boosts the meat, while the oysters' background saltiness gives an extra injection of flavor. With pubs in Ireland, London, and New York, The Porterhouse is good to go to for a few.

FARMHOUSE ALE

CENTURIES AGO, THESE BEERS DEVELOPED BECAUSE THEIR "LIQUID BREAD" SUSTENANCE KEPT FARMHANDS GOING THROUGHOUT THE HARD WORKING DAY AND WOULD KEEP THEM REFRESHED INTO THE EVENING. THEN, THEY WERE PROBABLY FAIRLY ROUGH BEERS MADE BY FARMERS AND NOT BREWERS. TODAY, FARMHOUSE ALES HAVE JUMPED FROM FARM TO BREWERY AND THEY ARE SOME OF THE BEST FOOD BEERS, AS THEY HAVE A GYMNASTIC VERSATILITY DUE TO THEIR BOLD BITTERNESS, ALLURINGLY FRUITY OR HERBAL FRAGRANCE, ROBUST BODY AND YET REFRESHING LIGHTNESS, AND DRY, ALMOST-SAVORY FINISH. SAISON IS THE MOST COMMON AND VARIED, AND IS A STYLE THAT'S BEEN MUCH DEVELOPED IN RECENT YEARS, WITH SOME BREWERS USING NEW WORLD HOPS, OTHERS ADDING SPICES, AND SOME USING WILD YEAST. BIÈRE DE GARDE IS A FRENCH FARMHOUSE ALE, WHICH TENDS TO BE SWEETER AND STRONGER THAN SAISON, WHILE YOU MIGHT ALSO SEE LOW-ABV (SUB-4%) TABLE BEERS LIKE MINI-SAISONS. IT'S AN ENORMOUSLY VARIED GROUP OF BEERS.

BRIDGE: VIETNAMESE, PEPPERED STEAK, HERB SAUSAGES

BALANCE: ROAST EGGPLANT (AUBERGINE), PROVENÇAL CUISINE, OILY FISH

BOOST: FALAFEL AND MOROCCAN FOOD, ROSEMARY FOCACCIA, DIM SUM

LOCAL: FARMHOUSE CHEESE

AVOID: CHOCOLATE

SAISON DUPONT

BEST WITH: SHRIMP PAD THAI

BREWED IN: TOURPES, BELGIUM
ABV: 6.5%

If *Beer and Food* were turned into a game of Top Trumps, Saison Dupont would be the best card in the pack. It has so many different qualities, which means it works with so many different foods: it's super dry and quenching; it's 6.5% ABV, so has malt body and alcohol depth; there's a kick of peppery bitterness, but you also get a hint of tartness from the way in which it's so dry; the hops are herbal and earthy, and then fruity with peaches, lemon, and apple, and also combine to be appetizing and freshly fragrant. Great with grilled meat, mighty with Mexican and Cajun spices, happy with hard herbs such as thyme and sage, and awesome with an array of Asian food, thanks to the shared citrus, spice, and herbs. Try pho, spring or summer rolls, nasi goring, or a classic Pad Thai. The beer brings more citrus zest and pepper, as well as a richness to go with the noodles, roasted nuts, and egg. Always have Saison Dupont in your refrigerator.

FUNKWERKS SAISON

BEST WITH: BRIE OR CAMEMBERT (OR SEAFOOD LAKSA)

BREWED IN: FORT COLLINS, COLORADO
ABV: 6.8%

Fort Collins is a must-visit on any US beer road trip. New Belgium and Odell are the headliners, but breweries such as Funkwerks—with its cosy taproom and cracking range of Belgian-inspired brews— make it worth sticking around. Funkwerks Saison pours a gold that looks as if it's illuminated from beneath, with a fluffy foam that catches all the amazing aromas of peach, pineapple, pepper, ginger, tart apples, and lemon. Carbonation is lively and fresh, plus there are some peppery spices and a tangerine fruitiness. The brewery also sells local cheeses and suggests a creamy, ripened cow's milk cheese to go with this beer. It's also good with laksa or creamy curries, where the fruit and fizz combine to be refreshing and light.

BRASSERIE DE SAINT-SYLVESTRE TROIS MONTS

BEST WITH: HERB ROAST CHICKEN

BREWED IN: SAINT-SYLVESTRE CAPPEL, FRANCE
ABV: 8.5%

From northern France, on the Belgian border, Bière de Garde is the country's main contribution to beer's style book and a classic farmhouse beer. The Champagne region might be better known for its grapes, but it's also the main grain growing area in the country and, with Bière de Garde, there's a cross-over of flavor between the two drinks: a nutty, toasty, doughy malt profile, loads of bubbles, and fresh stone fruit. The beer differs by being bulkier in the body, sweeter, richer, with a Belgian-beer spiciness, instead of Champagne's acidity. It's a complex beer, layered with depth. It's best with herb roast chicken (duck or pork, too), fresh veg, and roast potatoes. The malt depth bridges right to the chicken's sweetness, and the beer's herbal depth brings some additional seasoning.

PRAIRIE ALES PRAIRIE STANDARD

BEST WITH: VIETNAMESE SALAD

BREWED IN: KREBS, OKLAHOMA
ABV: 5.2%

This is a hoppy Farmhouse Ale and shows the way in which the style is evolving, taking the classic spicy dryness and throwing fruity hops on top. Brewed with New Zealand hops, Prairie Standard is a hazy gold and there's lime and mango, pineapple, and pepper. The bubbles are big and light, as they ping on your tongue, and there's complexity combined with bangability. A curry-like, coriander spiciness comes through and, with its lime-like fruitiness, it points toward Asian food. A Vietnamese salad of chicken, cucumber, shallots, mint, sweet basil, cilantro (fresh coriander), peanuts, carrots, and a dressing of lime, chili, sugar, and soy, gives lots of fresh, cool flavors to the beer's citrus and spice, particularly linking with the green herbs. Prairie Ales brewery was started by brothers Chase and Colin Healey because, in their own words, they wanted to do something that was awesome. High five to that!

WILD BEER CO EPIC SAISON

BEST WITH: FALAFEL AND HUMMUS

BREWED IN: SHEPTON MALLET, SOMERSET
ABV: 5.0%

Wild Beer brews on a farm, next to a cheese-maker, and has a range of fantastic Farmhouse Ales, many of which include fruit, wild yeast, and oak barrels. Epic Saison mixes a Belgian-style beer base with American Sorachi Ace hops, which are notorious for their lemony qualities. A copper-gold brew, with a big, white foam, the Sorachi Ace gets you first with lemon balm, pineapple, and tropical fruit. The body is dry and clean, there are earthy and peppery spices, which make it savory, and then a clinging, lemon-pith bitterness. The brewery suggests stir-fried lemon chicken or chicken satay. I think the lemon depth in the beer works best if it's regarded as a squeeze of citrus on the side—and with falafel and hummus, you boost the beer's lemon and earthy spice.

BELGIAN BLONDE, TRIPEL, AND STRONG GOLDEN

BLONDE AND GOLDEN ALES OF BELGIAN ORIGIN OR INSPIRATION, THE BEERS IN THIS FAMILY ARE SUPERSTARS OF *BEER AND FOOD*. THEY OFTEN HAVE ELEVATED ALCOHOL LEVELS AND YET THE MALT IS NEVER DOMINANT OR HEAVY AND THE HOPS GIVE A BITTER FINISH, WHICH COMBINES WITH THE DRYNESS PROVIDED BY THE VORACIOUSLY HUNGRY YEAST. THIS MIGHT ALSO KICK OUT SOME FRUITY ESTERS (APPLE, BANANA, ANISEED, AND PEPPER), WHILE A FEISTY, FAT-CLEARING CARBONATION KEEPS EVERYTHING LIGHT. BLONDES WILL BE THE LIGHTEST IN THE RANGE, SOMEWHERE BETWEEN 5.0 AND 7.0% ABV; TRIPELS AND STRONG GOLDEN ALES OVERLAP BETWEEN 7.0 AND 10.0% ABV. THEY ARE POWERFUL BEERS, AND YET STILL SOMEHOW DELICATE, WHICH MAKES THEM SO GOOD WITH A WIDE VARIETY OF DISHES.

BRIDGE: TOULOUSE SAUSAGE, SEAFOOD PASTA, APRICOT TART

BALANCE: ROAST PORK, OILY FISH, FOIE GRAS OR PÂTÉ

BOOST: ASPARAGUS, BEEF AND GINGER STIR-FRY, LEMON CHICKEN

LOCAL: MILD CHEESES, CURED MEAT

AVOID: HOT SPICE, CHOCOLATE

ORVAL

BEST WITH: WILD MUSHROOM RISOTTO

BREWED IN: FLORENVILLE, BELGIUM
ABV: 6.2%

Take a poll of brewers around the world and ask them which beers they'd want with them if they were stranded on a desert island, and I bet Orval would be the most popular choice. (Duvel, on the next page, would probably get in the Top 5.) It's a Trappist beer, but not like any of the others: it's a hoppy Belgian Pale Ale that's dosed with Brettanomyces yeast when it is packaged. As the beer ages, the hops mellow into the beer, and the peppery, lemony tartness of the yeast develops, meaning that every time you open a bottle, it's a little different, thus making it mysterious and intriguing. It's also a near-perfect food beer, with its savory, peppery quality, boozy strength that can stand up to big flavors, appetizing dryness, and tongue-tingling fizz. Paella, oily fish, cured meat, and pâté are all great food choices with this beer. With a wild mushroom risotto, finished with lemon juice, the beer zips through everything and zings with the added citrus. The ultimate pairing, if you can get it, is the cheese that they make at the Orval Abbey.

RUSSIAN RIVER DAMNATION

BEST WITH: CARIBBEAN-INSPIRED SALMON

BREWED IN: SANTA ROSA, CALIFORNIA
ABV: 7.5%

It might seem odd, but drinking a glass of this beer in a bar in Philadelphia made me think of the Caribbean... There's some banana, coconut, rum, lime, and pineapple in the aroma and this combines with a very clean malt body and a lingering bitterness. It's a complex, interesting, and massively drinkable Strong Golden Ale. Taking the tropical tastes, grill salmon with ginger, thyme, cayenne pepper, lime, honey, and garlic. The spices bridge to the beer's fruitiness, while the salmon's oily richness is softened by the beer's malt richness. Some coconut and cilantro (fresh coriander) rice on the side completes it. For dessert, make banana fritters or have a coconut chocolate bar.

OMNIPOLLO LEON

BEST WITH: ASPARAGUS AND PARMA HAM

BREWED IN: STOCKHOLM, SWEDEN
ABV: 6.5%

Omnipollo was founded by homebrewer and beer geek Henok Fentie in 2010, and Karl Grandin joined him soon after. Karl does the label artwork and all the bottles are so good-looking that they're worth saving after you've finished drinking their contents. Leon is a Belgian-style Golden Ale fermented with a Champagne yeast and uses whole cone Amarillo and Simcoe hops to be a mix of New World and Old World. There are lemons, grapes, peaches, and grapefruit in the aroma, the body is dry, the bubbles are sharp and refreshing, and it finishes like lime sherbert and peppercorns—it's superb. Wrap some asparagus spears in Parma ham and then roast them with freshly grated Parmesan cheese on top. The hops hit the asparagus's vegetal flavor and the fruit is great with the ham and cheese, while the saltiness is balanced by the dry beer.

WESTMALLE TRIPEL

BEST WITH: ROAST PORK WITH PEACH AND THYME

BREWED IN: WESTMALLE, BELGIUM
ABV: 9.5%

The website foodpairing.com is a fascinating resource that looks at how different foods and drinks work together, with webs of flavor showing the best ingredients to pair up. Being based in Belgium, the website looks at a number of different beers, including Westmalle's Tripel, and also gives recipes. One of these combines Westmalle Tripel with mango, almond, apricot, cumin, lemon, and mascarpone in a dessert, while another suggests pork with peaches, carrots, thyme, and ginger, and some of the beer: a wonderfully pleasing combination, which makes the most of the beer's stone fruitiness, peppery and herbal depth, spiciness, and elegant malt body. Very clever, just like the website. This is the classic and original Tripel and it's a Champions League food beer: also try it with apricot and thyme cheesecake or lemon-roast chicken with garlic and asparagus.

DUVEL

BEST WITH: FENNEL, OLIVE, AND PARMESAN GRATIN

BREWED IN: PUURS, BELGIUM
ABV: 8.5%

Duvel is the quintessential Strong Golden Ale. A bright blonde color, with a full, thick, foam, a glass of Duvel is a fine sight. The hops (Saaz and Styrian Golding) give citrus pith and aromatic spice, while fruity esters give almond, apple, and pear. It has a sharp carbonation, which combines with the hops, and a dryness to trick you into thinking it's bitter. But it's not, and this is one of those endlessly drinkable beers that it's hard to get bored with. It's also a really great food beer. Have it with a gratin of potato, fennel, olive, lemon, and Parmesan cheese. The beer does a remarkable job of emphasizing each individual ingredient. A pork chop is a good addition on the side.

BELGIAN BRUNE, DUBBEL, AND QUADRUPEL

THESE DARK BELGIAN BREWS INCREASE IN BODY, BOOZE, AND COMPLEXITY AS YOU MOVE FROM BRUNE THROUGH TO QUADRUPEL. BRUNES ARE EVERYDAY, EASY-DRINKING BEERS. THEY ARE DARK IN COLOR, WITH SOME CHOCOLATE, TOAST, AND PEPPERY HOPS, AND RARELY BREWED OUTSIDE OF BELGIUM. DUBBEL AND QUADRUPEL ARE LINKED TO ABBEY BREWING, AND REPRESENT CLASSIC BEER TYPES—SIMILAR RECIPES HAVE BEEN BREWED FOR CENTURIES. THESE ARE OFTEN RICH WITH CARAMEL, CHOCOLATE, DRIED FRUIT, FIGS, PLUMS, BANANA, AND PEPPER, BUT ARE RARELY SWEET; INSTEAD, MOST HAVE A SURPRISINGLY DRY FINISH. IT'S THE COMBINATION OF FRUITY FLAVORS, AN IMAGINED SWEETNESS, AND A DRY FINISH THAT MAKES THEM SO VERSATILE WITH DIFFERENT FOODS, FROM MAIN MEALS THROUGH TO DESSERTS AND SWEET SNACKS.

BOULEVARD BREWING THE SIXTH GLASS

BEST WITH: MOROCCAN LAMB CUTLETS

BREWED IN: KANSAS CITY, MISSOURI
ABV: 10.5%

Amber-red in color, with a thin lace of foam, The Sixth Glass is a classy tasting Belgian Quad. Caramel, tea bread, vanilla, earthy spice, figs, aniseed, orange liqueur, and roast apples—the first mouthful is like a shot of herbal spirit, as bitterness and sharp carbonation combine, and it ends with a very dry finish, while still leaving a pleasing sweetness on the lips, like a lipstick kiss. Moroccan-spiced lamb cutlets, cooked with cinnamon, coriander, pepper, cloves, salt, and paprika, and served with some raisin couscous (add some orange peel, too) is a very nice match. The spice in the beer is suddenly enhanced by the lamb, while the salt in the food lets the 10.5% ABV get through almost unnoticed.

BRIDGE: GAME BIRDS, MOROCCAN TAGINE, FRUIT CAKE

BALANCE: OATMEAL RAISIN COOKIES, BLUE CHEESE, SPAGHETTI AND MEATBALLS

BOOST: PULLED PORK, CHINESE DISHES, ROAST MEAT (ESPECIALLY GAME)

LOCAL: CARBONNADE, BELGIAN WAFFLES, BELGIAN CHOCOLATE

AVOID: CITRUS ACIDITY, WHITE FISH

UNIBROUE TROIS PISTOLES

BEST WITH: FIGS, BLUE CHEESE, AND PROSCIUTTO

BREWED IN: CHAMBLY, CANADA
ABV: 9.0%

Figs stuffed with blue cheese and wrapped in prosciutto might be more of a dinner-party starter than a beer snack, but make some when you want to drink a Dubbel or Quad, and you'll be glad you did. Trois Pistoles is rich with dried fruit, figs, some festive spices, toffee, cocoa, caramel, berries, and brown sugar, all with a vinous depth. The body is full and that combines with a refreshing carbonation to boost all of the flavors in the salty wrapped figs. Unibroue's website features food pairings and recipes for each of its beers; the brewery suggests using Trois Pistoles in a rabbit stew or brown sugar cookies and matching the beer with a variety of cheeses or a chocolate dessert.

PRETTY THINGS BABY TREE

BEST WITH: SHORTBREAD, MASCARPONE, AND ROAST APPLE

BREWED IN: CAMBRIDGE, MASSACHUSETTS
ABV: 9.0%

If you've read my other book, *Craft Beer World*, then you'll know that I've got a proper "brewmance" going on with Pretty Things—they can do no wrong. Beers with texture, body, depth that never seems to end, astonishing aromas, and just the most pronounced and wonderful flavors I've ever tasted. Baby Tree is another entry in my ongoing love letter. Vanilla, roast apples, and cola in the aroma; a big, smooth body, toasty and bready; candy sweetness in the background; and some spiciness alongside citrus pith. Try this beer with some salty shortbread biscuits topped with mascarpone and roast apple—there's some shared flavor and texture, and together the snack and beer create a perfect couple.

LEFFE BRUNE

BEST WITH: SWEET AND SOUR PORK

BREWED IN: DINANT, BELGIUM
ABV: 6.5%

Leffe Blonde and Brune are among the first Belgian beers many of us get to try, given their widespread distribution. The Blonde is frisky, fruity, and feisty, refreshing and nicely interesting without being challenging. The Brune, for me, has more going on, with a dose of dark sugar, caramel, dried fruits, and chocolate mixed with woody spices. Belgian Brune and Dubbel are surprisingly good with Chinese food, where the caramel depth and hint of spice in the beer is great with the salty-sweetness of the dishes. Sweet and sour pork (or whatever protein you prefer) works very well with Leffe Brune, where the beer can wrap right around all the bigger flavors and balance them, while also adding a flavor-boost of roast like the addition of soy sauce.

ROCHEFORT 6

BEST WITH: SAUSAGE, CHIPS, AND BEANS

BREWED IN: ROCHEFORT, BELGIUM
ABV: 7.5%

One day, for fun, two friends and I decided to try to find the perfect beer match for sausage, chips, and beans, a dinner that we all grew up eating as kids. They came to my house where I had a refrigerator filled with bottles, plus bangers on the grill (just a simple pork sausage, by the way). We had nine beers as we ate, and the best matches included Schlenkerla Rauchbier, which was as if we'd put liquid bacon with the meal, while Rodenbach's sweet-and-sour flavor was like a splodge of ketchup on the side. My favorite was Rochefort 6: the caramel and spice in the beer went straight for the bangers and beans; the carbonation lifted the meal, making it bounce around; and the beer also made the potatoes taste more potatoey. One of the geekiest meals I've ever had, but a lot of fun.

HOPPY SESSION BEER

THESE ARE THE KIND OF RELATIVELY LOW-ABV BEERS THAT HAVE BEEN BREWED IN THE UNITED KINGDOM FOR DECADES AND HAVE BEEN GIVEN A CRAFT-BEER MAKEOVER, TURNING THEM INTO BRIGHT, EXCITING, AND VIBRANT BEERS THROUGH THE USE OF AMERICAN, AUSTRALIAN, AND NEW ZEALAND HOPS, WHICH GIVE A BIG, BEAUTIFUL AROMA OF CITRUS AND TROPICAL FRUITS. THE EASIEST WAY TO THINK OF THEM IS AS MINI OR "SESSION IPAS." THEY ARE INCREASINGLY POPULAR WITH DRINKERS WHO WANT A BIG HIT OF HOPS WITHOUT A LEG-WOBBLING WALLOP OF ALCOHOL. THEY ARE GOOD WITH THE SORT OF FOOD THAT HELPS EXTEND YOUR DRINKING DAY, PARTICULARLY SALTY SNACKS, WHICH CAN SOFTEN THE BITTERNESS IN THESE BEERS.

BRIDGE: THAI TURKEY BURGERS, VIETNAMESE DISHES, CHILI PEANUTS

BALANCE: CHICKEN TENDERS, CHINESE FOOD, ASIAN FISH

BOOST: SMOKED MEAT AND FISH, CHICKEN TACOS, DIM SUM

LOCAL: GUACAMOLE AND NACHOS, BAR SNACKS, BARBECUE

AVOID: DESSERTS

DRAKE'S ALPHA SESSION

BEST WITH: FRIED VIETNAMESE SPRING ROLLS

BREWED IN: SAN LEANDRO, CALIFORNIA
ABV: 3.8%

A NorCal Bitter Ale is how Drake's describes this one. It's brewed with Bravo, Citra, and El Dorado hops, plus a hop so new that, at the time of writing, it doesn't even have a name, just a code—01210. Those hops give the beer a lovely aroma of lemon, grapefruit, bergamot, and lots of orange. It's clean, dry, and then bitter, and has the kind of pithy bitterness that really clings around, but also a savory kind of dryness. It's an excellent example of this new type of beer. With fried Vietnamese spring rolls, dipped in a sour-sweet-salty sauce, the hops are balanced by the deep-fried crunch, but the bitterness then comes back to refresh the mouthful and make you want more. There's a shared fruity, herbal quality between the two— mint, basil, lemon, and pepper—which works very well.

BRASSERIE DU MONT SALÈVE SORACHI ACE BITTER

BEST WITH: LEMONGRASS CRAB CAKES AND LEMON MAYONNAISE

BREWED IN: NEYDENS, FRANCE
ABV: 2.5%

Mont Salève makes some of the sexiest-looking beers in Europe. The brewery's range is broad and includes everything from this super-hopped light bitter to a French-hopped IPA to an Imperial Stout. After running the Paris Marathon, I went straight out drinking to try to find the best French beers and was happily surprised by both the range and quality, with all the beers sharing a dry finish and a lot of bitterness. Sorachi Ace Bitter is extraordinarily dry, bitingly and almost mineral bitter; there's a fierce carbonation; and it's loaded with lemony Sorachi Ace hops. Lemongrass crab cakes with lemon mayonnaise, plus an olive-oil-dressed salad—which is great with these hops—give some balance to go with the brew and boosts the lemony Sorachi Ace.

BREWDOG DEAD PONY CLUB

BEST WITH: PORK AND HOISIN WRAPS

BREWED IN: ELLON, SCOTLAND
ABV: 3.8%

Dead Pony Club has become like milk, muesli, and bananas to me; it doesn't need to go on the shopping list because I always remember to buy it. It's powerful, bold, and aggressive, yet only a modest 3.8% ABV, and remarkable for its hop aroma of roast citrus, tangerine juice, bitter herbs, and tropical fruit. The body is richer than a low-ABV beer should be, and then it's got the kind of bitterness that makes you drink more. I think it's excellent with hoisin sauce's fruitiness, with which it shares a kind of deep roast-citrus flavor. Roast some pork with hoisin and put it in a steamed bun or wrap it up, like a duck pancake, and top with some crushed peanuts.

EVIL TWIN BIKINI BEER

BEST WITH: SMOKED CHICKEN AND AVOCADO SALAD

BREWED IN: COPENHAGEN/BROOKLYN
ABV: 2.7%

A 2.7% hoppy pale beer packaged in cans—is there a more perfect thing to take along to the beach, music festivals, or summer barbecues? I don't think so. The beer's body is the equivalent of a tanned six-pack: it's an alluring bronze color, tight and toned, with no room for any excess flab. That light body holds up a big aroma of mandarin, melon, and grassy, floral hops before a dry bitterness. You finish one of these before your thirst is quenched, which is fine because, at 2.7% ABV, you can definitely drink a few. It's an outdoorsy beer and one for a healthy salad, I think. Smoked chicken and avocado is a very nice salad combination, which the juicy hops enliven with citrus, while the cooling avocado balances the beer's bitterness. This combination is also good in a sandwich.

THE KERNEL TABLE BEER

BEST WITH: SMOKED SALMON AND EGG BAGEL

BREWED IN: LONDON, ENGLAND
ABV: 3.0%

One of the most appealing things about The Kernel is that each new batch of beer tends to be deliberately a little different from the last one, with hop additions changing and grain bills being tweaked. The brewery does this because it isn't trying to match its beers to a standard taste and instead it's always trying and hoping to improve on the flavor. Table Beer is a really amazing drink, which varies between 2.7 and 3.3% ABV. It's hazy blonde, has a lemon, grapefruit, floral, and tropical hop aroma, and a dry finish. I took one sip of this beer and ordered a case of it—that's how much I liked it. At this low an ABV, it's fine to have for breakfast, so have it with some Eggs Benedict or London-smoked salmon on a toasted bagel with a poached egg.

BLONDE AND GOLDEN ALE

These are the spring and summer of the beer world: fresh and light, refreshing and fragrant, easy-going and enjoyable. They are louder than lager, but not as punchy as Pale Ales, and they arrived in Britain in the 1980s as sunny-weather ale alternatives to the ever-growing dominance of lager, with breweries aiming to entice drinkers away from ersatz Euro Pilsners. With a softness of pale malt and brightness from the hops, which could be European or New World, these are gently balanced beers that are approachable and designed to be uncomplicated and thirst-quenching.

BRIDGE: WHITE FISH AND SALSA, VEGETABLE BURGERS

BALANCE: CAESAR SALAD, DIM SUM, MEXICAN FOOD

BOOST: COCONUT-BASED CURRIES, THAI WEEPING TIGER SALAD

LOCAL: BARBECUE, PUB SANDWICH

AVOID: DESSERTS

DESCHUTES RIVER ALE

BEST WITH: PORK CHOP AND SWEET POTATO

BREWED IN: BEND, OREGON
ABV: 4.0%

Easy-drinking and interesting, sometimes you just want a beer like River Ale. Orangey gold in color, it has a simple and clean aroma of lime, marmalade, lemon, and grapefruit, plus some earthiness and toasty grain. The body feels classically English; there's a depth of chewiness and toast, and a really decent fullness that makes it very more-ish and good with food. Have this beer with a griddled pork chop—use some thyme and rosemary on top, because they are good with the hops—and some sweet potato fries. The char on the chop goes great with the suggestion of caramel in the beer and the sweet potato gives more sweetness. River Ale's citrusy American hops work well with all of this.

KROSS GOLDEN ALE

BEST WITH: CHURRASCO SANDWICH

BREWED IN: SANTIAGO, CHILE
ABV: 5.0%

One of Chile's best-regarded craft beers—although it's facing increasing competition from beers produced by other local breweries—Kross Golden Ale (which is more amber in color than golden, but we'll let that slip) uses American hops—Horizon, Cascade, and Chinook—to give a little pithy, floral, and herbal hop aroma to a beer that's rich with toasty malt, honey, and toffee. It's then light in bitterness, making this a good, balanced everyday gulper and something you'd be very happy to drink with dinner. Pizza is always a good choice with Golden Ale, but a better local choice would be empanadas or a churrasco sandwich. This is a bread roll filled with beef, avocado, tomato, and mayonnaise (not far off a hamburger). The beer's sweetness boosts the beef's flavor before the avocado gives some cooling balance.

STONE & WOOD PACIFIC ALE

BEST WITH: SEA BASS WITH SWEETCORN SALSA

BREWED IN: BYRON BAY, AUSTRALIA
ABV: 4.4%

Pacific Ale is brewed with Australian barley and wheat (this beer could also fit in the Wheat Ale category) and is then loaded up with Aussie Galaxy hops, which have a uniquely juicy mix of pineapple, peach, and mango. The beer is a hazy, unfiltered blonde and those hops immediately say hello with fresh, flirtatious, fleshy fruit. There aren't many beers with such an amazingly juicy aroma—I love it and it's the beer I've drunk the most while writing this book. With some sea bass and a sweetcorn, chili, lime, and cilantro (fresh coriander) salsa, the citrus in the beer lifts the sweet salsa and keeps it all very fresh. In both 2011 and 2012, Pacific Ale came second—behind Feral Brewing's Hop Hog—in the Critic's Choice Top 100 Beers of the year voted by *The Beer Lover's Guide to Australia*.

PURITY PURE GOLD

BEST WITH: SALMON AND LEMON BUTTER

BREWED IN: GREAT ALNE, ENGLAND
ABV: 3.8% ON CASK (4.3% IN BOTTLE)

Purity's Pure Gold is a smashing glass of sunshine refreshment from a modern brewery based in the Midlands. The cask version is 3.8% ABV and bottles are 4.3% ABV, and it's a Golden Beer brewed using German, English, and Slovenian hops. Chewy, with toasty malt in the middle, there's a little lemon, herbs, and tangy grapefruit in the aroma, plus a refreshing bitterness. It's great with food. You could try Caesar salad or veggie burgers, or even have it at brunch with some Eggs Benedict. I think it's delicious with grilled salmon, lemon butter sauce, and asparagus. The bright carbonation and subtle citrus in the hops balance the fish's richness and the butter sauce, while a hint of honey from the malt adds sweetness.

OAKHAM INFERNO

BEST WITH: CHICKEN SATAY

BREWED IN: PETERBOROUGH, ENGLAND
ABV: 4.0% ON CASK (4.4% IN BOTTLE)

If I owned a beer bar, Oakham's Inferno, Citra, and Green Devil IPA would always be in rotation through my taps. Oakham is a very good brewery that consistently brews excellent beers with a real clarity of flavor. They are very clean, and you can clearly taste the depth of malt and distinct fruity freshness from the hops. And hops are something this brewery is very good at adding in order to produce the best aroma. Cask Inferno is a favorite of mine: a little chewy biscuit malt and loads of zingy, fresh, grapefruity hops, plus a little floral aroma. In bottle, you get more carbonation, plus more alcohol and zestiness. Chicken satay is good with all the Oakham beers, where the nutty, citrusy sauce is boosted by the hops.

BRITISH ALES

BRITISH ALES ARE LIKE A WELL-TIMED COVER DRIVE COMPARED WITH THE BRUTAL HOME-RUN HIT OF AN AMERICAN IPA. THEY COMBINE HOP FRAGRANCE, DEPTH OF MALT, AND DRY BITTERNESS TO BE QUENCHING, EASY-GOING, SOCIAL DRINKS, WHICH ARE INTIMATELY TIED TO THE PUB. THEY ARE EVOCATIVE OF WOOD, SMOKE, AND NEARBY FIELDS OR FORESTS; EVOCATIVE OF CHARACTERS, COMFORT, PERSONALITY, AND SIMPLICITY, WHILE STILL HAVING GREAT DEPTH. AS VARIED AS THE BRITISH WEATHER, THEY COULD BE PALE BLONDE THROUGH TO VERY DEEP BROWN, LIGHTLY HOPPED OR BRACINGLY BITTER; THEY WILL PROBABLY BE BREWED WITH BRITISH HOPS, ALTHOUGH NEW WORLD HOPS ARE INCREASINGLY COMMON. INCLUDED IN THIS CATEGORY ARE MILD, BITTER, AND ESB. WITH FOOD, THESE ALES TEND TO HAVE A DRY BITTERNESS, SO SOME FAT IN THE DISH IS GOOD. SIMPLICITY IS OFTEN THE BEST MATCH FOR THESE EVERYDAY BEERS. YOU MAY FIND THAT A CHEESE SANDWICH IS JUST ABOUT THE PERFECT PAIRING.

BRIDGE: MEAT PIES, ROAST MEAT, ROAST VEGETABLES

BALANCE: BLACK PUDDING, THAI FOOD, VEGETABLE CURRY

BOOST: SAUSAGES, SMOKED FISH, WELSH RAREBIT

LOCAL: PLOUGHMAN'S LUNCH, FISH AND CHIPS, SCOTCH EGGS

AVOID: DESSERT, TOO MUCH CHILI

ILKLEY BLACK

BEST WITH: TOAD IN THE HOLE

BREWED IN: ILKLEY, ENGLAND
ABV: 3.7%

This is a Mild, although what a Mild is today is a little difficult to define. Once a beer that was served fresh—and hence had a milder flavor compared with aged beers—Mild evolved to become a beer associated with a low-ABV and a gentle flavor, which undermined many great examples of stronger and richer Milds. Yorkshire-brewed Ilkley Black is modest in ABV, but doesn't lack any depth, with black tea, berries, pungent English hops, and a little roast in the background, all very smooth and satisfying. Toad in the hole is a batter or, more appropriately for this beer, a Yorkshire pudding, that's baked with sausages in it. Serve with some thick onion gravy and you'll find that Ilkley Black adds a surprising sweetness and a balancing bitterness. You could also use some of this beer in the batter before cooking.

GOOSE ISLAND HONKER'S ALE

BEST WITH: CHICAGO-STYLE ITALIAN BEEF

BREWED IN: CHICAGO, ILLINOIS
ABV: 4.3%

The Chicago episode of Man vs. Food was our research on a trip to the Windy City. With an Al's Beef right by our hotel, this was our first stop for an Italian beef sandwich. The beef comes in a long roll and is seasoned, roasted, and then kept in gravy until it's piled into the bread and topped with hot peppers and giardiniera, a pickled mix of onions, celery, and carrots. Together, it's a hot, messy, glorious sandwich, which is great with a Honker's Ale. English-style, with bread and toffee in the malt base, the hops are Slovenian Styrians and give orange peel, pepper, and herbs with an earthy bitterness. That hop fragrance picks out the peppers on the sandwich and the malt adds sweetness. With that combination, man definitely won.

FULLER'S LONDON PRIDE

BEST WITH: PORK PIE

BREWED IN: LONDON, ENGLAND
ABV: 4.1% ON CASK, 4.7% IN BOTTLES

Pork pies are weird. They have a firm, hot-water pastry on the outside and a center that's thick with pork cuts and set in a jelly. It's a park and picnic regular, and often seen in pubs sitting next to the Scotch eggs. I wouldn't have one on its own (like I said, they're weird), but with a pint of London Pride, a pork pie almost becomes essential. The beer is a classic: pale amber with an aroma of English hop sacks, berries, and gardens; the body is biscuity, complex, and clean, with a dry, quenching finish. It's exactly what a British Bitter should be. The earthy English hop bitterness balances the fat in the pie, while the addition of chutney or mustard adds a pleasant fruitiness.

NYNÄSHAMNS ANGBRYGGERI BEDARÖ BITTER

BEST WITH: GRAVAD LAX

BREWED IN: NYNÄSHAMN, SWEDEN
ABV: 4.5%

Lots of lovely floral and forest fruits dominate the aroma of Bedarö Bitter, Nynäshamns Angbryggeri's best-selling beer. Those hops suggest Englishness, but the beer is also supercharged with some American hops. A lightly hazy golden color, there's a waft of dried citrus and some earthiness; the body is tight and dry, and yet still robust and strong; and the bitterness is the sort that makes you think of dry herb liqueurs. Gravad lax is salmon cured with salt, sugar, pepper, and dill, which is best served on bread. The beer has a mineral-like cleanness that slices through the fish's richness, while the hops reveal a herbal depth that you hadn't noticed earlier.

HOLGATE ESB

BEST WITH: SAUSAGE ROLL

BREWED IN: VICTORIA, AUSTRALIA
ABV: 5.0%

ESB stands for Extra Special Bitter. Think of it as a regular Bitter, only bigger in all directions: more malt, more alcohol, and more hops. With this you should expect a deep malt depth with toast or caramel and then a defined and lingering hop flavor and bitterness. Holgate's ESB is a properly English take on the style, so it's got toasty malts, earthy hops, and some dried fruit, plus a hint of an Aussie accent coming from the late addition of peachy Galaxy hops. Try it with a really good sausage roll for an unpretentious pairing. The hops and sausage herbs match up and the beer gives sweetness to cut through the fat. Like a pork pie or Scotch egg, Holgate ESB is made for the pub or a picnic.

AMERICAN PALE ALE

PALE ALE DEVELOPED ALONGSIDE AMBER LAGER AND AMBER ALE AS THE CRAFT ALTERNATIVE TO THE LACKLUSTER LAGERS DOMINATING THE MARKET. THE AROMA OF AMERICAN HOPS— CITRUS, FLORAL, AND PINE—AND A DEEP GOLDEN BODY OF MALT DEFINE THE STYLE, WHICH CAN BE VERY BROAD IN HOW IT TASTES, RANGING FROM LIGHT AND DELICATE TO BRASH AND BOLD. IT'S THE QUINTESSENTIAL CRAFT BEER STYLE AND YOU CAN GET HOLD OF PALE ALE FROM ALASKA TO AUCKLAND, SHANGHAI TO SÃO PAULO, AND EVERYWHERE IN BETWEEN: IT'S THE WORLD'S LOCAL CRAFT-BEER STYLE AND FRESH IS ALWAYS BEST, SO CHOOSE A LOCAL BEER AND LOCAL FOOD TO GO WITH IT. THE BEST MATCHES ARE CASUAL, EVERYDAY FOODS IN WHICH THE SALT, CHARRED MEAT, OR FAT WILL HELP TO BALANCE THE HOPS IN THE BREW.

BAIRD RISING SUN PALE ALE

BEST WITH: CHICKEN KARAAGE

BREWED IN: NAMAZU, JAPAN
ABV: 5.3%

Run by husband and wife Bryan and Sayuri Baird, you'll find a range of American-inspired beers brewed to suit local tastes, focusing on a supreme balance of flavors. Rising Sun Pale Ale pours a copper color and immediately gives loads of fresh and pithy citrus: lime, yuzu, and oranges, plus orange candy. The malt is full-bodied and carries the citrus hop flavor through to its lasting, clean bitterness. It's a beer for izakaya food—casual snacks that you eat while drinking. Have a bowl of salted edamame beans, yakitori, or chicken karaage—pieces of chicken are marinated in garlic, ginger, sake, soy, and sesame oil, coated in flour, and then deep-fried to give hot, crispy nuggets. With some lemon on top, this is the ideal snack to go with Rising Sun. Baird's Suruga Bay Imperial IPA is a great Double IPA if you want to try something bigger.

BRIDGE: ROTISSERIE CHICKEN, MEXICAN FOOD, PULLED PORK, OR RIBS

BALANCE: BLACKENED FISH AND SALSA, FRIED CHICKEN, BURGERS AND SANDWICHES

BOOST: BARBECUED SEAFOOD, GRILLED MEAT, PIZZA

LOCAL: FRIED POTATOES, BAR SNACKS

AVOID: DESSERT

LITTLE CREATURES PALE ALE

BEST WITH: BARBECUED SHRIMP

```
BREWED IN: FREEMANTLE, AUSTRALIA
ABV: 5.2%
```

Like Sierra Nevada's Pale Ale, Little Creatures Pale Ale is a style-defining beer. It can be credited with kick-starting Australian craft brewing and is a clever mix of Aussie and American hops to give subtle citrus and juicy tropical fruit. It's a relaxed, easy-going kind of beer and the ultimate antipodean refreshment. We look to Paul Hogan, better known as Crocodile Dundee, for this match. In TV ads for the Australian Tourism Commission in the mid to late 1980s, he said: "I'll slip an extra shrimp on the barbie for you," and created a legendary catchphrase. Clichéd, for sure, but with Creatures, it's a bloody good match for shrimp, mate. The Pale Ale's hint of caramel makes the shrimp taste sweeter, while the malt deals with the barbecue's char and the hops add a citrusy seasoning.

KOCOUR CATFISH SUMEČEK

BEST WITH: BRAMBORÁKY

```
BREWED IN: VARNSDORF,
CZECH REPUBLIC
ABV: 4.2%
```

Kocour is one of the Czech Republic's modern breweries, producing a range of updated takes on Euro classics, such as its bacony V3 Rauchbier, Kiwi-hopped Haka NZ Lager, and an impossible-to-pronounce cherry lager called Višňový Ležák, plus some hoppy brews with a clear American influence. The brewery's American-style beers—Catfish Sumeček Pale Ale, IPA Samuraj, and the Double IPA 70 Quarterback—are all very good and show off the smooth, soft drinkability of a classy Czech beer, plus the juicy, fragrant aroma of American hops with a very clean, precise bitterness. Order a mug of Catfish and carefully approach the Czech menu, which is dominated by dumplings and meat. Eschew those and choose bramboráky. This is a fried potato pancake and we all know how well Pale Ale works with fried potatoes.

SIERRA NEVADA PALE ALE

BEST WITH: PORK WITH ORANGE AND THYME

```
BREWED IN: CHICO, CALIFORNIA
ABV: 5.6%
```

The first Pale Ale and still one of the best, this is a classic craft beer that has inspired and converted countless brewers and drinkers. It was first brewed in November 1980, although it took 11 batches before Ken Grossman and Paul Camusi, the brewery's founders, were happy enough to release it in the spring of 1981. Deep gold in color, the aroma is pure Cascade hops, with grapefruit pith and flesh, and a floral background that is so fresh and gently appealing. The body is satisfyingly malty, and then you get a dry, quenching bitterness, which gives more grapefruit flavor. I love this beer with roast pork with orange and thyme—the hops bridge to the fruit and herbs, and cut through the pig fat. A veggie alternative would be Glamorgan sausages made with cheese, leeks, and breadcrumbs.

WAY AMERICAN PALE ALE

BEST WITH: PÃO DE QUEIJO (CHEESE BUNS)

```
BREWED IN: PINHAIS, BRAZIL
ABV: 5.2%
```

Brewed with Cascade, Citra, and Amarillo hops, Way's APA, which the brewery describes as being for "Lupulomaníacos" (hop maniacs), has a pithy, floral, resinous hop aroma and a toasty malt body with a gentle, smooth bitterness—it's definitely in the American style, but what makes it different is how the bitterness is restrained to suit local tastes. Pão de Queijo are little buns, crisp and chewy, super cheesy, and unbelievably light; you could eat about a million of them. The shared fruitiness in the cheese and hops makes this an addictive match because, when they're together, you never want your plate to be clear or your glass to be empty. Pao de Queijo is a snack for any of the Way beers, which also include a Double IPA, a Cream Porter, and a strong wood-aged lager.

AMERICAN IPA

IPA IS THE BEST-SELLING CRAFT BEER STYLE IN AMERICA AND ONE THAT'S BEEN COPIED AROUND THE WORLD. IT ALL STARTED WITH A BEER BREWED CENTURIES AGO, ONE WHICH TRAVELED FROM ENGLAND TO INDIA AND GAINED THE NAME INDIA PALE ALE. THAT STORY EVOLVED WHEN CRAFT BREWING KICKED OFF IN AMERICA IN THE 1980S AND THE STYLE HAS SINCE BECOME DOMINATED WITH THE FLAVOR, BITTERNESS, AND AROMA OF AMERICAN-GROWN HOPS. NOW, IF YOU SEE THOSE THREE LETTERS—AND IF YOU DRINK A LOT OF BEER, THEN YOU'LL SEE THEM A LOT—YOU CAN GENERALLY EXPECT SOMETHING BURSTING WITH CITRUSY HOPS AND WITH A DEFINITE, BOLD BITTERNESS. THE FLAVORS INHERENT IN IPAS CREATE NATURAL BRIDGES TO FOOD, WITH HOP OILS CONTAINING SIMILAR COMPOUNDS TO WOODY HERBS, GARLIC, ONIONS, AND CITRUS, WHILE THE STRONG MALT BODY GIVES THE BALANCE OF SWEETNESS.

BRIDGE: VIETNAMESE, ANYTHING WITH KETCHUP, ROAST GARLIC AND WOODY HERBS

BALANCE: ONION RINGS, CHICKEN TENDERS, CHEDDAR CHEESE

BOOST: BARBECUE, MEXICAN FOOD, CARROT CAKE

LOCAL: CHEESEBURGER, MAC 'N' CHEESE

AVOID: DELICATE DISHES, DESSERTS

TOCCALMATTO SKIZOID

BEST WITH: ARANCINI

BREWED IN: FIDENZA, ITALY
ABV: 6.2%

Hopped with Columbus, Centennial, and Chinook, Skizoid is a copper-colored Italian IPA that's got all the citrus you'd expect, plus some ripe peaches and apricots, pine, flowers, and grapes. Put it with arancini, which are breadcrumbed and fried rice balls filled with ragù sauce and mozzarella. This combination works because the richness in the rice bridges to the fullness in the beer's body; the meat and cheese middle is super with the malt and hops; and the bitterness does its job of keeping things refreshing, meaning that you've always got room for more arancini. Toccalmatto makes some of Italy's best beers: Zona Cesarini is a superlative IPA, Stray Dog is a banging Bitter, Surfing Hop is a monster Double IPA, and B Space Invader is a beauty of a Black IPA.

BREWDOG PUNK IPA

BEST WITH: DEEP-FRIED HAGGIS

BREWED IN: ELLON, SCOTLAND
ABV: 5.6%

This was the beer that made me realize I was a beer geek. As I was starting to get interested in beer, BrewDog launched and was making beers unlike anyone else in Britain: big flavor and a bold use of hops, plus a regular range of new brews that I was thirsty to try. Punk IPA is BrewDog's flagship beer. Golden in color, the aroma is a mix of citrus and tropical fruits, with a load of dank, resinous pine in the background. The body has a little roundness, which helps with food, and a bitterness that is dry and clings on. The pairing may be parochially Scottish—and perhaps clichéd owing to the Scottish love of battering food— but with deep-fried haggis, Punk IPA is a lot of fun, as the citrus hops burst through all the rich meat. The non-Scottish alternatives would be onion rings or onion bhajis.

CENTRAL CITY RED RACER IPA

BEST WITH: SMOKED BACON MAC 'N' CHEESE

BREWED IN: SURREY, CANADA
ABV: 6.5%

This copper-colored canned Canadian IPA (try saying that after a six-pack...) is brewed with German Magnum hops and American Amarillo, Centennial, and Simcoe hops, which combine to give classic grapefruit, orange, and pine, plus bitter herbs and berries. The body has some lip-sticking sweetness and is toasty with caramel, which carries more hop flavor before the 80 units of bitterness kick out a citrus-pith bite. A 2010 survey of Canadians revealed that 43 percent would choose bacon over sex, so let's satisfy those urges with smoked bacon mac 'n' cheese. Smoky, salty bacon balances bitterness and highlights sweetness in the beer and cheese, plus those hops love cheese.

BELLS TWO HEARTED

BEST WITH: SMOKED TROUT TART

BREWED IN: KALAMAZOO, MICHIGAN
ABV: 7.0%

Ernest Hemingway once wrote a story called "Big Two-Hearted River," named after the eponymous river in Northern Michigan. In this story, the protagonist catches a couple of fish and enjoys an onion sandwich and a cigarette for lunch on the river's edge. You could use that as food inspiration, but onion sandwiches sound disgusting, so, alternatively, look to the rainbow trout on the beer's label for a better match, especially if the fish is smoked and baked in a tart with leeks and served with a watercress, fennel, and orange salad. Two Hearted is a quintessential American IPA, and is rightly regarded as one of the best. Hazy orange in color, with a fluffy, white foam, it's a symposium of Centennial hops, giving oranges and blossom. The body is smooth and balanced, and carries loads of hop flavor, while the juicy orange works so nicely with the richness of smoked fish.

RUSSIAN RIVER BLIND PIG IPA

BEST WITH: GARLIC AND MOZZARELLA PIZZA DOUGH

BREWED IN: SANTA ROSA, CALIFORNIA
ABV: 6.1%

The sight of that smartly dressed, portly pig is enough to get beer geeks very excited. Russian River is known for its incomparable IPAs, beers with astonishing balance and depth, as well as an awesome aroma. Pliny the Elder is the Double IPA, an 8.0% beauty, while Blind Pig is the everyday drinker that I wish was always in my refrigerator. A luminous orange-gold, you get grapefruit, tangerine, floral hops, and pine needles. It's a beer made for gulping with its super-smooth body and quenching bitterness. At the brewpub in Santa Rosa, you can get Beer Bites, which are hunks of pizza dough topped with garlic and mozzarella (ask for extra Cheddar cheese, if you can—it's even better). The garlic brings out a savory-like hop flavor and the cheese is excellent with both the malt and hops. Beer snacks are the best thing for Blind Pig.

PALE ALE AND IPA FAMILY

THE IDEA OF AN IPA GIVES US A BEER THAT'S FAIRLY STRONG AND BOLDLY HOPPED. TAKING THAT TEMPLATE, IT'S EASY TO DEVELOP THIS STYLE IN MANY DIFFERENT DIRECTIONS AND THIS SECTION BRINGS A BUNCH OF THEM TOGETHER ALONGSIDE VARIATIONS OF PALE ALES. WHAT WE HAVE HERE ARE BEERS THAT BYPASS THE AMERICAN HOPS AND INSTEAD USE ENGLISH (LIKE THE ORIGINAL PALE ALES AND IPAS), AUSTRALIAN, NEW ZEALAND, AND CENTRAL EUROPEAN HOPS. ALSO INCLUDED ARE HOPPY BEERS BREWED USING BELGIAN YEAST TO GIVE A MIX OF FRUITY HOPS AND FRAGRANT, SPICY YEAST. IPA IS A BROAD STYLE OF BEER AND THIS SELECTION DEMONSTRATES ITS RANGE.

The flavors from different hops and yeast strains naturally align to different culinary ingredients, so here's a quick cheat sheet based on where each hop grows or yeast strain is produced.

GERMAN AND CZECH: Lemon, black pepper, mayonnaise, European mustard
ENGLISH: Parsley, thyme, chutney, curry spices, English mustard, meat gravy
NEW ZEALAND AND AUSTRALIA: Lime, cilantro (coriander), mint, sweet chili, soy sauce
AMERICAN: Ketchup and American mustard, salsa, rosemary, fried onions
BELGIAN YEAST: Black pepper, aniseed, basil, mint

CISCO BREWERS WHALE'S TALE

BEST WITH: WELSH RAREBIT

BREWED IN: NANTUCKET, MASSACHUSETTS
ABV: 5.5%

Made with Maris Otter malt and Golding hops, this is as English as an American-brewed beer can be. I had a can of this with Welsh rarebit for brunch in Hawthornes, Philadelphia. It's like a restaurant meets a beer store, and you can walk to the huge refrigerators, choose your beer, and then take it back to your table to drink with your food. The beer is deep amber in color and has a marvelously marmaladey aroma, with floral and roast citrus. The body is chewy and mouth-filling (a bit like marmalade on toast), it's clean and easy-drinking, and the hops lead to an earthy, clinging bitterness. This beer is excellent with some Welsh rarebit, as it becomes like a lovely chutney on the side and is excellent with the cheese. The best thing about Whale's Tale is that it has the great skill of making the Golding hop sexy.

RATSHERRN PALE ALE

BEST WITH: FRIED FISH ROLL

BREWED IN: HAMBURG, GERMANY
ABV: 5.6%

If you're in Hamburg, Germany, you have to visit Ratsherrn, a modern brewery next to Altes Mädchen, which is a beer bar with a large range of brews on tap and in bottle. Ratsherrn brews a Pils, a Rotbier, and a Pale Ale, plus some interesting specials. The Pale Ale is brewed with German Hercules, Hallertauer Tradition, Hallertauer Mittelfrüh, and Sapphire hops, plus some American Cascade at the end. It's a classy Pale Ale that shows off the stone fruit and herbs of German hops, plus the floral, citrus Cascade, and they combine wonderfully. As a port city, there's lots of fish in Hamburg. A local lunch is fried fish in a bread roll with some tartare sauce, and the beer's fruitiness and bitterness is exactly what you want with this.

FLYING DOG RAGING BITCH

BEST WITH: HONEY AND
ROSEMARY ROASTED PARSNIPS

BREWED IN: FREDERICK,
MARYLAND
ABV: 8.3%

Raging Bitch is a Belgian-style
IPA, which means it's like an
American IPA in its malt base
and mix of citrusy hops, but
then a Belgian yeast rips
through it and adds a spicy
depth—in this case, the spice is
like cloves and pepper. Unusual
at first, then intriguing, and
then you're hooked. The aroma
gets all the nice citrus, plus
tropical fruit, even some banana
and pear esters, and then it dips
down into a woody, almost smoky,
spiciness. Roasted parsnips have an earthy,
herbal, aniseed-like spiciness and adding
honey also brings out some banana fragrance.
By throwing on the woody, phenolic, resinous
rosemary (which shares aromatic compounds
with American hops), you complete a perfect
dot-to-dot between yeast, vegetable, and hops
and then fill it in with sweet honey and malt.

NOMÁD KAREL

BEST WITH: SMAŽENÝ SÝR OR
NAKLÁDANÝ HERMELÍN

BREWED IN: PRAGUE, CZECH REPUBLIC
ABV: 7.6%

This is a Czech-hopped IPA and probably the
best beer I drank in 2013. It's brewed only
with Czech hops, although I assumed it was
all-American hops due to its outrageously
delicious aroma of peaches, apricots, lemon,
and tangerine. I drank this IPA while on a
stag-do in Prague, and all I can remember is
sitting at a long table, surrounded by 16
blokes, and shouting out (repeatedly) how
this is the best beer I've ever tasted in the
whole damn world. I went back to another
bar the next day just to make sure that I
hadn't been tricked the night before: I hadn't
been. You can only get this beer in the Czech
Republic, but it's worth traveling for and,
when you're there, order some smažený sýr
(fried cheese) or nakládaný hermelín (pickled
cheese with chili). These taste odd on their
own, but are great with this beer's fruitiness
and soft hop bitterness.

MAGIC ROCK CLOWN JUICE

BEST WITH: SZECHUAN PEPPER BEEF

BREWED IN: HUDDERSFIELD, ENGLAND
ABV: 7.0%

This is an India Wit Ale and is somewhere between an
IPA and a Witbier, meaning that it's a Belgian Wheat
Beer, brewed with the classic orange peel and
coriander, fermented to 7.0% ABV with a classic
Witbier yeast, and then heavily hopped and dry-
hopped with American Cascade and Amarillo, just
like an IPA. It's an astonishing beer: all kinds of
different citrus fruits, banana, clove, savory-like
coriander, peppery spice, and tropical fruit. All of
that spiciness, plus the juicy citrus, pushes it
toward your plate. Stir-fry beef with some
szechuan peppers, soy sauce, and sugar, and then
add some green vegetables where the combination
of spices, heat, pepper, and citrusy hops will leave
you with a big, painted-on smile.

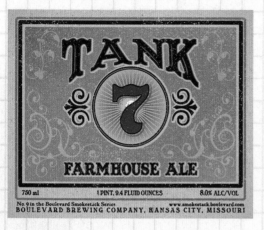

BOULEVARD BREWING TANK 7

BEST WITH: FISH BANH MI

BREWED IN: KANSAS CITY, MISSOURI
ABV: 8.5%

"I'm drinking Boulevard Tank 7. Buy one!" That's the text I sent my mate Mark after my first taste of this beer—he was at the Great British Beer Festival and I knew they had bottles there. He replied soon after: "Holy shit. Tank 7 is ridiculously good!" When you drink a lot of different beers, it's easy to get complacent about them. Then, sometimes you taste something that's so exciting, so interesting, and just so damn good that it makes you jump up and down. Tank 7 has amazing, intoxicating aromas of roast pineapple, rhubarb, and mango, a light and clean body, then a peppery, spicy bitterness. Although not technically an IPA, it's hoppy enough to count, I reckon. It's so good that my mate Matt took a bottle with him on his honeymoon to Vietnam where he had it with a banh mi and said it was one of the best beer matches he'd ever had. The mint and cilantro (fresh coriander) in the sandwich work so well with the yeast and hops.

ADNAMS INNOVATION

BEST WITH: MUSHROOMS ON TOAST

BREWED IN: SOUTHWOLD, ENGLAND
ABV: 6.7%

"Brew something to wow me!" was the instruction from Jonathan Adnams, brewery chairman, when he wanted a new beer to celebrate the opening of Adnams' new brewhouse in 2007. Innovation was the result and it's proved so popular that a beer intended as a one-off has become a permanent brew in the Jack Brand range. It's a worldly IPA that uses English Boadicea, Slovenian Styrian Goldings, and American Columbus hops to give grapefruit, flowers, lemon, herbs, and berries. Fry some mushrooms in butter with lots of black pepper, some garlic, and thyme leaves, then finish with crème fraîche, and serve on a slice of toasted bread. The hops bridge to the pepper, earthy mushrooms, and thyme, and then the bitterness refreshes it. A good breakfast or brunch.

8 WIRED SUPER CONDUCTOR

BEST WITH: PORK AND PINEAPPLE SKEWERS

BREWED IN: BLENHEIM, NEW ZEALAND
ABV: 8.88%

8 Wired's HopWired is the quintessential Kiwi IPA. It is made only with local grain and hops, giving the beer an amazing aroma of passion fruit, gooseberry, and grapes, and a general greenness. Super Conductor is the brewery's Double IPA, a mix of Aussie and Kiwi hops, with a helluva lot more added compared with the already-hoppy HopWired. You get a beer that's unbelievably dry and boldly bitter, with a huge, juicy, fruity aroma of exotic fruit, resinous citrus pith, gooseberries, lime, and Thai basil, and a whiplash of lasting bitterness. Alternate pieces of pork and pineapple on a skewer, and then roast or barbecue. Put the pork and pineapple in a soft taco and throw on some lime and fresh green chili. The fruitiness of the beer is utterly perfect with the roast pineapple and caramelized meat.

MURRAY'S ICON 2IPA

BEST WITH: THAI TURKEY BURGERS

BREWED IN: PORT STEPHENS, AUSTRALIA
ABV: 7.5%

An Aussie Double IPA, which is brewed next to a vineyard about 322 km (200 miles) north of Sydney, Icon 2IPA is part of Murray's year-round beer range. Murray's also has a restaurant where you can try the beers and work through some of the interesting seasonal offerings, which include a pumpkin ale, Hopfenweisse, a 2.8% ABV Red IPA, and a smoked, Belgian-yeast-fermented Stout brewed with mussels and oysters. The menu suggests a beer and wine match for each item and they reckon that the cheeseburger is the best thing for Icon 2IPA. And it's a great choice. The beer has a banging aroma of tropical fruit, grapes, passionfruit, lime, blood oranges, and sweet grapefruit. The body is big, but not boozy, there's a caramelized fruit sweetness, and the bitterness bites, but doesn't hurt. A Thai-spiced turkey burger also loves all of those tangy tropical fruits.

SIERRA NEVADA ESTATE ALE

BEST WITH: APPLE CAKE

BREWED IN: CHICO, CALIFORNIA
ABV: 6.7%

As soon as hops are harvested, they are typically dried to reduce their water content and ensure they remain good for brewing for a whole year. But, for a very short period around the hop harvest each year, and for those breweries based near hop farms, there's the opportunity for the only truly seasonal brew: the green, fresh, or wet hop beer. For this, the hops bypass the drying process and go direct from bine to brew kettle in a few hours, aiming to capture all the delicate oils that are lost during the drying process. Sierra Nevada's Estate Ale is unique, as the brewery grows its own hops and barley for the brew, and they combine to give a beer with a melon-like, grassy, blossomy freshness. Make sure you drink green-hops beers fresh and eat something similarly seasonal with them. As apples come just after hops in the harvest calendar, the apples will be picked by the time the beers are ready. Bake an apple cake and open the beer.

WORTHINGTON'S WHITE SHIELD

BEST WITH: KEDGEREE

BREWED IN: BURTON-UPON-TRENT, ENGLAND
ABV: 5.6%

India Pale Ale originated in London, but it was when brewers in Burton-upon-Trent, in Staffordshire, started making beers for export to India that the style really developed. They combined pale malts with the local hard water to give a brighter beer than seen in the capital, as well as brews that emphasized hop and malt flavor. Breweries such as Bass and Allsops became enormous brewing entities, while Worthington Brewery was a significant other in the famous brewing town. Much has changed in the town since then, although Worthington's White Shield has stayed in production as a genuine India Pale Ale. Deep bronze in color, the hops give roast apples, hop sacks, and a deep woody earthiness. It's rich in texture and then the bitterness is deep and quenching. It's bottle-conditioned and ages well, giving more fruit and a sherry character over time. With kedgeree, a rice dish of smoked fish, curry spices, and boiled egg, the hops play with the smoke and earthy spice and the malt brings a balancing sweetness.

DOUBLE IPA

You might immediately think that Double IPA (or Imperial IPA—it's the same thing) is a terrible or terrifying style for food, being so big, bold, and often aggressively overpowering, but there are some wonderful ways to match it up with different dishes. What you'll get from a Double IPA is a beer on the golden-amber color spectrum with a booming hop aroma, a deep and perhaps sweet malt body, and then a hefty bitterness at the end. The best are teasing and somehow elegant, balancing massive malt and heroic amounts of hops (the worst taste like nail polish mixed with honey and hop juice). Fat and salt are the best tricks with DIPA, but the beer's naturally high sweetness does create its own spice-softening qualities.

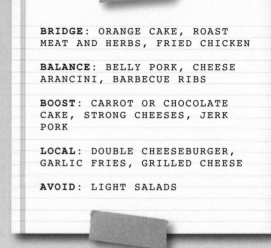

BRIDGE: ORANGE CAKE, ROAST MEAT AND HERBS, FRIED CHICKEN

BALANCE: BELLY PORK, CHEESE ARANCINI, BARBECUE RIBS

BOOST: CARROT OR CHOCOLATE CAKE, STRONG CHEESES, JERK PORK

LOCAL: DOUBLE CHEESEBURGER, GARLIC FRIES, GRILLED CHEESE

AVOID: LIGHT SALADS

THORNBRIDGE HALCYON

BEST WITH: GRILLED APRICOTS, MASCARPONE, AND PROSCIUTTO HAM

BREWED IN: BAKEWELL, ENGLAND
ABV: 7.4%

Have you ever seen a cage-fighter doing ballet? Me neither, but this beer is the equivalent of that sight. It has a serious 7.4% ABV, but the body, while muscular, is also deft and light; a pale gold, a hint of sweetness, but mostly just strong in the sense that it holds all the hops in place. And those hops aren't an olfactory assault; they are the ballet's orchestra to the cage-fighter's thrash metal. With tangerine, floral, peaches, and apricots, it's juicy and wonderfully clean and pronounced. It's an excellent beer and, given its dual personality of softness and power, it can handle some big flavor. Grill some fresh apricots with rosemary and put them on toast with mascarpone and prosciutto. The cheese cuts the bitterness, the fruit teases the hops, and the meat gives salty sweetness.

ALPINE EXPONENTIAL HOPPINESS

BEST WITH: MANGO OR STRAWBERRY, ROSEMARY, CHEESE

BREWED IN: ALPINE, CALIFORNIA
ABV: 11.0%

Hops contain terpenes, including myrcene, citral, linalool, pinene, and more, which produce woody, resinous, floral, citrus, and herbaceous qualities. These terpenes are naturally found in the essential oils of many other plants and ingredients, such as rosemary, bay, thyme, sage, mint, lemongrass, and mangoes, meaning that hoppy beers are naturally aligned to these flavors. Combine mango, rosemary, thyme, and strong cheese (the cheese balances big bitterness) in a tart or quesadilla, or try roasting strawberries with some rosemary and have them with triple cream cheese on a salty shortbread for a great match to very hoppy beers. Exponential Hoppiness is a Tripel IPA, so even bigger than a Double IPA, and gets its name because each hop addition is double the previous amount, making it exponentially hoppy. It's a monster of a beer, brutal and brilliant, exploding with hops, piney, and resinous. It has citrus pith and roasted fruit, and then a slick, full, boozy body. Yet, somehow, it's enormously drinkable. Herby lamb burgers with mango chutney are also good with this.

EPIC HOP ZOMBIE

BEST WITH: SPICED LAMB CUTLETS

BREWED IN: AUCKLAND, NEW ZEALAND
ABV: 8.5%

Need... More... Hops... is the tagline for Hop Zombie, a beer that will satisfy even the most savage hop-lover, leaving them zombified and soporific before kicking them in the backside with its bitterness. At 8.5% ABV, it's a beastly brew made with a mix of American and New Zealand hops, giving grapefruit, pineapple, mango, passionfruit, and resinous pine needles. The malt body is pretty light, but hardy enough to handle those hops before waving the white flag and letting the bitterness power through. Bake some well-seasoned lamb cutlets with garlic, pepper, chili, and rosemary, and finish off with some cilantro (fresh coriander) and lime juice. It's a great snack—which, if you wish, let's you pretend that you're a carnivorous zombie—giving fat and salt for the bitterness and herbs to bridge to the hops.

CAPTAIN LAWRENCE CAPTAIN'S RESERVE IMPERIAL IPA

BEST WITH: JERK CHICKEN AND COLESLAW

BREWED IN: ELMSFORD, NEW YORK
ABV: 9.0%

I don't generally like chili heat with lots of hops, but this is one of the rare and wonderful exceptions. The beer has a lush mix of apricots, peaches, mango, and orange blossom, which is really fresh and enticing, and it's backed up with an almost-sweet and soft-bodied caramel depth. With jerk spices, the malt wraps right around the heat, smothering it in a good way, while the citrusy herbs are enhanced by the hops, bringing out shared woody, spicy flavors. The coleslaw on the side helps to keep everything balanced and cools down any potentially combustible combinations. This is also great with some belly pork covered with the classic jerk seasoning, which includes thyme, garlic, ginger, chili, and allspice.

OMNIPOLLO NEBUCHADNEZZAR

BEST WITH: GRILLED CHEESE

BREWED IN: STOCKHOLM, SWEDEN
ABV: 8.5%

Nebuchadnezzar was King of the Neo-Babylonian Empire and credited with the creation of the Hanging Gardens of Babylon. This is also the name of the multi-award-winning Imperial IPA, conceived (successfully) to be Sweden's best IIPA. Omnipollo trials its beers at home and then scales up the recipes and makes them in different breweries around the world. Neb is an enormous hanging garden of fruit—it's big, bold, and bursting with grapefruit, oranges, roasted tropical fruit, and pine. It's somehow balanced, and the bitterness is powerful and yet not brutal. Upgrade a grilled cheese sandwich with some caramelized onion and garlic, and all the fruity flavors in the dairy come out, while the browned bread gives more toasty sweetness and balances the bitterness. In the wine world, a nebuchadnezzar is a 3-gallon (15-liter bottle); I wish this beer came in bottles that big.

RED ALE

There are two main types of Red Ale: hoppy American Reds and malty Irish Reds. Not many breweries make the Irish versions, so featured here are those that are vibrant, fruity, and bitter as a result of the hops. Think of these beers as Red IPAs because they have the same characteristics: richness and depth of malt, some alcohol, and loads of hops. The extra color comes from using specialty malts and these could bring caramel, nutty, and toasty flavors and often some additional sweetness—crystal malt would be a common grain to use, giving caramel and, sometimes, even a hint of raisin or smoke. As a broad group this could also take in hoppy Amber Ales. Food matches follow similar suggestions to those for the IPAs and Pale Ales, plus these beers work well with caramelized food (think of the Maillard Reaction, see page 25), smoke, sweetness, and deeply savory dishes.

BRIDGE: CHAR SUI PORK, NUT BURGER, GRILLED EGGPLANT (AUBERGINE)

BALANCE: GAME MEAT, CRAB CAKES WITH CHIPOTLE MAYO, KOREAN CHICKEN WINGS

BOOST: SMOKED BRISKET, BELLY PORK, SPICY ROAST CHICK PEAS

LOCAL: PEPPERONI PIZZA, CHILI MAC 'N' CHEESE

AVOID: SIMPLE WHITE FISH, SWEET DESSERTS

GREEN FLASH HOP HEAD RED

BEST WITH: JAMBALAYA

BREWED IN: SAN DIEGO, CALIFORNIA
ABV: 7.0%

This is an essential Red IPA to try. The color of an old copper coin, it's a blast of American hops, giving apricot, pine, orange peel, and grapefruit. The redness in the body translates as toffee on toast, filling the beer with malt depth and a little sweetness, but nothing that gets in the way of the big hops and their bitter finish. I love this beer with jambalaya or gumbo because they share some unexpected qualities: sweetness between grain and onion, as well as bitterness from hops and green bell (sweet) peppers. Plus, there's malt richness in the beer that balances the deep savory flavors in the pot. If you like heavily hopped beers, then Green Flash should be one of your go-to breweries, especially its Palate Wrecker and Imperial IPA, which will leave you seeing green hoppy flashes.

SUMMER WINE BREWERY ROUGE

BEST WITH: BARBECUE BELLY PORK

BREWED IN: HOLMFIRTH, YORKSHIRE
ABV: 5.8%

SWB's Red Hop Ale is a remarkable, bangable, hop explosion. Take one gulp and your senses are flooded with mandarin, orange candy, floral hops, and grapefruit, while the malt body grips hold of all those hops, keeping that citrus flavor dominant throughout and tasting fresh and bold. At the end, you're left with a little whisper of sweetness, which is blasted away by a peppery, pithy bitterness. They brew a lot of hoppy beers at SWB and I also recommend Maelstrom, which is the brewery's Double IPA, for the most intense hop hit. Rouge needs some fat and I've always liked belly pork with hoppy Reds. Get the best match by marinating the pork in classic barbecue spices and brown sugar, and then slow-cooking or smoking it—smoke loves hops.

NAPARBIER ZZ+

BEST WITH:
PATATAS BRAVAS

BREWED IN:
NOAIN, SPAIN
ABV: 5.5%

Naparbier is one of
the better Spanish
craft breweries. It
produces a dry,
quinine-like Pilsner;
a dark, roasted, and tiny-bit-tart Janis Porter,
which rocks with black pudding; a brilliant
Black IPA called Back in Black, which is
smooth, lush with chocolate orange, brashly
bitter in the best of ways, and great with
grilled octopus in oil and paprika; and ZZ+
Amber Ale, which is a hazy red color with
subtle and inviting tangerine, grapefruit, and
floral aromas, leading to a dry, quenching
bitterness. Patatas bravas are chopped and
fried potatoes covered in a spicy tomato sauce,
and then served with a mayonnaise or garlicky
aioli. A hidden sweetness in the beer cools the
sauce and keeps it a refreshing, casual match.

SIREN LIQUID MISTRESS

BEST WITH: WILD BOAR BURGER

BREWED IN: FINCHAMPSTEAD,
ENGLAND
ABV: 5.8%

With four core beers, plus more
specials and collaborations than
you could even attempt to
count, Siren is a brewery to
look out for and its beers
ordered when you see them.
Never boring, never lacking in
flavor, story or interest, this
brewery—led by brewer Ryan
Witter-Merithew—produces
some seriously great stuff. Since
starting in 2013, there's been a
soured Double IPA inspired by
limoncello, a
2.8% ABV "quarter IPA," an idea
for a rainbow of IPAs with seven
breweries taking part and each taking a
different color, plus a cellar stacked with
barrels. Liquid Mistress is a year-round, hoppy
red that's got a depth of dried fruit, caramel,
roast, and berries, and then a burst of pithy,
grapefruity hops. The malt depth in this beer
makes it great with strong meats, such as
venison and wild boar, especially with some
chili inside a burger.

BROUWERIJ 'T IJ COLUMBUS

BEST WITH: BITTERBALLEN

BREWED IN: AMSTERDAM, NETHERLANDS
ABV: 9.0%

I like the bottle design of Brouwerij 'T IJ's IPA so much
that I have an empty bottle of it on my bookshelf. Unlike
the diamond design with the ostrich and windmill, the IPA
is a tattooed pin-up with India Pale Ale running right up
her leg. That's my kind of girl. The beer is good, too: a
classic fruity, floral, and bitter IPA. Columbus is a big 9.0%
ABV hoppy red beer, which definitely feels Dutch, but has
an American accent, as if it's been watching too much
American TV. Deep red, with a big, frothy foam, there's
floral, pithy hops, and stone fruit and malt sweetness,
although a lively carbonation keeps it light before a knock-
out, drily bitter finish. Try with ossenwurst, a Dutch ox
sausage, or bitterballen, which are Dutch deep-fried
meatballs and a classic beer snack.

BROWN ALE

A LOT OF BEER STYLES ARE NOW
EXTENDED AND PREFIXED WITH THE WORD
"AMERICAN." ESSENTIALLY, THESE BEERS
HAVE COME TO MEAN A BOLDER, PERHAPS
STRONGER, AND DEFINITELY HOPPIER
VERSION OF A MORE TRADITIONAL STYLE;
THINK OF THEM AS THE IPA-SATION OF
THAT OLD STYLE. THERE'S AMERICAN
STOUT, AMERICAN WHEAT, AMERICAN
RED, AND AMERICAN BARLEY WINE, AND
THE SAME WORKS WITH BROWN ALE.
THIS MEANS THAT THE BROWN ALE
CATEGORY SPLITS INTO TWO GROUPS: THE
CLASSIC ENGLISH STYLE, WHICH IS
TOASTY, CLEAN, AND DRILY BITTER, AND
THE HOPPY AMERICAN BROWN, WHICH IS,
IN MANY WAYS, LIKE A BROWN IPA, BUT
JUST WITH MORE MALT BODY AND A
NUTTY, PERHAPS ROASTED, DEPTH.
BRITISH BROWNS ARE NOT THE HIPPEST
STYLE AROUND, BUT THE AMERICAN
VERSIONS DEFINITELY GIVE THEM AN
APPEALING MAKEOVER. WITH FOOD,
THINK GRILLED MEAT, BREAD, AND
EARTHY FLAVORS, AND THE WAY IN WHICH
MALT SWEETNESS INTERACTS WITH IT.

BRIDGE: TOASTED CHEESE
SANDWICH, LAMB STEW, GARLIC-
ROAST CHICKEN

BALANCE: CHINESE FOOD,
MEATLOAF, MUSHROOM RISOTTO

BOOST: NORTH AFRICAN CUISINE,
KEBABS, CREAMY CHICKEN PIE

LOCAL: GAME BIRDS OR MUSHROOM
SWISS BURGER

AVOID: FRUITY DESSERTS

UPSLOPE BREWING BROWN ALE

BEST WITH: ROAST
CHICKEN OR FALAFEL
WRAP

BREWED IN: BOULDER,
COLORADO
ABV: 6.7%

Designed for the on-the-go beer lover,
Upslope beers come in cans, so you can
chuck some in your backpack and take them
hiking or biking or whatever other outdoor
activity you're doing. The brewery is based in
Boulder, Colorado, a cool university town
with an astounding number of breweries
(and also the home of the Brewers
Association)—it's a fit, healthy, outdoor-
loving sort of place, so the beers are a hit.
Upslope's Brown Ale is like a can of coffee,
cocoa, and toast, with a bitter and dry finish,
making it simultaneously satisfying from the
grain and refreshing from the hops. If
you're on a hike, you need suitable food to
fuel you. For lunch, take a wholemeal wrap
and stuff it with some roast chicken, peanut
butter, roasted red bell (sweet) pepper, and
arugula (rocket), or go with falafel instead.
A flapjack is the sweet choice.

OPPIGÅRDS BREWERS BROWN

BEST WITH: ONION SOUP AND GRUYÈRE CROUTONS

BREWED IN: HEDEMORA, SWEDEN
ABV: 5.5%

Hopped with American Cascade, Amarillo, and Chinook, plus Pacific Gem from New Zealand, this Oppigårds brew sits on the hoppier side of the style, although it keeps hold of the classic British beer, thanks to the dry, malty base. With toast and chocolate, roasted nuts, licorice, and even some coffee hints, the hops come through herbal, floral, and berry-like, but not overpowering. The brewery suggests hard cheese, such as Gruyère, as a great match, plus I love Brown Ale with onion soup. There's a shared caramelized flavor between onion and malt, plus the beefy stock loves the sweetness in the grain before the hops hit the garlic and herbs. The cheese crouton on top is the perfect addition, as it gives more caramelized flavor to boost the brew's malt depth.

8 WIRED REWIRED BROWN ALE

BEST WITH: PORK BAO

BREWED IN: BLENHEIM, NEW ZEALAND
ABV: 5.7%

The words "boring brown beer" have got stuck in the British drinking lexicon to pass judgment over generic ales that taste like twigs and cold tea. Brown Ale isn't the sexiest style in the world, getting left behind as others are glamorized and pushed forward, but Brown Ale is capable of many great things, especially with food, given its mix of chewy, toasty, roasted grain, and then its hops. Rewired Brown Ale rewrites what the style can achieve: the body is so tasty, as it's full with some nutty sweetness before the hops give grass, berries, lime, and roasted tropical fruit. With pork bao, which are pillow-soft, steamed buns stuffed with pork, hot sauce, cucumber, and scallions (spring onions), the malt sweetness in the beer enhances the pork's meatiness, the fruity hop aromas match the sauces, while the green veg bridge with the green flavors in the hops.

PORT BREWING BOARD MEETING

BEST WITH: CHOCOLATE CHIP MUFFIN

BREWED IN: SAN MARCOS, CALIFORNIA
ABV: 8.2%

Made with Ryan Brother's coffee beans from San Diego and cocoa nibs from TCHO, in San Francisco, Board Meeting has a deep fresh-coffee flavor, a creamy cocoa richness, a little caramel and vanilla sweetness, and a long, deep, mouth-filling texture. There's bitterness, too, and when you put that with a chocolate chip muffin, the cake's sweetness gives a great balance, plus a boost, to all the roasted flavors. Port Brewing and Lost Abbey make beers in the same brewhouse; Port Brewing pumps out the American-styles, while Lost Abbey go for Belgian-inspired beers. Both are excellent and it's a brewery that should definitely be visited if you're nearby. I really love all of the Port Brewing beers, by the way: Wipeout and Mongo are two of the best IPAs I've tasted.

SAMUEL SMITH'S NUT BROWN ALE

BEST WITH: BANGERS AND MASH

BREWED IN: TADCASTER, ENGLAND
ABV: 5.0%

Founded in 1758, Samuel Smith's is Yorkshire's oldest brewery and still very traditional, employing a cooper, using horses to deliver beer nearby, drawing brewing water from a well beneath the brewery, and using slate "Yorkshire squares" for fermentation. The beers are all traditional as well, with classic Pale Ale, Stout, Porter, and this Nut Brown Ale. Chestnut-amber in color, it's toasty; there are berries, roast apple, and vanilla; and it's an easy-drinking beer with a dry, quenching finish. The beer's malt sweetness loves a sausage sandwich, or you could have a classic pub lunch of bangers and mashed potato with a rich onion gravy.

BLACK ALE

BLACK ALE IS OTHERWISE KNOWN AS BLACK IPA OR INDIA BLACK ALE OR EVEN CASCADIAN DARK ALE (NAMED AFTER THE CASCADIAN MOUNTAINS AND THE SURROUNDING REGION WHERE MANY AMERICAN HOPS GROW AND THE STYLE SUPPOSEDLY ORIGINATED). THEY ARE VERY DARK BEERS, WHICH ARE MADE WITH A LOT OF HOPS. FOR ME, A GREAT BLACK ALE IS A BEER THAT YOU SHOULD BE ABLE TO DRINK WITH YOUR EYES CLOSED AND SAY "THAT'S AN IPA!"—ONLY TO BE SURPRISED WHEN YOU LOOK AND SEE A BLACK BEER. THE SKILL IN THIS STYLE IS GETTING THE BALANCE OF FRUITY AMERICAN HOPS WITHOUT THE BITTER CHOCOLATE OR COFFEE POWERING THROUGH. YET, THE DARK MALT IS DEFINITELY IN THERE, AND IT ABSOLUTELY HAS AN IMPACT ON FOOD PAIRINGS AND, LIKE BACKGROUND MUSIC, CAN CHANGE AN ATMOSPHERE, SO THE DEPTH OF DARKNESS IS ABLE TO ENHANCE ROASTED FLAVORS AND SWEETNESS WHEN PUT WITH FOOD. THE STYLE WAS ONCE A FAD, A BREW THAT SEEMED TO ALMOST MAKE FUN OF ITSELF BY POINTING OUT THE DICHOTOMY OF ITS NAME (A BLACK PALE ALE), BUT IT'S BECOME A VERY POPULAR BEER.

BRIDGE: CHAR-GRILLED MEAT, MEXICAN MOLE, LAMB AND ROSEMARY STEW

BALANCE: MOROCCAN FOOD, VIETNAMESE NOODLES, OILY FISH

BOOST: GARLIC-ROAST MEAT, ROAST TOMATOES, SMOKED SALMON

LOCAL: OREGON BLUE CHEESE, SMOKED BACON BURGER

AVOID: ANYTHING DELICATE

BEAR REPUBLIC BLACK RACER

BEST WITH: ORANGE SPONGE CAKE

BREWED IN: HEALDSBURG, CALIFORNIA
ABV: 8.1%

Bear Republic's Racer 5 is one of my favorite beers. It reminds me of a few great nights that turned into a trip to California to drink the beer fresh from the brewery, so it brings back great memories whenever I see or drink it. My love for Racer 5 meant I had to buy Black Racer when I saw it. It's a great beer: there are loads of lush floral and orangey hops, something that reminds me of roast melon, plus herbs and grapefruit zest. The body is big and full, yet it somehow has a lightness and a mesmerizing freshness, hiding some dark malt way in the background. Have it with an orange sponge cake (carrot cake or pineapple-upside-down cake are both good alternatives) and the combination is like eating a chocolate orange.

BUXTON BREWERY BLACK ROCKS

BEST WITH: SPICY SAUSAGE PASTA

BREWED IN: BUXTON, ENGLAND
ABV: 6.0%

Based high in the hills of the Peak District, Buxton Brewery's beers are bold, hop-forward, exciting, and yet always balanced and very easy-drinking, even in the biggest, most bitter beers. The brewery makes Hoppy Session Ales, Pale Ales, IPAs, and Stouts, plus some interesting barrel-aged beers and experiments with wild yeast and sour beer. Black Rocks is a 6.0% ABV beer that says berries, citrus, and some faraway fresh coffee beans. The brewery also makes Imperial Black, a 7.5% ABV Black IPA that's full-on citrus and resinous pine, with some burnt smokiness. With spicy sausage pasta, the dark malt is sweetened by the acidity of tomatoes (it's even better if you roast the tomatoes), and then the meaty sausage adds hop-loving fat.

FERAL KARMA CITRA

BEST WITH: CAJUN BLACKENED STEAK WITH MANGO SALSA

BREWED IN: SWAN VALLEY, AUSTRALIA
ABV: 5.8%

Feral's Hop Hog IPA is routinely named as Australia's best craft beer by *The Beer Lover's Guide to Australia*. It's a super beer, loaded with so much hop aroma and flavor, grapefruit, pine, oranges, mangoes, and herbs, and then balanced and refreshing to finish. Knowing the brewery's skills with hop sacks, it comes as no surprise that its India Black Ale, Karma Citra, is also a winner. The body is creamy and smooth, more so than you'd expect, and then dries right out at the end, as the bitterness and some dark malt kick out. But what makes it so good is how the Citra hops flood tropical fruit through the whole thing, making it juicy and fresh. Cajun blackened steak (or chicken or mackerel) picks out the roast grain and the bitter hops, and then a mango and lime salsa enhances the fruity aroma, so you get a few boosting bridges of flavor.

21ST AMENDMENT BACK IN BLACK

BEST WITH: BEER-BRAISED RIBS

BREWED IN: SAN FRANCISCO, CALIFORNIA
ABV: 6.8%

On 17 January 1920, the 18th Amendment to the United States Constitution came into effect and mandated a nationwide prohibition on the production, transportation, and sale of alcohol. This remained in place, and America was dry of legal alcohol until 5 December 1933 when the 21st Amendment to the United States Constitution repealed the previous change and booze could be made once again. In 2000, that historic change inspired the name of this brewpub in San Francisco, where they now use Back in Black to braise ribs. The beer has a fragrant depth of resinous hops and citrus pith, and then a dry, long finish—bringing it back together with the ribs makes for a great combo.

MATUŠKA ČERNÁ RAKETA

BEST WITH: SMOKED MACKEREL WITH POTATO AND WATERCRESS SALAD

BREWED IN: BROUMY, CZECH REPUBLIC
ABV: 6.9%

Black Rocket, as the name translates, is an Intercontinental Black Ale, meaning that it uses Czech grain and a mix of Czech and American hops. That combination works so well and so naturally because the delicate lemony, floral, and peppery flavor in Czech Saaz gives a boost to the bolder, juicier citrus of American Cascade and Amarillo. Together, they give a bitterness akin to a classic Czech Pils, as it lingers for a long time, and then comes a great layer of hop flavor, which blasts forward from the base of toffee and a hint of semi-sweet (dark) chocolate. It's excellent with smoked mackerel, giving some malt sweetness to balance the oily richness. Have that with a potato and watercress salad, with lots of fresh lemon as the dressing—it's the lemon that brings everything together and gives it a boost of flavor.

SMOKED BEER

IF YOU WANT TO FILL YOUR REFRIGERATOR WITH FOOD-FRIENDLY BOTTLES, THEN LOOK FOR SMOKED BEERS BECAUSE THEY CAN PRODUCE SOME OF THE MOST SENSATIONAL AND UNEXPECTED BEER-AND-FOOD MATCHES. MANY YEARS AGO, MALT WAS PRODUCED OVER DIRECT HEAT FROM WOOD-BURNING FIRES AND, LIKE CHARRED SPONGES, THE GRAIN SUCKED UP THE SMOKE FLAVOR, WHICH WAS THEN TRANSFERRED TO THE BEER DURING THE BREWING PROCESS. BY THE 19TH CENTURY THE SPREAD OF NON-DIRECT KILNING MADE IT POSSIBLE TO PRODUCE MALT WITHOUT THE SMOKE. RAUCHBIER FROM BAMBERG, IN GERMANY, IS THE FAMOUS STYLE AND ESPECIALLY NOTED FOR ITS SMOKED-SAUSAGE SCENT, WHICH SUGGESTS A SAVORY DEPTH. YOU WILL ALSO FIND A MORE GENERICALLY NAMED "SMOKED BEER," WHICH CAN RANGE FROM A SUBTLE AND DISTANT WAFT OF SMOKE TO A BONFIRE IN YOUR GLASS. ANY BEER STYLE CAN USE SMOKED MALT: THE BAMBERG CLASSICS ARE MALTY LAGERS, WHILE STOUTS AND PORTERS ARE ALSO POPULAR. IT'S THE WAY THEY HAVE A MEATY, BARBECUE-LIKE DEPTH THAT SEEMS TO ADD A BOOST OF FLAVOR TO EVERYTHING THEY GO WITH.

JACK'S ABBY SMOKE & DAGGER

BEST WITH: PORK AND SPICY ROAST PUMPKIN

BREWED IN: FRAMINGHAM, MASSACHUSETTS
ABV: 5.8%

Run by the Hendler brothers Jack, Eric, and Sam, Jack's Abby was founded in January 2011. With a deliberately mindful approach that looks at the local land, the Hendlers use hops that they grow on their family farm in Vermont, which also provides pumpkins for a seasonal beer. They specialize in lagers, developing their own styles, such as hoppy "India Pale Lagers" (including the phenomenal Hoponious Union) and American-hopped session lager. They brew Fire in the Ham, a Bamberg-style Rauchbier, and Smoke & Dagger, a black lager, which uses some beech-wood-smoked malt to give a richly full body that hangs hints of smoke all the way through the beer, making it simultaneously appetizing and satisfying. Have it with pork and spicy roast pumpkin (use chipotle and smoked paprika). The creamy sweetness in the gourd is excellent with the dark grain and the smoke is like an injection of flavor.

BRIDGE: CHIPOTLE, SMOKED MEAT AND FISH, SPIT-ROAST CHICKEN

BALANCE: POTATO SALAD, LEMON DRESSINGS, ROAST VEGETABLES

BOOST: BLUE CHEESE, PORK SAUSAGES, GRILLED MACKEREL WITH LEMON

LOCAL: ROAST PORK, BAMBERG ONION

AVOID: DELICATE WHITE FISH, MOST DESSERTS

ALASKAN BREWING SMOKED PORTER

BEST WITH: ROASTED CHESTNUTS
OR TOASTED MARSHMALLOWS

BREWED IN: JUNEAU, ALASKA
ABV: 6.5%

This is a quintessential smoked beer. It's a robust Porter that uses malt smoked over alder wood. The beer was first brewed in 1988 and is a once-a-year vintage, which is annually released on 1 November. It's a remarkable beer to drink: a light-sucking black in color, with a mocha foam, the smoke comes out immediately with earth, bonfires, and wood. The body is rich and thick, very bitter semi-sweet (dark) chocolate laces through it and weaves around the char of smoke; there's some vanilla and berries and the kind of nice acidity that's found in good coffee. It's a powerful beer, but great with food such as steak and blue cheese, barbecue, roast salmon, or I like toasted chestnuts and marshmallows—you can't beat the way the smoke lingers through everything.

AECHT SCHLENKERLA RAUCHBIER MÄRZEN

BEST WITH: BAMBERG ONION
(AND SO MANY OTHER THINGS)

BREWED IN: BAMBERG, GERMANY
ABV: 5.4%

Bamberg is an incredible city that's both beautiful and lined with breweries. It's the home of Rauchbier, but only two places make it year-round: Schlenkerla and Spezial. Both have their own malting, using beech wood to produce the smoke, which gives an unmistakable smoked bacon and charred wood aroma. Schlenkerla's Märzen is deep red and full-bodied with malt, giving toasty sweetness beneath the pervasive and savory smoke. It's unequivocally a love-hate beer, but I always have some at home because it's capable of some amazing food combinations: remarkably intense with Stilton; superb with roast meats; a lot of fun with chocolate; and lemon-dressed oily fish is a surprise winner. Bamberg onion is the classic local match: this dish comprises slow-roasted onion stuffed with smoked pork and cooked in the beer.

NILS OSKAR RÖKPORTER

BEST WITH: DUCK AND PLUM SAUCE

BREWED IN: NYKÖPING, SWEDEN
ABV: 5.9%

Made with 80 percent beech-wood-smoked malt, plus some dark grains, Rökporter is a deep red-black, like the color of dying embers, and, while the smoke is immediate, it's also surprisingly subtle given the proportion used. You get the characteristic smoked-meat aroma, plus tobacco, bonfires, and the berry fruitiness of semi-sweet (dark) chocolate. The body is full, soft, and smooth, with smoke, vanilla, licorice, roasted plums, and coffee, plus the hops add their own berry and stone-fruit flavor. It's good with anything that has roast, meaty flavors and hints of aniseed (think fennel or star anise): Chinese char sui, beef chili, Italian fennel sausages, or duck and plum sauce.

WESTBROOK GRÄTZER

BEST WITH: BARBECUED
MACKEREL, LEMON

BREWED IN: MOUNT
PLEASANT, SOUTH CAROLINA
ABV: 3.4%

The ongoing interest in looking at the history of brewing has brought back some fairly obscure and unusual beers, and few are stranger than Grätzer or Grodziski. It's a Polish style that went out of fashion until craft brewers somehow rediscovered it and thought it sounded tasty. It's made only with smoked wheat (or a very large percentage) and brewed to a low ABV with lots of hops. Westbrook's is pale blonde and hazy; it's very woody in the aroma, chewy despite its low ABV, bready, a little sweet, and then dry and bitter to finish—it's hard to understand this beer and yet you'll drink it really fast trying to figure it out. Some simple grilled or barbecued oily fish with lemon and garlic is very good. The smoked beer boosts the fish and the lemon adds a citrus counterpoint. Westbrook makes a range of these heritage beer styles, including a Gose and a smoky-sour Lichtenhainer.

OATMEAL STOUT AND MILK STOUT

THESE STOUTS GET THEIR OWN SECTION, THANKS
TO THEIR SPECTACULAR FOOD-FRIENDLINESS.
STOUTS ARE DARK BEERS WITH A BITTER ROASTED
QUALITY. OATMEAL AND MILK STOUTS DIFFER IN
THAT THEY HAVE SMOOTHER, CREAMIER TEXTURES
AS A RESULT OF THE EXTRA INGREDIENTS THAT
GIVE THE STYLES THEIR NAMES—OATS OR MILK
SUGAR/LACTOSE. YOU STILL GET THE
CHOCOLATEY, ROAST-MALT FLAVOR IN THESE
BEERS, BUT THEIR BODIES ARE SOFTER, PLUMPER,
AND SWEETER (THEY ARE SOMETIMES CALLED
SWEET STOUTS), WHICH MEANS THAT THEY WORK
REALLY WELL TO BALANCE STRONG FLAVORS,
ESPECIALLY CHILI HEAT WHERE THE BEER'S
SWEETNESS AND SMOOTHNESS COMBINE TO
SOOTHE AGAINST THE SCOVILLE SCORCH. THEY
ALSO LIKE A BIT OF SWEETNESS, AND BALANCE
FAT. CHOCOLATE AND COFFEE ARE COMMON
ADDITIONS TO THESE BEERS, WHICH COULD RANGE
FROM LOW IN ALCOHOL TO IMPERIAL-STRENGTH
VERSIONS.

BRIDGE: FLAPJACKS, RICE PUDDING, JAPANESE CUISINE

BALANCE: CHILI HEAT, ROAST VEGETABLES, INDIAN COCONUT CURRIES

BOOST: SMOKED MEAT, FRIED RICE, STEAK AND HORSERADISH

LOCAL: HOMEMADE OATMEAL COOKIES, BACON SANDWICH

AVOID: NOTHING! THESE BEERS ARE GREAT ALL-ROUNDERS

MIKKELLER BEER GEEK BREAKFAST

BEST WITH: BACON CROISSANT

BREWED IN: COPENHAGEN, DENMARK
ABV: 7.5%

Beer geeks tend to like Mikkeller. It's a
brewery without physical walls, but also
without a limit to its creativity, as Mikkel
Borg Bjergsø brews at many different
breweries around the world. It's the
combination of being experimental,
extreme, and prolific in producing new
brews that gets the geeks (myself
included) interested. Beer Geek Breakfast
is an Oatmeal Stout brewed with good
coffee. It pours like black ink and then
erupts with a thick, dark foam. It smells
like a coffee shop, it's intensely roasted,
yet smooth, and loaded with semi-sweet
(dark) chocolate, before American hops
leave bitter citrus pith. As a coffee-lover,
as well as a beer geek, this beer is what I
want for breakfast (although I tend to
save it for special occasions, such as
birthdays and Christmas). A croissant
works, as does a bacon sandwich, so—just
because you can, as no regular rules
apply if you have beer with breakfast—put
smoked bacon in a croissant.

NAIL BREWING STOUT

BEST WITH: PORK FRIED RICE

BREWED IN: BASSENDEAN, AUSTRALIA
ABV: 6.0%

Hammer down a Nail is the appropriate tagline for a brewery that focuses on just a few quality beers, which are all utterly bangable. There's Nail Ale, which is a refrigerator-filling Aussie Pale Ale that's floral, fruity, and fresh. Golden Ale is ripe with juicy fruit and another one to knock back. Once a year, you'll find Clout Stout, a beastly 10.0% ABV Imperial Stout that's bulging with chocolate, coffee, and dark fruits, but, watch out, because a few of these will leave you hammered. Nail's Stout is a lush oatmeal brew: classically creamy (even oily) and smooth, it's like dark-chocolate porridge and a mug of black coffee, which leaves its bitterness. Totally nail the pairing by serving this beer with pork fried rice—the nuttiness of the sesame-oil-fried rice, plus the sweet-savory ingredients mixed in with it, is bang on.

HITACHINO NEST SWEET STOUT

BEST WITH: TERIYAKI

BREWED IN: IBARAKI, JAPAN
ABV: 4.0%

Brewed with lactose, this Japanese Stout is almost like a chocolate smoothie: cocoa, roasted nuts, licorice, berries, and plenty of sweetness, with virtually no roast or bitterness. The beer's body is really nice and creamy smooth, and, in spite of how it sounds, it definitely isn't oversweet and has a great balance of flavors. The beer works well with teriyaki sauce's sweetness and soy saltiness, so use that on beef, in a chicken stir-fry, over mackerel, or as a dipping sauce. The Hitachino Nest beers are some of Japan's best and most widely available. The brewery's White Ale is a wonderful Witbier, while Nipponia is a true, indigenous, Japanese brew that uses traditional Kaneko Golden barley and Sorachi Ace hops, which were developed in the country.

LEFT HAND MILK STOUT NITRO

BEST WITH: CHILI CON CARNE

BREWED IN: LONGMONT, COLORADO
ABV: 6.0%

Left Hand's best-seller comes in a standard version and Nitro— meaning that nitrogen is pushed into the beer during production, which gives a creamy, full body. To pour properly, you need to take the cap off and dump the beer into your glass in one go, which is both thrilling and worrisome. Somehow it all combines into the perfect pour with a creamy tan foam. Made with milk sugars, it has a creamy smoothness, a lovely sweetness in the middle, plus berries and vanilla. It's great with food, especially spice, because the beer can wrap around it, cool it down, but still let the flavor pass through the other side. It works almost universally with Tex-Mex or Southwest food, particularly a big bowl of slow-cooked chili.

SAMUEL SMITH'S OATMEAL STOUT

BEST WITH: STEAK, ROAST PARSNIPS, HORSERADISH

BREWED IN: TADCASTER, ENGLAND
ABV: 5.0%

I think this beer is the reason that I now put Oatmeal and Milk Stouts in my list of favorite beer styles. A style that was once famously promoted as healthful, it virtually disappeared until Sam Smith resurrected it in 1980. It has creamy chocolate and licorice, cocoa, gentle roast bitterness, some sweet berries, even a little floral hint, and a soothing, smoothly full mouthfeel. It's great with five-spice chicken wings and surprisingly good with fried snacks, such as onion bhaji, but I think it's best with some steak, roast parsnips (kind of like baked fries), and horseradish sauce. This makes for an amazing combination, with the hint of aniseed in the parsnips enhancing the beer, which then cools the heat of the horseradish and makes the meat's char tastier. Forget steak, chips, and ketchup, have this instead— it's one of my favorite beer-and-food pairings.

STOUT AND PORTER

WHAT'S THE DIFFERENCE BETWEEN STOUT AND PORTER? WELL, PORTER CAME FIRST. IT WAS LONDON'S BEER. A DARK ALE, MATURED FOR A LONG TIME, AND DRUNK BY THE WORKING CLASSES. STOUT WAS A NAME APPLIED TO EXISTING BEER TYPES TO SIGNIFY THAT IT WAS STRONGER, SO THERE WAS BROWN STOUT OR STOUT PORTER, FOR EXAMPLE. OVER TIME, STOUT CAME TO MEAN A STRONG DARK BEER AND THEN, AS THAT EVOLVED, IT STUCK AS SIMPLY A DARK BEER. WHEN WARTIME RATIONING HIT BREWERS, THE OLD-FASHIONED PORTERS GOT LEFT BEHIND, WHILE STOUT, WHICH HAD A REPUTATION FOR BEING WHOLESOME AND HEALTHY, PROGRESSED. PORTER WAS NEARLY EXTINCT UNTIL CRAFT BREWERIES IN THE UNITED KINGDOM AND UNITED STATES BROUGHT IT BACK TO PROMINENCE. THERE ISN'T REALLY A DEFINABLE DIFFERENCE BETWEEN THESE TWO STYLES TODAY, ALTHOUGH ONE WAY OF SEPARATING THEM IS TO SAY THAT STOUT WOULD PERHAPS HAVE MORE ROASTED BARLEY BITTERNESS THAN PORTER. VARIATIONS EXIST, SUCH AS SWEET STOUTS, DRY STOUTS, AMERICAN STOUTS (HOPPY, STRONGER VERSIONS), AND ROBUST AND BROWN PORTERS.

BRIDGE: GREEN VEGETABLES, SLOW-COOKED STEWS, LIVER

BALANCE: ROAST CHICKEN, GRILLED ONIONS, OILY FISH

BOOST: GRILLED MEAT, TOMATO-BASED PASTA OR PIZZA, OYSTERS AND MUSSELS

LOCAL: GOOD LOCAL MEAT AND SEAFOOD

AVOID: THIN STOUTS AND PORTERS; THEY WON'T GO WITH ANYTHING.

CARLOW BREWING O'HARA'S IRISH STOUT

BEST WITH: **CHAR-GRILLED STEAK**

BREWED IN: CARLOW, IRELAND
ABV: 4.3%

An alternative to the ubiquitous Irish Dry Stout, O'Hara's is a handsome beer, pouring black and settling with the distinctive creamy foam on top—there's something utterly appealing about beer that looks like this. The body is darkly delicious, bitter with roast barley, coffee grounds, some smoke, and the berry fruitiness of semi-sweet (dark) chocolate before it gets earthy and dry to finish. That dark flavor and the bitter dryness want some flavorsome fat, which is where a good steak comes in. Steak is great with almost all beers, but especially Dry Stout: the shared charred flavor makes both the beer and the beef taste fuller, sweeter, richer. O'Hara's also brews Leann Folláin, which is Gaelic for "wholesome ale," and it's an Extra Irish Stout.

BOGOTÁ BEER COMPANY CHAPINERO PORTER

BEST WITH: BLACK PUDDING OR PIZZA

BREWED IN: BOGOTÁ, COLUMBIA
ABV: 5.0%

With a large number of pubs in Columbia's capital, Bogotá Beer Company is the name to look out for if you want to drink local craft beer. BBC makes a wide range of European-inspired styles, such as Kölsch, Hefeweizen, Witbier, and Stout, plus an American IPA. Chapinero Porter looks and smells like Columbia's celebrated coffee, pouring black with a mocha foam, then giving an intense aroma of ground coffee, semi-sweet (dark) chocolate, and berries. A surprisingly light body, it starts with sweet cocoa and then the roast bitterness comes out and hangs on through to the end. The BBC pubs sell pizza, which is a great choice for Porter since it's very nice with tomato and cheese. But if you're drinking a Columbian beer, you want Columbian food, so have morcilla, a local black pudding, or bandeja paisa, which is an enormous meat platter.

FULLER'S LONDON PORTER

BEST WITH: TANDOORI LAMB CHOPS

BREWED IN: LONDON, ENGLAND
ABV: 5.4%

Porter is London's beer style. Developed at the beginning of the 18th century, it was a hoppier and longer-aged dark beer that was intended to stand out from the standard brown beers of the day. It was matured in massive barrels and brewed in enormous volumes. Porter's downfall came with the World Wars, when it was hugely impacted by grain rationing, and Stout was seen as more wholesome. Fast-forward to 1996 and Fuller's brewed a new beer based on an old recipe and, despite its relative newness, this London Porter is a textbook-illustrating classic: it is black with a thick foam and there's chocolate, roast, smoke, and earthy fruit. London loves a curry, and tandoori lamb chops, served with roti or naan bread, give a smoky, grilled darkness to match the beer and allow some malt sweetness to play with the spices.

HILL FARMSTEAD EVERETT PORTER

BEST WITH: LOBSTER THERMIDOR

BREWED IN: GREENSBORO, VERMONT
ABV: 7.5%

Rarity combined with rarely rivaled quality has made Hill Farmstead one of the world's most sought-after breweries. The bucolic brewery location and the farmhouse setting add to the hype, with drinkers making pilgrimage journeys there to try the beers. Shaun Hill brews on a farm that has been in his family for over 230 years and most of the beers are named after his ancestors—Everett is Shaun's grandfather's brother. The beer is an American Porter, brewed with American hops and the farm's well water. I'm convinced that the water has magic qualities because the texture and mouthfeel of all Hill Farmstead beers are peerless—cloud-like and ethereal, and yet they carry so much flavor. Everett is rich with dark malt, a nutty and sweet creaminess, chocolate, and a long, dry bitterness. It's much revered, so it needs foods with similar qualities: wagyu (Japanese) beef, foie gras, Iberico ham, or lobster thermidor, for example.

RIVERSIDE 88 ROBUST PORTER

BEST WITH: OILY FISH AND ROAST POTATOES

BREWED IN: PARRAMATTA, AUSTRALIA
ABV: 6.0%

Set up by homebrewer-turned-pro Dave Padden, and his business partner Stephen Pan, in a suburb of Sydney, Riverside Brewing has sped off to a rapid start since first filling its tanks in the middle of 2012. With good-looking bottles and great-tasting beers, it's easy to see why this brewery has been so popular. It makes six core beers, including a boldly hopped American Amber called 44; 69 is an all-Aussie Wheat Ale, and 77 is a voluminous and feisty IPA—88 is the brewery's robust Porter, with classic chocolate and coffee, an easy-drinking lightness, and lots of roast, which lasts at the end and mixes with some hop fruitiness. This kind of beer is great with smoked or oily fish, where the roast grain gives balance. Have the fish with roast new potatoes and bitter green leaves with a lemon dressing.

IMPERIAL STOUT AND PORTER

THE PREFIX IMPERIAL WAS ORIGINALLY USED BY BREWERIES FROM AROUND THE 18TH CENTURY TO DENOTE THE STRONGEST OR FINEST BEER THEY PRODUCED. THE MOST FAMOUS, OR AT LEAST THE BEERS THE HISTORY BOOKS LIKE TO TALK ABOUT TODAY, WERE SHIPPED TO RUSSIA, AND SO BECAME KNOWN AS RUSSIAN IMPERIAL STOUTS. AS WITH INDIA PALE ALE, THE HOOK OF A GOOD STORY, PLUS THE CHANCE TO BREW A BIG BEER, HAS CAPTURED THE ATTENTION OF BREWERS. STOUT AND PORTER COMBINE BECAUSE THERE REALLY IS LITTLE DIFFERENCE BETWEEN THE TWO WHEN THE BEER GETS TO 8.0% ABV AND WAY BEYOND (SOME WILL PASS 12.0% ABV). THEY ARE FULL-BODIED, MASSIVELY MALTY, VERY DARK, AND BITTER-SWEET. SIPPING BEERS, WHICH ARE ALMOST THE EQUIVALENT OF ALCOHOLIC MOCHA, THEY TEND TO BE BEST WITH DESSERT AND CHEESE, THANKS TO THEIR ALREADY-HIGH SWEETNESS AND A LARGE BITTERNESS.

BRIDGE: SEMI-SWEET (DARK) CHOCOLATE, SLOW-COOKED MEATS, COOKIES

BALANCE: BLUE CHEESEBURGER, CHILI CHOCOLATE, TIRAMISÙ

BOOST: STRONG AND BLUE CHEESE, CHEESECAKE

LOCAL: FRESHLY BAKED CAKES, LOCAL CHOCOLATE

AVOID: DELICATE DISHES, SALADS

PARTIZAN FOREIGN EXPORT STOUT

BEST WITH: PULLED PORK

BREWED IN: LONDON, ENGLAND
ABV: 8.6%

Partizan's beers are made under a cozy railway arch, not far from London Bridge, which opens every Saturday so that you can drink the many magnificent creations, including peerless Pale Ales, stunning hoppy Saisons, and delightful dark beers like this Foreign Export Stout. The winning thing about the Partizan FES is that it has an unreal depth of malt, thick and full-bodied, which is yet light to drink, where the dark malt is really dark but not brutally bitter, and there's also chocolate and hazelnut sweetness. I think that Partizan is one of the best breweries in the United Kingdom and its beers are also some of the best-looking, thanks to Alec Doherty's bottle designs. FES is great with pulled pork—it loves slow-cooked meat, plus the barbecue sauce's sweetness is sucked into this black hole of a beer.

DE STRUISE BLACK ALBERT

BEST WITH: BELGIAN CHOCOLATE

BREWED IN: OOSTVLETEREN, BELGIUM
ABV: 13.0%

Black Albert is the sort of beer you could never tire of drinking. It's astonishingly complex, so full of many flavors, layered, textured, powerful, and just damn interesting, with chocolate, coffee beans, berries, rum, vanilla, roasted nuts, port, caramel, licorice, bitter plums, and more. A bottle of this is rich and satisfying enough to be dessert on its own, but you can boost it by serving local Belgian chocolates, particularly praline ones. The Struise Black Damnation Series uses Black Albert as a base beer and then does different things to it. Some of the beers have coffee, some are intensely strong (using the Eisbock method of freezing the beer to increase alcohol levels), and some are barrel-aged, like Black Mes. This goes into Caol Ila whisky barrels and pulls in their woody, smoky, salty flavors—it's incredible.

NORTH COAST OLD RASPUTIN

BEST WITH: BLUE CHEESE

BREWED IN: FORT BRAGG, CALIFORNIA
ABV: 9.0%

This beer has become a classic Russian Imperial Stout. Midnight black, with a cappuccino foam, it has roasted flavors, coffee, chocolate, vanilla, and dried fruits. The body is full and chewy, and it has a remarkable balance of flavor between sweet malt, roast malt, and bitter hops, meaning that the beer keeps coming at you with more flavor. Imperial Stouts are superb with blue cheeses— Stilton, stichelton, Gorgonzola, Roquefort, Oregon blue—as the beer has an unctuously full body, sweetness, and bitterness, and a berry-like fruitiness, all of which boost the cheese's richness. Plus, there's a shared creamy, chocolatey flavor between the two. The simplicity of one good beer with one good cheese is hard to beat and unnecessary to try and overcomplicate.

TO ØL GOLIAT

BEST WITH: NEW YORK CHEESECAKE

BREWED IN: COPENHAGEN, DENMARK
ABV: 10.1%

There are few Davids capable of standing up to this Goliat. It's a giant 10.1% Imperial Stout that's brewed with coffee, giving an oily, inky-black pour with a handsome dark foam. Viscous, soft, sweet and yet bitter, a big roast, loads of chocolate and vanilla, and the most intoxicating aroma. It's like walking into a coffee shop just as they've brewed a fresh cup and taken some muffins out of the oven. And baked goods give the best matches: brownies, blondies, or a baked cheesecake, where the creamy cheese and bitter barley roast are balanced and sweetened. If you want to drink To Øl beer, go to Mikkeller & Friends in Copenhagen (To Øl are one of the friends). It's a small, neat bar with a tap list that could make a beer geek weep with joy.

MINOH IMPERIAL STOUT

BEST WITH: KOBE STEAK

BREWED IN: OSAKA, JAPAN
ABV: 8.5%

When Masaji Oshita told his daughters that he'd bought them a brewery, it was undoubtedly a bit of a surprise. Masaji ran a liquor store for many years before deciding to make the move to producing the booze, as well as selling it. A few years later, in 1997, the first Minoh beers were sold. Jump forward to today and Minoh makes some of Japan's best-regarded and most-awarded beers. The brewery's Imperial Stout is a superb drink: inky black with a handsome dark foam; it's thick with cocoa, vanilla, a bitter roast like good coffee, a deep savory taste, and a nice fruity sweetness. For a big beer, it's very drinkable, as it balances the dark roast with a lip-sticking sweetness. In Osaka, you'll find Beer Belly bars, all serving up the superb Minoh beers alongside pub food. A loaded hamburger works really well, as the beer gives sweetness to balance the beef. A well-marbled and well-loved kobe or wagyu steak would be worthy of this beer, too.

STRONG ALE AND BARLEY WINE

A BIT OF AN ARMS-OPEN GROUP, THIS COLLECTS TOGETHER BEERS THAT ARE HIGH IN ALCOHOL AND PULLS THEM FROM A RANGE OF DIFFERENT BEER STYLES. INTO THIS WE WELCOME: SCOTCH ALES, DEEP RED BEERS, WHICH ARE GLASSES OF MALT WITH JUST A TICKLE OF HOPS; BARLEY WINE, A TRADITIONAL OLD ENGLISH BEER STYLE, WHICH IS A VINOUS AND WINE-STRONG BREW THAT BECAME UNFASHIONABLE, BUT WAS BROUGHT BACK WITH THE CRAFT-BEER REVOLUTION; OLD ALE OR VINTAGE ALE, WHICH ARE BEERS THAT HAVE EITHER BEEN AGED BEFORE RELEASE OR ARE DESIGNED TO LAST A WHILE IN BOTTLE. YOU MIGHT ALSO SEE WHEATWINE, A BARLEY-WINE-LIKE BREW THAT'S MADE WITH A LARGE AMOUNT OF WHEAT; CHAMPAGNE BEER, WHICH IS BETWEEN GRAPE AND GRAIN, BEING A LIVELY PALE BREW THAT'S STRONG AND YET ELEGANT; AND, FINALLY, STRONG ALE, WHICH PRETTY MUCH MEANS THOSE STRONG BEERS THAT DON'T REALLY FIT IN ANYWHERE ELSE AND CAN TASTE LIKE ANYTHING FROM A STRONG BITTER TO AN IMPERIAL IPA.

BRIDGE: FRUIT CAKE, CHOCOLATE TRUFFLES, POACHED FRUIT

BALANCE: FATTY MEATS, PÂTÉ, CHINESE SWEET AND SOUR

BOOST: AGED AND BLUE CHEESE, GAME MEATS

LOCAL: HEARTY STEWS AND LOCAL CHEESES

AVOID: ANYTHING DELICATE, MOST CHILI HEAT

ORKNEY BREWERY SKULL SPLITTER

BEST WITH: COARSE PORK PÂTÉ, CHUTNEY, AND BREAD

BREWED IN: ORKNEY, SCOTLAND
ABV: 8.5%

The 7th Viking Earl of Orkney, Thorfinn Einarsson, had the nickname of Skull Splitter, although it seems that not many people know why... Some suggest he was very tall, while others believe it's from a childhood event when he split open another child's head. Orkney Brewery's Skull Splitter is a Scotch Ale made on an island north of the Scottish mainland. It's a deep red-brown beer, which has a chewy malt flavor, without being sweet, and then leaves a hearty, oaky, whisky-like complexity. Roast pork works well with it, but the gamey richness in a coarse pork pâté, served with some chutney and fresh bread, is best. The beer works like an additional sweetener and can also balance the fatty richness of the food. It's a fireplace evening snack to warm you up.

THE ORKNEY BREWERY

Skull Splitter

THE AUTHENTIC ORCADIAN ALE
HAND CRAFTED IN SMALL BATCHES

ABV 8.5%

THE ORKNEY BREWERY

SIERRA NEVADA BIGFOOT

BEST WITH: BLUE CHEESE AND MANGO CHUTNEY

BREWED IN: CHICO, CALIFORNIA
ABV: 9.6%

Barley Wine was a virtually extinct style before Anchor Brewing's Old Foghorn and Sierra Nevada's Bigfoot brought them back into brewhouses. In the 1970s and '80s, nothing like this was brewed in America, a beer market dominated by pale, light-tasting brews, so these powerful, boozy, well-hopped beers blasted a way past preconceptions and provided a very different drink. Bigfoot has a strong base of malt, giving caramel, bread, and dried fruit, and is heavily hopped with Cascade, Centennial, and Chinook to give floral, resinous, and citrus-pith aroma. The beer ages well, with the bright hoppiness fading and the rich malt pushing forward, although I prefer it fresh (because I love hops). Blue cheese and mango chutney are best. The bitterness and rich malt sweetness is unbelievably good with the powerful cheese, while the mango chutney gives fruit and fragrant, earthy spices.

DE MOLEN BOMMEN & GRANATEN

BEST WITH: ALMOND CAKE

BREWED IN: BODEGRAVEN, NETHERLANDS
ABV: 15.2%

Not many beers are like Bommen & Granaten (which means Bombs & Grenades). It's a monster 15.2% Barley-Wine-ish beer that's fermented with a Champagne yeast. Amber in color and a syrupy pour, the aroma is like a fermented fruit bowl, with candied citrus, roast pineapple, honey, and sherry. Thick and sweet, yet dry and bitter, there's insane richness throughout, masses of fruit, and a bitter-orange-liqueur depth. This beer has a cake-like quality and so an almond cake's nutty sweetness is superb with it, combining to become like the booze-soaked base of a trifle (in fact, a peach trifle would be a great alternative pairing). Or, have the beer with the smelliest cheese you can find, like Stinking Bishop, where one is the bomb, the other the grenade, and they explode together with unexpected loveliness.

BARLEY BB10°

BEST WITH: PECORINO ROMANO OR GAMEY MEATS

BREWED IN: SARDINIA, ITALY
ABV: 10.0%

All the Barley beers come in wine bottles and share a flair and flavor that make them stand out: Friska is a refreshing Witbier, Toccadibo is Tripel-esque, and BB10° is an unusually strong beer that gets a boost from Sardinian Cannonau grapes (Grenache), which are boiled up in the brewery and then blended with the more traditional barley base. The beer yeast rips through all of the malt and fruit sugars, and leaves you with something that's, quite literally, a Barley Wine. There's vinous fruit, strawberry, brown sugar, semi-sweet (dark) chocolate, and figs, plus a tannic-tea and citrus-pith bitterness. It's an intriguing beer, and one that works well with a variety of local Sardinian foods, especially Pecorino Romano, where the beer's dark-fruit flavors are excellent with the salty cheese.

DOGFISH HEAD BURTON BATON

BEST WITH: PINEAPPLE-UPSIDE-DOWN CAKE

BREWED IN: MILTON, DELAWARE
ABV: 10.0%

Dogfish Head Burton Baton starts out as two separate beers—a strong Old Ale and an Imperial IPA—made in two different stainless-steel tanks and then blended together into a 10,000-gallon oak tank and left to mature. What you get is a richly hoppy ale, deep amber in color, with loads of pithy citrus, caramel, toast, and vanilla. It's perfect with pineapple-upside-down cake's juicy, caramelized fruit and sweet softness of sponge. The hops say "hi" to the pineapple, while the subtlety from the large oak tank gives a bridge of vanilla and spice, as well as a depth of creaminess. Any big Barley Wine or Double IPA that mixes citrusy hops and a caramel-like malt depth works well with this cake.

BARREL-AGED BEER

BEFORE SHINY STAINLESS STEEL GOT BREWMASTERS SWOONING IN ADMIRATION AND ADULATION, ALL BEER WOULD'VE BEEN AGED IN WOODEN BARRELS. THE WOOD WASN'T THERE TO ADD FLAVOR; IT WAS SIMPLY THE BEST MATERIAL BREWERS HAD TO MATURE THEIR BEERS. TODAY, BARRELS ARE BACK IN BREWERIES, OFTEN VIA A VINEYARD OR DISTILLERY, AND THEY ARE USED DELIBERATELY TO PUSH MORE FLAVOR INTO BEERS. LEAVING A BREW IN A BARREL ENABLES IT TO PICK UP THE FLAVOR, AROMA, AND TEXTURE OF WHATEVER WAS PREVIOUSLY KEPT IN THERE AND THAT INTEGRATES THROUGH THE DRINK TO CREATE NEW DEPTH AND CHARACTER. WHISKY AND BOURBON BARRELS ARE IN THE MOST DEMAND, OFTEN BEING USED TO AGE IMPERIAL STOUTS, WHILE WINE BARRELS ARE FREQUENTLY EMPLOYED TO MAKE SOUR BEERS. YOU MIGHT ALSO SEE MADEIRA, TEQUILA, RUM, SHERRY, AND OTHER BARRELS, AND EACH WILL GIVE DIFFERENT QUALITIES TO THE BEER STORED INSIDE THEM. THE WOOD ALSO BRINGS QUALITIES AND FLAVORS TO THE BEER, SUCH AS VANILLA, BROWN SUGAR, SMOKE, COCONUT, AND NUTS, PLUS A DRY TANNIC MOUTHFEEL.

BRIDGE: VANILLA DESSERTS, CHOCOLATE TRUFFLES, BARBECUE DISHES

BALANCE: STRONG CHEESES, COOKIES, CHEESECAKE

BOOST: BREAKFAST PASTRIES, STRAWBERRIES AND CLOTTED CREAM, BANANA DESSERTS

LOCAL: A CHASER WITH THE SPIRIT PREVIOUSLY INHABITING THE BARREL

AVOID: LIGHT DISHES, SALADS

FIRESTONE WALKER SUCABA

BEST WITH: CRÈME BRÛLÉE

BREWED IN: PASO ROBLES/BUELLTON, CALIFORNIA
ABV: 13.0%

When Firestone Walker started experimenting with a few old barrels to age some beers, the brewery didn't anticipate that a few years later it would have over 1,500 barrels and an entirely new facility in which to house them. Now 100 miles away from the Paso Robles brewery, next to the taproom in Buellton, the Firestone Walker Barrelworks focuses on wood-aged beers, including some sour projects and strong ales that mature before being blended into finished beers. Sucaba is a bourbon-barrel-aged Barley Wine—fiery red with a glorious coconut and cherry aroma, vanilla, and figs. The body is warming and full, laced with barrel texture and flavors that marry perfectly with the burnt cream and vanilla of a crème brûlée. Firestone Walker beers are extraordinary in their balance of barrel flavor and base beer; always intense and yet never overdone.

CAPTAIN LAWRENCE GOLDEN DELICIOUS

BEST WITH: CALVADOS APPLES WITH CREAMY BLUE CHEESE

BREWED IN: ELMSFORD, NEW YORK
ABV: 10.0%

This starts out as a Tripel brewed with lots of American hops, including a hefty dose of Amarillo dry hops. It's then aged in oak barrels, which used to hold apple brandy, meaning you get a drink that's somewhere between a Tripel, a cider, and a complex, crazy cocktail of fruit and booze. The yeast and the hops give peachy stone fruit, which is poked at by tart apples, vanilla, a savory woody flavor, and spice, and then there's a long, boozy finish with plenty of apple brandy—there aren't many beers like this one. You could have belly pork and roasted apple, but the beer fits better with dessert or an after-dinner nibble. Apples flambéed in calvados and served with a creamy blue cheese (try Gorgonzola) and shortbread is my choice, where the cheese's saltiness softens the brandy and enhances the fruitiness.

THE BRUERY BLACK TUESDAY

BEST WITH: COCONUT AND PEANUT M&MS

BREWED IN: PLACENTIA, CALIFORNIA
ABV: 19.0%

In Vietnam you can get peanuts roasted in coconut oil and they are amazing: salty, crunchy, and then sweet. I had some one night with some mates, while drinking a few beers, and they were incomparably perfect with bourbon-barrel Imperial Stout. They aren't easy to find, however, so an alternative would be to buy a packet each of coconut and peanut M&Ms and combine them in a big bowl—the savory peanut, the sweet coconut, and the chocolate are superb with strong barrel-aged Stouts, sharing vanilla, cocoa, caramel, and coconut. These are especially good with rare beers that have outrageous volumes of bourbon flavor, such as The Bruery's once-a-year, limited-release, long-time-aged monster Imperial Stout. The beer is also very good with a PB&J sandwich. Most other barrel-aged Imperial Stouts work, just in case you can't get this one.

HARVIESTOUN OLA DUBH 12

BEST WITH: A HIGHLAND PARK 12 CHASER

BREWED IN: ALVA, SCOTLAND
ABV: 8.0%

Breweries in Scotland are fortunate to be surrounded by distilleries and some make use of old whisky barrels to mature their beers. With whiskies ranging enormously from sweet and spicy through to smoky and intense, any beers that go through the barrels pick up many different qualities. Harviestoun Brewery works closely with Highland Park distillery and takes the same base beer—a roasty, smooth, chocolately Porter—and matures it in different whisky vintages. You might find Ola Dubh 12, 16, 18, 30, and 40, where the number tells you the age (in years) of the whisky. The 12 has an oily texture, there's salted caramel, a hint of smoke and earth, vanilla, sherry, and berries. It's mature, complex, and very interesting. Forget the food on this one because the best match is a Highland Park whisky chaser, where you can see how the flavor moves from dram via a barrel into a brew.

MALHEUR DARK BRUT

BEST WITH: A CHOCOLATE BOARD

BREWED IN: BUGGENHOUT, BELGIUM
ABV: 12.0%

This is a Champagne Beer, a style that Malheur can likely be credited with creating with its superlative Bière Brut. It comes in a Champagne bottle, at Champagne strength, and its production uses Champagne methods. Malheur Dark Brut is made with dark malts and aged in oak barrels before it reaches the bottle. This lengthy production produces a unique and spectacular beer that's effervescent and yet bold, malt-rich and yet elegant, and nutty, spicy, and chocolatey. There's also vanilla and citrus—and it's all just remarkable. It's definitely an after-dinner beer and I've always loved the idea of serving a chocolate board instead of a cheese board: different truffles, different types of chocolate, fruit. That'd be deservingly decadent and perfect with Dark Brut.

CIDER

A WORLDWIDE RESURGENCE IN CIDER HAS SEEN IT GO FROM A FUNKY, LEFTFIELD, FARMHOUSE DRINK, TO SOMETHING MARKETED FOR DRINKING OVER ICE, TO SOMETHING SOUGHT-AFTER AND CLOSELY ALIGNED TO THE STORY OF CRAFT BEER, WITH A LITTLE BIT OF WINE'S HARVEST SEASONALITY. TO MAKE CIDER, THE APPLES ARE PICKED, CRUSHED TO A PULP, THEN PRESSED TO EXTRACT ALL OF THE JUICE. THIS JUICE COLLECTS IN A FERMENTATION VESSEL (A TANK OR BARREL) AND THE YEAST NATURALLY PRESENT ON THE APPLES STARTS THE FERMENTATION. IT'S LEFT TO MATURE UNTIL IT'S READY TO GO. CIDER IS A COMPLEMENTARY DRINK ALONGSIDE CRAFT BEER AND THEY OFTEN SHARE SHELF SPACE AND BAR TOPS. THE FLAVOR RANGE IS HUGE, FROM SWEET TO ACIDIC, FROM LIGHT IN ALCOHOL TO FEARSOMELY STRONG, FROM PALE AND CRISP TO SOUPY AND THICK. IT'S A GREAT DRINK FOR FOOD, AS IT'S NATURALLY FRUITY, OFTEN DRY AND TART, AND REFRESHING AGAINST BIG FLAVORS AND FAT.

BRIDGE: APPLE CAKE, THAI FOOD, ORIENTAL SALADS

BALANCE: FRIED FISH, COCONUT CURRIES, SUSHI AND SASHIMI

BOOST: ROAST PORK AND CHICKEN, CHEDDAR CHEESE, CURED SAUSAGES AND MEAT

LOCAL: FARMHOUSE CHEESES

AVOID: TOMATO-BASED CURRIES

ZEFFER BREWING CO DRY APPLE CIDER

BEST WITH: SMOKED MACKEREL AND BEETROOT SLAW

BREWED IN: MATAKANA, NEW ZEALAND
ABV: 5.0%

With an abundance of apples, it makes sense that New Zealand produces some super ciders to sit beside their cracking craft beers and wonderful wines. Just like those drinks, the ciders are clean and full-on fruity, giving vibrant freshness, sharpness, and all-round drinkability. Zeffer gets its apples from around New Zealand and then crushes them in its cidery, using just juice and no sugar. The brewery also makes Dry Pear Cider, which has a floral, fruity, honey quality but is still dry; a fancy "Slack Ma Girdle" Cider, which is like a glass of Sauvignon Blanc, with tropical fruit, tart apples, and then a tannic dryness; while its Dry Apple Cider is like biting into a fresh, crisply tart apple. Try it with barbecued or smoked mackerel, as the dry cider gives a brilliant boost to the oily, rich fish. Serve with a beetroot, apple, and cabbage slaw.

TRABANCO SIDRA NATURAL

BEST WITH: CHORIZO COOKED IN CIDER

BREWED IN: GIJÓN, SPAIN
ABV: 6.0%

Spain is a star of the cider world. It's made in the north of the country and Asturias is the main region, a place so famous for its cider, or sidra, that it has a Protected Designation of Origin, complete with a regulatory board. It's there that you might encounter "cider throwing," which involves holding the glass in one hand and the bottle in the other, putting as much distance between the two as your arm-span allows, and pouring the sidra from a height. As the flat cider hits the glass, it aerates and sparkles like Champagne. Trabanco is one of the most common Asturian sidras and a pale hazy color; there are woody aromas, lemons, and apples, and it finishes sour, tannic, and wild—much more acidic and acetic than other ciders. It's great with the richness of chorizo, and a popular tapas dish has the spicy sausage cooked in cider. Black pudding is also great.

BURROW HILL FARMHOUSE CIDER

BEST WITH: ROASTED OR GRILLED PORK

BREWED IN: MARTOCK, ENGLAND
ABV: 6.0%

Did you know that 1.5 billion pints of cider and perry were drunk in Britain in 2012, which is nine percent of all alcoholic drinks? And, did you know that 57 percent of the apples grown in Britain (about 250,000 tonnes) are used to make cider? There's no doubt that a recent surge in growth was helped by big brands advertising the refreshing quality of drinking cider over ice, but this has helped the whole industry to grow, drawing attention to more traditional British ciders. Burrow Hill makes some superb cider brandies, and drives the Cider Bus to Glastonbury Festival each year, pouring endless pints of its crisply refreshing drink. Farmhouse Scrumpy is tannic, tart, and yet as sweet as a fresh apple, dry with apple-skin bitterness, and uncarbonated, so you drink it like juice. I don't think you can beat a sausage, pork chop, or roast belly pork with a glass of scrumpy.

ASPALL PREMIER CRU

BEST WITH: PORK TERRINE

BREWED IN: DEBENHAM, ENGLAND
ABV: 7.0%

In 1728, Clement Chevallier moved from Jersey to Aspall Hall, in Suffolk. He was unsuccessful in his plan to grow grapes and turned to apples instead, making Aspall the oldest cider-maker still around. Aspall produces some of the most readily available ciders in the UK (not at the expense of quality). Premier Cru shares similarities with sparkling wine; it's clean, bright, and refreshing; there's crisp apple, a dry finish, an apple-skin earthiness, and a pleasing balance. That makes it a great appetite-arouser. It's good with a chunky pork terrine starter where the cider balances the fat and is delicious with the pig flavor. Serve with chutney made with Aspall Cyder vinegar, and it's even better.

WOODCHUCK GRANNY SMITH HARD CIDER

BEST WITH: THAI CURRY

BREWED IN: MIDDLEBURY, VERMONT
ABV: 5.0%

If you're in an American craft beer bar, then Woodchuck is a cider you're likely to see. Started in 1990, this has grown to be a major cider brand, with a range of different and interesting products, where its ultra-limited edition Private Reserve Series features a pumpkin cider, a bourbon-barrel-aged cider, and one fermented with a Belgian Witbier yeast. The brewery's Granny Smith Hard Cider is a single-varietal cider, showcasing the apple's sharp-sweet tartness to give a very pale drink with tangy apples and a dry and quenching finish. The acidity and freshness lets it burst right through a creamy Thai curry, pinging the spices with fruit and then giving a great tang to the combination.

MAINSTREAM BEERS

Just because it's made by a big brewery doesn't make it the enemy. Sure, these beers might not be overflowing with flavor, boldly hopped, or aged for weeks to develop depths of deliciousness, but they deserve to be taken into consideration, even if just for the fact that they are sold in huge volumes. None of these beers are bad; they wouldn't sell millions of cases a year if they were really awful, would they? I think there's an unfair snobbishness toward these beers and, surely, even the most hardcore craft-beer lover can sit down and drink a bottle of Bud every now and again? Or, if not a Bud, then I'm sure all of us have one or two mainstream beers that mean something to us: the beer we first tasted, the beer we pounded through college, a holiday beer, a guilty pleasure. As major worldwide brands, they have a ubiquity that means we're likely to see them somewhere, at some time, and, if that happens, what do you want to eat with those beers?

BRIDGE: TO LOCAL FOODS AND LOCAL ACTIVITIES

BALANCE: THERE'S MORE TO LIFE THAN CRAFT BEER

BOOST: YOUR BANK BALANCE (THESE ARE DEFINITELY CHEAPER THAN CRAFT BEERS)

LOCAL: LOCAL FOOD IS DEFINITELY THE BEST CHOICE FOR THESE BEERS

AVOID: SNOBBERY; IT'S JUST BEER

BUDWEISER

BEST WITH: A BALLGAME AND A HOT DOG

BREWED IN: ST LOUIS, MISSOURI
ABV: 5.0%

Budweiser is my mass-produced beer of choice. Super-clean, ultra-refreshing, quenching, simple, and, to me, it's a good beer. Looking on RateBeer.com, Budweiser scores 0 out of 100. Not many beers get a zero. And I think it's unfair snobbery to give it that low a score. No, it isn't as wonderful as a classic Czech Pilsner, for sure, but it's very drinkable and it's got a good story, too (which it's worth reading, although it is interspersed with bullying and they do tend to come out as the bad guys). Brewed for the first time in 1876, Bud contributed to America's change in taste from dark ales to pale lagers. It's now a backyard barbecue beer, an I-just-want-a-beer beer, and postcard-ready as a ballgame beer with a hot dog. Budweiser isn't exciting, but it's not a bad beer. And I always, unashamedly, have Bud in my fridge.

DESPERADOS

BEST WITH: FRIENDS, PLUS BARBECUED CHICKEN AND LIME SALSA

BREWED IN: SCHILTIGHEIM, FRANCE
ABV: 5.9%

I have three general beer-drinking rules: never drink a "flavored" beer; never drink a beer from a clear bottle; and never drink something that requires lime stuffed in the bottle neck. However, there is one notable exception to this: Desperados, which is a "tequila-flavored beer" that comes in a clear bottle and is served with lime. I don't know how it happened, or where it started, but Desperados was my university beer. You couldn't easily get it back then (around 2005), so it was always a special treat and, at one house party, we even had two 1-gallon (5-liter) mini-kegs of it (and a bag filled with limes, obviously). The beer is very sweet, quite strong, and a bit weird. Sure, I don't drink much of it, but, for me, it's a party beer: best drunk with friends, outside, in the sunshine. And, it's really good (honestly) with barbecued chicken with lime, tomato, chili, and cilantro (fresh coriander) salsa—put it in a burger bun or tortilla, and relax.

MYTHOS

BEST WITH: SUNSHINE AND FRIED FISH

BREWED IN: THESSALONIKI, GREECE
ABV: 5.0%

Holiday beer is probably the most delicious beer there is. Sun-kissed, sitting on the beach and thirsty, a glistening glass of ice-cold beer arrives and tastes like perfection. My holiday beer is Mythos because I go to Greece most years. Mythos means holidays, sandy beaches, blue seas, and blue skies, and I immediately feel warm and relaxed when I think about it. When there, I love the local fresh fish, particularly little fried fish with a squeeze of lemon—it's my perfect beer snack, where the lager's sweetness and refreshing coldness cuts through the salt and fat on the fish. Simple holiday beer is the best, but, like a summer fling, it's not the sort of thing to bring home and it's best left in the hazy, happy glow of memories (until you return next year).

GUINNESS

BEST WITH: MEAT PIE AND RUGBY

BREWED IN: DUBLIN, IRELAND
ABV: 4.1%

In 1759 Arthur Guinness signed a 9,000-year lease on a disused brewery at St James's Gate, in Dublin, where he started to produce dark ale and Porter. By 1800, the focus was on Porter and his beer's ascension to worldwide dominance of the dark tap started from there. Now, Guinness is the most iconic beer in the world. A black beer with a creamy foam, it's smooth, there's a little roasted bitterness, some dark fruit, but not much more; it's surprisingly subtle. A beef and Guinness stew is a classic recipe. Put the stew inside a pie and have it with a Guinness, while watching a game of rugby. Interesting fact: the Guinness Storehouse in Dublin is Ireland's most-visited tourist attraction.

TSINGTAO

BEST WITH: ALL-YOU-CAN-EAT CHINESE BUFFET

BREWED IN: QINGDAO, CHINA
ABV: 4.7%

Tsingtao is one of the top-selling beer brands in the world. The brewery was founded in 1903 by German and British settlers, but has changed ownership many times since then. Tsingtao is brewed with barley from various places around the world, plus rice, and hops from China, a major hop growing country (the hops are mostly used in ultra-high-volume domestic brews). Some Tsingtao is made with pure spring water from the Laoshan Mountains (but not all the breweries where it's made have access to this water). As for the taste? It's clean, a little sweet, and then dry to finish. This is relevant because it's widely exported, so there's a chance that you'll find it in bar fridges and Chinese restaurants around the world. The simple flavor and clean, dry bitterness mean that it works to balance most Chinese food, so have it with an all-you-can-eat buffet and see if anything really stands out.

3 MATCHING FOOD AND BEER

BREAKFAST

BEER WITH THE FIRST MEAL OF THE DAY? WHY THE HELL
NOT? OF COURSE, YOU AREN'T GOING TO DO THIS EVERY
DAY—IF YOU CURRENTLY DO, THIS ISN'T THE BEST BOOK
FOR YOU TO READ. BUT, OCCASIONALLY IT'S NICE TO POUR
A BEER AND TREAT BREAKFAST A LITTLE DIFFERENTLY.
THE TYPICAL BREAKFAST DRINKS OF ORANGE JUICE AND
COFFEE HAVE CLOSE EQUIVALENTS IN WITBIER OR PALE
ALE AND STOUT, WHILE HEFEWEIZEN CAN HAVE A BANANA-
MILKSHAKE QUALITY, SO WE'VE ALREADY GOT SIMILAR
THINGS TO WORK WITH.

WEISSWURST

GREAT WITH: **GERMAN-STYLE WHEAT BEER**

PERFECT PAIR: BAYINGER BRÄU-WEISSE
BREWED IN: AYING, GERMANY
ABV: 5.4%

One Saturday in Munich, it took ages to find
somewhere that wasn't busy for weisswurst and
Weissbier at 11:00am and, as we hungrily went
from place to place, we were taunted with
tables covered with plates of white sausage and
pints of Hefeweizen. Finally, we found a table at
Ayingers Wirsthaus. The sausage is unusual:
it's ugly, pale gray, and subtly spiced, and has a
rubbery skin that you don't eat. The beer is
creamy and smooth, and has all of the banana
aromas you'd expect, plus some lemon, pepper,
and vanilla. Put them together and the beer's
soft sweetness teases out the peppery spices in
the sausage as they perk each other up. When
you order, you choose the number of sausages
you want—get at least three, plus a pretzel,
because when you start drinking beer at
11:00am, you need a substantial breakfast.

FULL ENGLISH BREAKFAST

GREAT WITH: **SMOKED PORTER**

PERFECT PAIR: BEAVERTOWN SMOG ROCKET
BREWED IN: LONDON, ENGLAND
ABV: 5.4%

You might want to drink a Bloody Mary with
this, so why not go for the beer equivalent: a
Flemish Red such as Rodenbach Grand Cru,
which has a tomato-like richness, a beefy
savory side, and an acetic edge. But that feels
like an unnecessarily fancy match for what is
an intense, greasy, incredibly unhealthy, and
obviously delicious first meal of the day. With
sausages, bacon, eggs, beans, mushrooms,
potato, and toast, a cup of tea is an excellent
choice, which is only bettered by a beer with
smokiness that works really well with the meat
and beans. Don't go all out Rauch; you want a
sweetish, smoky-edged, dark beer, such as
Smog Rocket, which is smooth like good coffee
and has a flavor-boosting, smoked-meat depth.
Alaskan Smoked Porter is an excellent
alternative here.

BLUEBERRY PANCAKES, BACON, AND MAPLE SYRUP

GREAT WITH: SWEET STOUT

PERFECT PAIR: YARDS CHOCOLATE LOVE STOUT
BREWED IN: PHILADELPHIA, PENNSYLVANIA
ABV: 6.9%

Think of American breakfasts and most people surely imagine a huge stack of buttermilk pancakes and a side of bacon, all drizzled with maple syrup. I like the addition of blueberries, as they burst and bleed deep purple juice around your plate. Yards Chocolate Love Stout, which is aged with cocoa and vanilla, is a breakfast-in-bed kind of beer. It looks sexy as it pours a thick black. Then, you take a sip and it's smooth, sweetly chocolatey, luscious, a little smoky to kiss the bacon, plus there's some fruitiness to complement the blueberries. It's like pouring chocolate syrup over the pancakes. I reckon a Double IPA is the rock 'n' roll choice if you are eating these for breakfast before you've gone to bed.

BREAKFAST BURRITO

GREAT WITH: PALE AND HOPPY SESSION BEER

PERFECT PAIR: FOUNDER'S ALL DAY IPA
BREWED IN: GRAND RAPIDS, MICHIGAN
ABV: 4.7%

If you're going to start drinking early, then you want something that will help you last until supper. While this is more like a Half Day IPA—a few 4.7% ABV brews will hit you pretty quickly unless your burrito is the size of a kayak—it makes a mean combo with a breakfast wrap of a tortilla filled with potato, egg, and cheese, plus some kind of spicy sausage. The fresh citrus hop aroma in the beer is like a glass of orange juice before the bitterness works like an alarm clock for your tongue, waking it up after every gulp and kicking away the cover of cheese and meat fat. I wish I could justify having this combination every day.

PAIN AU CHOCOLAT

GREAT WITH: CHOCOLATE STOUT OR IMPERIAL STOUT

PERFECT PAIR: SAMUEL SMITH'S
IMPERIAL STOUT
BREWED IN: TADCASTER, ENGLAND
ABV: 7.0%

Think coffee and croissants. Sweet buttery pastry is able to soften even the most bitter of coffees, and it's one of those combinations that is so simple and yet so superbly wonderful. Put some chocolate in the middle of that pastry, and it's even better. Pour a full-bodied Stout and it becomes sensational. Sam Smith's Imperial Stout is a relatively modest 7.0% ABV, but it's luscious with smooth chocolate, some toffee, sweet bread, chocolate-covered raisins, and vanilla. It works because it flirts with sweetness to begin with and then goes dark and bitter at the end with a savory roast that loves the pain au chocolat's savory sweetness. It's a great Imperial Stout and a fun food pairing, which also works as dessert.

SMOKED SALMON BAGEL

GREAT WITH: PORTER OR SAISON

PERFECT PAIR: BROOKLYN SORACHI ACE
BREWED IN: BROOKLYN, NEW YORK
ABV: 7.6%

This is a decadent breakfast that you shouldn't rush. It should take a while to prepare, you should have the morning papers ready, and you should eat slowly. This isn't something you throw down in three minutes. And that's why it works with a beer. You could pour a Porter, as its roast flavor makes everything taste sweeter, but I love the elegance of Brooklyn's Sorachi Ace. Golden, hazy, dry, and fragrant, you get lemon zest, floral honey, and a crack of pepper that balance the big flavors in the salmon and the richness of the cream cheese, while adding a juicy boost of freshness to the match. The beer is like Champagne, only it tastes way better.

SALAD

More than a boring bowl of green stuff that we eat because we feel we should, the best salads are an interesting mix of textures, flavors, and tastes, which combine to create either a great addition to a meal or a dish in their own right. When it comes to finding a beer to go with a salad, think about creating a bridge to its dominant flavors: if the salad contains lime juice, look for New Zealand hops; balsamic vinegar wants a Cherry Beer or Belgian Red; peppery green leaves call for the spiciness of a Saison; and heavy mayonnaise wants some sharp, dry hops to cut through it.

CAESAR SALAD

GREAT WITH: KÖLSCH, SAISON, OR CIDER

PERFECT PAIR: ANTHEM HOPS
BREWED IN: SALEM, OREGON
ABV: 5.5%

Hail Caesar Cardini! He's the man credited with creating this classic salad dressing in the 1920s. Today's recipe involves pounding a garlic clove and a couple of anchovies (and/or Worcestershire sauce) in a pestle and mortar, and then adding a few spoons of mayonnaise, some lemon juice, freshly grated Parmesan cheese, and pepper. Pour that over crisp Romaine lettuce and top with croutons and more Parmesan, and you're done. It's a sturdy salad that can handle a drink with a lot of depth. Pilsner's peppery bitterness works, Kölsch's crispness and love of saltiness works, and Saison's spiciness loves the cheese, anchovy, and lemon. But I want apples. Anthem Hops is a cider aged with Cascade hops—very clean, lots of lively bubbles, the tartness of a good Granny Smith, a dry finish, and the fresh citrusy fragrance of Cascade hops. It's a clever coming together of cider and beer, and it gives a zing of sharpness to the salad.

VIETNAMESE CHICKEN SALAD

GREAT WITH: SAISON, NEW WORLD LAGER, OR PACIFIC PALE ALE

PERFECT PAIR: 8 WIRED SAISON SAUVIN
BREWED IN: BLENHEIM, NEW ZEALAND
ABV: 7.0%

Finely chopped white cabbage, iceberg lettuce, scallions (spring onions), cucumber, and carrot, plus a handful of beansprouts, Thai basil, cilantro (fresh coriander), and crushed salted peanuts with a dressing of fish sauce, lime juice, sugar, a clove of crushed garlic, and one hot chili pepper. This is a super salad that's light, fragrant, spicy, and fresh—and you need a beer with a similar vibrancy, ideally aiming at the citrusy herbs and the lime. 8 Wired's Saison Sauvin gets its juicy, tropical, gooseberry, and lime fragrance from Nelson Sauvin and Motueka hops. It's got a brisk carbonation to keep it light and there's some yeast spice to play with the aniseed-like flavors in the carrot and basil. New Zealand hops and a light body of malt is the way to go with this salad.

MOZZARELLA, BASIL, AND TOMATO

GREAT WITH: DARK LAGER OR SOUR BEER

```
PERFECT PAIR: LINDEMAN'S FARO
BREWED IN: VLEZENBEEK, BELGIUM
ABV: 4.75%
```

The key to this match is the umami in the tomato. Umami is a savory, meaty taste that is high in foodstuffs such as soy sauce, aged cheeses, and meats. It works as a natural flavor booster and balancer, which can make acidity less acidic and meatiness more meaty. The cheese is like a sponge to soften acidity and a microphone to amplify salt, as well as the herbal, peppery flavor of the olive oil and basil. For me, two flavors pull tomato and mozzarella together: lemon and caramel. So, I want to eat this salad with an appetite-boosting Sour Beer, but nothing too tart. Faro is a sweetened Sour Beer and so you get a little lemon juice, some apples, cherries, and a balanced sweet-sourness, which whispers caramel. Add some grated Parmesan cheese on top and it's even better. It's also good with the caramel depth of Dark Lager.

POTATO AND BACON SALAD

GREAT WITH: DARK LAGER OR PORTER

```
PERFECT PAIR: NOTCH ČERNÉ PIVO
BREWED IN: IPSWICH, MASSACHUSETTS
ABV: 4.0%
```

This reminds me of Pizza Hut and their salad buffet. Growing up, whenever we ate there, I'd always fill a bowl with as much potato salad as possible and then top it with those indeterminate, crispy-bacon-flavored sprinkle things. Improve on that with diced new potatoes, mayonnaise, Dijon mustard, chives, and slow-cooked smoked bacon. I can eat this salad on its own, but it's also great with some barbecued steak. While not exactly the same, you get potato salad with a lot of Central European dishes, such as schnitzel, and that location gives us the beer pairing of Schwarzbier. Notch's Černé Pivo is inspired by Czech Black Lagers and it's got just a hint of dark malt, which plays with the bacon, and then there's a smooth creaminess before a dry, herbal finish. It's also a brilliant beer with grilled meat.

ASPARAGUS, POACHED EGG, CURED HAM, PARMESAN CHEESE

GREAT WITH: BELGIAN BLONDE OR BELGIAN TRIPEL

```
PERFECT PAIR: EXTRAOMNES BLOND
BREWED IN: MARNATE, ITALY
ABV: 4.4%
```

Belgian Tripel, particularly Westmalle, is a classic match for asparagus and egg where the beer's subtle, background, sulfurous note bridges to the asparagus spears and egg whites, while the brisk carbonation eases through the creamy yolk. I like that match, but think it's a bit powerful, so I prefer a lighter Belgian beer. Extraomnes Blond is pale gold; the aroma is fresh and fragrant with a hint of yeast fruitiness and lemon; the body is simple; the carbonation is sharp; and the bitterness cuts through everything. By adding the caramel and fruity richness of both the Parmesan cheese and cured ham, you get an extra bridge of flavor over to the beer. It's a perfect spring lunch combo.

QUINOA, GOATS' CHEESE, PISTACHIO, AND POMEGRANATE

GREAT WITH: SOUR FRUIT BEER

```
PERFECT PAIR: GOOSE ISLAND LOLITA
BREWED IN: CHICAGO, ILLINOIS
ABV: 7.0%
```

This is a Middle-Eastern-inspired salad of dark green leaves, such as arugula (rocket) and spinach, some pomegranate seeds, toasted pistachio nuts, quinoa, salty-sour and crumbly goats' cheese, some mint and parsley, all with a dressing of pomegranate juice, olive oil, and red wine vinegar (or Sour Raspberry Beer). Goose Island Lolita is aged in wine barrels with raspberries, giving a blushing pink beer that has a berry-fruit aroma and an elegant, dry, and tart finish. With the pomegranate, it mellows and blends seamlessly into the dish, while the pistachio nuts mirror the oak-barrel depth. But it's the way in which the beer gets creamy and sweeter with the goats' cheese that lifts the match and makes it into something completely wonderful and exciting.

FISH AND SHELLFISH

IF YOU'RE EATING OILY FISH, THEN YOU WANT TO BALANCE ITS FATTY RICHNESS; SMOKED FISH NEEDS SWEETNESS OR ACIDITY; SHELLFISH CAN RANGE FROM LITTLE SWEET COCKLES TO SALTY OYSTERS; AND CRUSTACEANS ARE MEATY AND SWEET. ALSO, THE WAY IN WHICH YOU PREPARE THE FISH MAKES A HUGE DIFFERENCE. CATCH A COD, FILLET IT, AND THEN CUT EACH FILLET INTO TWO: GRILL ONE JUST WITH SALT AND PEPPER; BATTER AND DEEP-FRY ONE; STEAM ONE WITH ASIAN SPICES; AND USE THE OTHER IN A MEDITERRANEAN FISH SOUP. EACH OF THESE DISHES WANTS A VERY DIFFERENT BEER. SO, BASICALLY, FISH IS A BROAD GROUP AND NO SIMPLE RULES APPLY: IT'S EVERY FISH FOR HIMSELF.

STEAMED LOBSTER

GREAT WITH: **PILSNER OR KÖLSCH**

PERFECT PAIR: SOUTHAMPTON PUBLICK HOUSE KELLER PILS
BREWED IN: SOUTHAMPTON, NEW YORK
ABV: 5.0%

"I'll have lobster and fries and a pint of beer, please." There is something wonderfully cheeky about ordering that. It feels good, though. And it tastes great. Lobster is sweet and meaty, and it takes on a toasty hazelnut quality when you dip it in melted butter. Fries feel like a natural choice to me, as they give a saltiness and crunch that adds texture to the soft crustacean. Southampton's Keller Pils is an unfiltered Pilsner that's great with lobster: there's a creamy smoothness to the body, some subtle nuttiness, a mix of lemon and floral hops, and then a lemon-pith and pepper bitterness, which works like seasoning on the lobster. It's got a lot of depth of flavor without being overpowering—it's a kickass kellerbier.

SPICY CRAB CAKES

GREAT WITH: **PALE ALE OR NEW WORLD LAGER**

PERFECT PAIR: MAINE BEER CO MO
BREWED IN: FREEPORT, MAINE
ABV: 6.0%

Garrett Oliver, the brewmaster at Brooklyn Brewery, is "The Man" when it comes to beer and food. His *Brewmaster's Table* is the book that every beer lover should read. When he hosts beer dinners around the world, spicy crab cakes always tend to feature on the menu and he pairs them with Brooklyn's East India Pale Ale. It's a cracking combo. I like my spicy crab cakes with an orange or grapefruit mayonnaise (just mix the fruit juice into some mayo), as this jumps right across to a Pale Ale. Putting Maine's MO with crab cakes is the equivalent of wrapping them in brioche and squeezing citrus juice over them. The beer has loads of orange, plus softer, ripe stone fruits like mango, apricot, and peach. It's smooth and easy-to-drink, the sweetness brings it all together, and just a little nip of bitterness boosts the curry spices.

MOULES À LA BIÈRE

GREAT WITH: WITBIER OR BELGIAN BLONDE

PERFECT PAIR: UPRIGHT BREWING FOUR
BREWED IN: PORTLAND, OREGON
ABV: 4.5%

Moules à la bière are mussels cooked in beer, often Witbier or Blonde, with shallots and garlic. To match the juicy, salty, little molluscs, you want a beer that's light and fruity. Upright's Four is a Witbier that's elegant and zesty, and has a slight citrus depth running through it, which balances the sea saltiness in the dish and keeps it tasting fresh and light. It's a beer that seems to get increasingly tasty as I drink it, which is exactly how I feel when eating a big bowl of mussels: the more I eat, the more I enjoy them and hope that the bowl will never get empty. If you've got mussels cooked in white wine, then Witbier still does a great job—it's got a bridging acidity between wheat and grape.

FISH PIE

GREAT WITH: SMOKED BEER

PERFECT PAIR: 8 WIRED THE BIG SMOKE
BREWED IN: BLENHEIM, NEW ZEALAND
ABV: 6.2%

Smoked fish is important in fish pie; it pushes a waft and depth of appetizing meatiness through the thick white sauce, which is then balanced with sweet little prawns or leeks that combine to give the dish a big boost of flavor. Choose a beer with a gentle smokiness to bridge to the smoked fish—it works like a loudspeaker amplifying all the wonderful flavors. 8 Wired's The Big Smoke uses smoked malt in combination with dark grains to give a soft chocolate and dark fruit depth, plus some fragrant hops. But it's the way in which the wood-smoked malt—which is subtle and not like a bonfire in your glass—mirrors the smoke in the fish that doubles up the depth and impact. Alaskan Smoked Porter is also great here, as is Okell's excellent Aile or Birrificio Lambrate's Ghisa.

BAKED SEA BASS WITH LEMON, ROSEMARY, AND OLIVES

GREAT WITH: NEW WORLD LAGER OR PILSNER

PERFECT PAIR: SEPTEM FRIDAY'S PALE ALE
BREWED IN: EVIA, GREECE
ABV: 4.7%

Septem's Friday's Pale Ale is not like those heavy-handed, American-style Pale Ales; this is one of the most elegant Pales there is. Biscuity malt is surrounded by a gentle hop fruitiness (Saaz and Nelson Sauvin), with peach, lychee, lemon, and tangerine, plus some earthy herbs— it's sensational in its fresh subtlety. It's able to pirouette past the olives, lift the lemon, play with the rosemary, and allow the fish's natural sweetness to come through. To me, it's the smell of Greek seafront restaurants; hence, going for a Greek brew. If you can't find this beer, then a New World Lager or aromatic, herbal Pilsner, such as Jever or Firestone Walker Pils, both work well.

SEAFOOD PAELLA

GREAT WITH: PILSNER OR BELGIAN BLONDE

PERFECT PAIR: PILSNER URQUELL
BREWED IN: PILSEN, CZECH REPUBLIC
ABV: 4.4%

I cook paella when I want to feel like it's sunny outside. Its bright yellow color makes me think of the sun, as I stand in its radiant glow hoping to catch a tan and trying to get a Proustian flashback to huge paella pans wafting their aromas around Spanish streets. Seafood paella is salty, strong, and full of umami, which a big squeeze of lemon can lighten and lift, so the best thing a beer can do is to add sweetness to balance this, which is why sweetish Spanish lagers like San Miguel or Estrella work so well. I prefer a Pilsner Urquell for its fuller body and hint of buttery caramel (it's great with the seafood) and then the citrusy, grassy lift of hops.

CHICKEN AND TURKEY

EVERYONE KNOWS CHICKEN AND TURKEY, RIGHT? I'M FAIRLY CERTAIN THAT NO ONE WILL SIT DOWN WITH JUST A PLAIN POULTRY BREAST AND TRY TO FIND A GOOD BEER MATCH (THOUGH I'D RECOMMEND A KÖLSCH OR DARK LAGER). INSTEAD, THE BIRDS WORK LIKE A BLANK CANVAS TO COVER WITH LOTS OF DIFFERENT FLAVORS, SO, WHEN YOU LOOK TO MATCH BEERS TO THEM, IT ALL DEPENDS ON HOW THE BIRD IS COOKED AND WHAT IT'S COOKED WITH. ONE OF THE VERY BEST BEER AND FOOD COMBINATIONS EVER IS CHICKEN SKIN ROASTED WITH LOTS OF SALT AND SERVED WITH A GLASS OF GUEUZE—IT'S AN AMAZING SNACK.

SPANISH TORTILLA

GREAT WITH: KÖLSCH OR BLONDE ALE

PERFECT PAIR: DRAKE'S BLONDE ALE
BREWED IN: SAN LEANDRO, CALIFORNIA
ABV: 4.8%

Not technically chicken, I know, but close enough to count. Spanish tortilla is a dish that is way greater than the sum of its humble ingredients of eggs, potato, onion, and seasoning—and you get a dish that's salty, savory, and yummy with umami. Drake's Kölsch-esque Blonde Ale is clean, there's sweetness from the malt, a little earthy hops, and a floral aroma; and it's able to pick out the sweetness in the onions and keep everything light and fresh. If you pimp the tortilla with chorizo, this beer still works really well, as its biscuit-malt depth is excellent with the spicy sausage. Eggs generally work well with pale, low-hopped beers, including Hefeweizen.

GARLIC, HERB, AND LEMON ROAST CHICKEN

GREAT WITH: NEW WORLD LAGER OR BELGIAN TRIPEL

PERFECT PAIR: BIRRA DEL BORGO MY ANTONIA
BREWED IN: BORGOROSE, ITALY
ABV: 7.5%

In the film "Amélie," Dominique Bretodeau buys a chicken every Tuesday morning. He roasts it with potatoes. After carving the legs and wings, he then loves to pick at the rest of the carcass with his fingers, starting with the oysters. Bretodeau is a wise man; the oysters are the reason to raise your hand and offer to carve the bird. Just make sure that you open a bottle of My Antonia before you begin. Finish the beer with the rest of the bird, and you'll see how good this Imperial Pilsner is with the garlic, herbs, and lemon on the chicken. It's hopped with Simcoe, Warrior, and Saaz, which give a mix of lemon pith, peaches, dried flowers, and fresh herbs, as well as a botanic kind of bitterness that really emphasizes the herbs and the chicken's natural sweetness.

FRIED CHICKEN

GREAT WITH: PILSNER OR PALE ALE

PERFECT PAIR: URBAN CHESTNUT ZWICKEL
BREWED IN: ST LOUIS, MISSOURI
ABV: 4.8%

My dream beer with fried chicken is Unfiltered Pilsner because it's got a creamy depth that enhances the buttery richness of the meat, a floral-citrus aroma that bridges the spices in the crumb, and a sharp bitterness to balance the fat. There's one problem: most Unfiltered Pilsners or Kellerbiers are draft only. Urban Chestnut's Zwickel is a very good example of one of the few bottled versions: soft-bodied, smooth, with a biscuity malt sweetness, and then a bracing bitterness giving citrus pith and peppercorns. If, like me, you need to get your Kellerbier and fried chicken fix, then buy a bucket and sneak it into your local lager brewery. FYI: Zwickel is the German name for the sample tap on a beer tank, so, see that mentioned, and you're getting the good beer straight from the cellar.

CURRY-ROASTED CHICKEN

GREAT WITH: HOPPY SESSION BEER

PERFECT PAIR: MOOR NOR'HOP
BREWED IN: PITNEY, ENGLAND
ABV: 4.1%

This recipe involves coating a whole chicken in curry spices and lots of salt, and then stuffing it with a bulb of garlic and a bunch of cilantro (fresh coriander) before roasting it on a bed of onions, fennel, carrots, and potato. Fruity hops work really well here, as they tease out the spices, sweeten the saltiness, and bridge to the roasted vegetables. Moor's Nor'Hop is very pale and very hoppy, with orange, floral, and tropical aromas from the American hops. It has a softness in the middle, thanks to it being unfiltered, a little background of pale malt, a clean, quenching finish, and it's able to boost all of the chicken spices in a brilliant way. If you see their So'Hop, it's the same beer, but brewed with Southern Hemisphere hops. Both are excellent.

COQ À LA BIÈRE

GREAT WITH: AMBER ALE OR BELGIAN BLONDE

PERFECT PAIR: DE KONINCK
BREWED IN: ANTWERP, BELGIUM
ABV: 5.2%

This is chicken slow-cooked in beer (Bière de Garde or Blonde) with smoked bacon, mushrooms, shallots, and some herbs (usually thyme, bay, and rosemary). Cream goes into the finished sauce before the dish is served with mashed potato or fries. A Belgian-style Blonde or Amber, such as De Koninck, with its ping of carbonation, caramel maltiness, and spicy, herbal, stone-fruit finish, is able to lift the dish's savory richness and also bridge to some of the herbal and sweet flavors. It's not the most complex of beers, but it's very good with this chicken, plus—and I apologize in advance for this one—De Konink's distinctive spherical glass is called a "bolleke," so, in this unique instance, you can order a coq and a bolleke.

CHRISTMAS/THANKSGIVING DINNER

GREAT WITH: BELGIAN DUBBEL OR QUADRUPEL

PERFECT PAIR: CHIMAY GRANDE RÉSERVE
BREWED IN: CHIMAY, BELGIUM
ABV: 9.0%

Christmas dinner is my favorite meal of the year and so it deserves a special bottle. With roast turkey, roast potatoes, herby stuffing, and many vegetables, all covered in thick gravy, it's a mountainous meal and a tough one to tackle with a beer. My trick is to match the beer to the gravy, which, in my kitchen, is made with the cooking juices, port, and chicken stock. Chimay Grande Réserve comes in a 25 US fl oz (750ml) bottle that's made for sharing. (Chimay Blue is the same beer in a small bottle.) Pouring a red-brown, it gives us dried fruit, chocolate, port, caramel, figs, cinnamon, and herbs. It smells of Christmas to me and, with the food, is able to wrap everything up together. It's the very best beer I've found to go with the festive fowl.

GAME
AND OFFAL

PERHAPS NOT TO EVERYONE'S TASTE, BUT GAME AND
OFFAL HAVE SOME GENEROUS QUALITIES WHEN YOU'RE
CHOOSING BEERS TO DRINK WITH THEM. GAME ANIMALS
TEND TO HAVE STRONGER, RICHER FLAVORS THAN THEIR
NON-GAME EQUIVALENTS (THINK PHEASANT VERSUS
CHICKEN, BOAR VERSUS PORK, AND SO ON), WHILE OFFAL
OFTEN HAS A RICHNESS OF TEXTURE OR, LIKE HAGGIS
AND BLACK PUDDING, COMES BOLSTERED WITH LOTS OF
SEASONING. GIVEN THE FULLER AND EARTHIER FLAVORS
OF GAME AND OFFAL, THE BEERS TEND TOWARD DARKER,
EARTHIER DRINKS. THE MORE SQUEAMISH CAN SIMPLY
REPLACE THE FURRY OR FLYING GAME WITH CHICKEN AND
THE BIGGER BEASTS WITH BEEF OR PORK.

LAPIN À LA GUEUZE

GREAT WITH: FLANDERS RED OR STOUT

PERFECT PAIR: BRASSERIE DE
LA SENNE STOUTERIK
BREWED IN: BRUSSELS, BELGIUM
ABV: 4.5%

If rabbits were the size of pigs, aside from
being unbelievably scary, they'd also be my
favorite animal in the kitchen. I love them for
their tender sweetness, which is somewhere
between chicken and pork. Lapin à la Gueuze is
classic cuisine à la bière. It's a slow-cooked,
one-pot dish with rabbit, prunes, onion, herbs,
and Gueuze, and you get soft meat and a rich
sauce that's a little lighter than the other
classic Belgian meat-and-beer stew, known as
Carbonnade. Stouterik, a Belgian-brewed Dry
Stout, has a background of dark malt, a little
sweetness, some prune-bridging dried fruit,
and some smoke, which teases the sharp
earthiness in the Gueuze. It's a surprising
match and also a very good one.

HAGGIS, NEEPS, AND TATTIES

GREAT WITH: PORTER OR SCOTCH ALE

PERFECT PAIR: WILLIAMS BROS FRAOCH
HEATHER ALE
BREWED IN: ALLOA, SCOTLAND
ABV: 5.0%

Fraoch harks back to the days when hops
weren't the main ingredient used to give beer
its bitterness or flavor. Williams Bros continue
an old Scottish tradition of adding heather,
which grows abundantly around the country,
to this beer, along with bog myrtle—they don't
add any hops to Fraoch. Haggis is a classic
Scottish dish made from sheep's offal (liver,
lungs, heart), oatmeal, and spices, including
nutmeg and pepper, and it's served with neeps
and tatties (rutabaga/swede and potato). Put
Fraoch and haggis together and something
uniquely evocative happens, as the floral
aroma in the beer nudges the similar flavors
in the neeps and then breezes through the
spices and the savory richness of the meat,
making it lighter, more floral, sweeter, and
less like eating a gray ball of guts.

CHICKEN LIVER PÂTÉ
WITH HONEY-ROAST FIGS

GREAT WITH: BELGIAN DUBBEL

PERFECT PAIR: ST BERNARDUS PRIOR 8
BREWED IN: WATOU, BELGIUM
ABV: 8.0%

The most successful pâté pairings come when
you bridge to whatever you are serving
alongside it because, given the fatty richness
of the dish, most beers work pretty well: for
example, berry compote works with Cherry
Beer, a semi-sweet (dark) chocolate sauce with
Sweet Stout, and roast pineapple with Pale
Ale. I like honey-roasted figs and Belgian
Dubbel. The fruity, floral figs balance the
richness in the pâté before the full-bodied beer
boosts it all with extra dried-fruit flavor, sweet
doughy bread, brown sugar, festive spice, tea,
and toasted nuts, plus big bubbles that lift the
buttery texture. Foie gras works in a similar
way, although you'll want a more Champagne-
like brew—Saison works very well with
whatever goes with the goose liver.

ROAST PHEASANT
AND ROOT VEGETABLES

GREAT WITH: BEST BITTER

PERFECT PAIR: ADNAMS GUNHILL
BREWED IN: SOUTHWOLD, ENGLAND
ABV: 4.0%

I went pheasant shooting once and hit
nothing but clouds all day. I was with my
Grandad, who is much better at it than I am,
and he got a couple of birds for me to take
home and cook. I like pheasant simply roasted
with fragrant woody herbs and root
vegetables, especially carrots, parsnips, and
celeriac, as their sweetness works really well
with the meat. It's great with Adnams
Gunhill, which has a toasty body, with forest
fruitiness and caramel through it, all of which
enhances the bird's gamey flavor, while the
floral, earthy hops find the herbs on the
vegetables and seem politely to announce
their presence. It's the beer and food
equivalent of a scene from "Downton Abbey."

SWEDISH REINDEER STEW

GREAT WITH: PORTER OR BELGIAN DUBBEL

PERFECT PAIR: CARNEGIE STARKPORTER
BREWED IN: FALKENBERG, SWEDEN
ABV: 5.5%

This is kalops, a slow-cooked Swedish stew
in which the traditional beef is replaced with
reindeer meat. White peppercorns and allspice
give a warming, fragrant flavor to the rich,
meaty stew, which also contains plenty of onion
and big chunks of carrot (reuniting Rudolf with
his Christmas Eve snack). Kalops is served
with potatoes and pickled beetroot. Carnegie
Starkporter is made by Carlsberg and is the
oldest registered trademark in Sweden, having
been brewed since 1836. It's black, but doesn't
have a heavy roast bitterness; instead, you get
a smooth, full body of malt, which gives toffee,
toast, and a little chocolate. The sweetness in it
takes the edge off the pickled beetroot, pokes
the carrots, plays with the allspice, and lets
the meat's gamey depth come right through.
It's also good if the kalops is made with beef...

DUCK CONFIT AND RED CABBAGE

GREAT WITH: SAISON OR WITBIER

PERFECT PAIR: SOUTHAMPTON PUBLICK
HOUSE DOUBLE WHITE
BREWED IN: SOUTHAMPTON, NEW YORK
ABV: 6.6%

Double White isn't like other Witbiers. It
doesn't have the same lemonade-like quench.
Instead, you get a beer with body, depth,
and complexity, which is enhanced by the
coriander, lemon, and orange used in the brew.
It's able to handle heaviness in a way that
other beers struggle to do, making Double
White good with duck confit (which is duck
marinated in herbs and spices, and then
cooked in duck fat for a few hours). Double
White's spicy yeast and coriander cleverly
bridges glass to plate, while its carbonation is
able to balance all the fattiness. Use some
fennel seeds in the red cabbage and it makes
everything taste lighter, adding a teasing
faux-sweetness. A classic Saison can be
a good alternative.

PORK

When I started writing this book, I filled a notebook with ideas, recipes, and tasting notes. I gave each beer style a page where I listed potential brews to write about with possible dishes that would be great with the style. On every single one of those style pages, I'd included some kind of pork dish. The pig is a generous animal with its very many cuts and what chefs can do with them. The good news for beer is that pork contains fat, so can handle hops, sweetness, spices, and acidity, plus the meat also picks up caramelized cooking flavors to mirror the malt. The pig is probably beer's best mate.

ROAST BELLY PORK, MASHED POTATO, AND APPLE SAUCE

GREAT WITH: CIDER OR PALE ALE

PERFECT PAIR: TUATARA AOTEAROA PALE ALE
BREWED IN: KAPITI, NEW ZEALAND
ABV: 5.8%

Pork contains lactones, which give subtle fruity flavors such as apricots, peaches, and coconut. Also, pork works really well with apples, which can cut through the fatty richness, so serve belly pork with stewed apples on the side, preferably made with rosemary and orange peel (just to point toward the beer match). I want to drink this with a Pale Ale— namely Tuatara's APA, which is made only with New Zealand hops and gives a stone-fruit flavor of peach, apricot, and mango that is great with pork and apple. The beer's bitterness balances the fat by lifting it, the hops pick up on the wood-citrus of the herbs, and the base of sweet malt carries the meat flavor. Pale Ale and belly pork are always a good pairing.

PORK JUNGLE CURRY

GREAT WITH: BELGIAN-STYLE WHEAT BEER

PERFECT PAIR: WESTBROOK WHITE THAI
BREWED IN: MOUNT PLEASANT, SOUTH CAROLINA
ABV: 5.0%

One day, you might find yourself in Northern Thailand's jungles. If you do, then I hope you had the foresight to pack a few cans of Westbrook's White Thai in your rucksack to go with the jungle curry you'll be cooking on your campfire. Unlike other Thai curries, this doesn't use coconut and that's because, if you look around the jungle, there aren't many coconut trees. Instead, there are bamboo shoots and eggplants (aubergines), chili peppers, ginger, lemongrass, lime leaves, and basil (it's a fortunate bounty of jungle spices). There's also jungle meat, such as wild boar, frogs, and snails, although, of course, you also cleverly had the foresight to pack some pork. With White Thai—a Witbier brewed with lemongrass and ginger, which uses the lemony Sorachi Ace hops—you get a double hit of citrusy herbs, while the creamy smooth body provides some cooling balance. Pack wisely when you go to the jungle.

TOULOUSE SAUSAGES AND BEANS

GREAT WITH: BELGIAN BLONDE,
SAISON, OR BROWN ALE

PERFECT PAIR: BELLEROSE BIÈRE
BLONDE EXTRA
BREWED IN: SAINT-AMAND-LES-EAUX, FRANCE
ABV: 6.5%

This is a kind of cassoulet minus the rib-
sticking duck fat. It's made with garlicky
sausages (also made with smoked bacon, red
wine, and thyme), white beans (butter,
cannellini, flageolet), garlic, onion, smoked
bacon, tomatoes, and herbs (thyme, rosemary,
bay). It's a versatile beer dish and a few brews
step forward, such as Brooklyn Brown in which
the toasty notes and woody, herbal hops bring
everything together really well. However, I
prefer Bellerose, which is like a hoppy Bière de
Garde. It's got a smooth body of malt, which
pokes caramel into the porky parts, and then
lots of fragrant, floral, and peppery hops that
pick out the herbs and the garlic running
through the dish. The dry bitterness is then like
a period, or full stop, before the next mouthful.

SMOKED HAM

GREAT WITH: FRUIT BEER OR WITBIER

PERFECT PAIR: UNIBROUE ÉPHÉMÈRE APPLE
BREWED IN: QUEBEC, CANADA
ABV: 5.5%

Guaiacol, which is a smoky compound and the
main flavor found in smoked ham, is a precursor
to eugenol. Eugenol is what gives cloves their
smoky phenol aroma and peppery, spicy flavor.
Guaiacol and eugenol both have a little vanillin in
them. Witbier typically has a clove-like spiciness,
some smoke, and hints of vanilla, so Wit naturally
enhances the flavor of smoked ham. By adding
fruit, it just gets even better. Unibroue's
Éphémère Apple is a Witbier made with apple
must. It's got a tart apple taste, some lemon and
orange citrus, a full body and bright carbonation,
a sweet lift of vanilla candy, and a background
nudge of smoky spice, which brings the whole
thing together into a wonderful pairing. A barrel-
aged cider works well here, too, as many contain
hints of guaiacol, eugenol, and vanillin.

MUSTARD PORK CHOPS
WITH FENNEL-ROAST POTATOES

GREAT WITH: BELGIAN BLONDE

PERFECT PAIR: SHARP'S CHALKY'S BITE
BREWED IN: ROCK, ENGLAND
ABV: 6.8%

Chalky's Bite is made with Cornish fennel
and takes its inspiration from classic Belgian
brews. It's a golden beer with bright
carbonation. It has a little honey sweetness
and a floral hop aroma, and, when you put it
with mustard-glazed pork chops with fennel-
roasted potatoes, you really pick out the
sweet aniseed in the beer. It's a great food
beer with pork and fish, as the fennel gives
it a savory and appetizing kind of depth
with a cheeky hidden sweetness. The beer
is named after chef Rick Stein's little Jack
Russell dog, who caused mischief running
around the camera crew as they tried to
film his television shows. Sharp's Brewery
is located across the River Camel from
Padstow, where Rick Stein has a number
of restaurants.

HOG ROAST ROLLS

GREAT WITH: ESB OR BEST BITTER

PERFECT PAIR: FULLER'S ESB
BREWED IN: LONDON, ENGLAND
ABV: 5.5% (BOTTLE VERSION IS 5.9%)

This little piggy went to market, this little
piggy stayed home, this little piggy had roast
beef, this little piggy had none, and this little
piggy went "wee wee wee" all the way to the
pub where he was impaled on a massive spit
and roasted for hours over a fire before being
ceremoniously carved and placed inside huge
bread baps with a piece of crunchy crackling
and some apple sauce. He was then greedily
eaten by someone drinking a pint of Fuller's
ESB, which is rich with bready malt, some
caramel sweetness, herbal hops, marmalade,
and even a roast-apple depth before a dry
bitterness that lingers. Poor little piggy, he
should've stayed at home...

RED MEAT

A KEY FEATURE OF COOKED MEAT IS THE MAILLARD REACTION, WHICH OCCURS WHEN AMINO ACIDS IN THE MEAT REACT WITH CERTAIN SUGARS ON BEING HEATED AND GIVE COLOR AND FLAVOR TO THE OUTSIDE OF THE FOOD (CARAMEL, TOAST, ROASTED). THIS HAPPENS WITH GRILLED MEAT, BAKED BREAD, FRENCH FRIES, AND MORE. JUST CONSIDER THE DIFFERENCE BETWEEN A POACHED STEAK AND A GRIDDLED ONE, AND YOU'LL UNDERSTAND THE DIFFERENCE. THE MAILLARD REACTION ALSO INFLUENCES THE COLOR OF MALTED BARLEY DURING ITS PRODUCTION, SO THIS CREATES A NATURAL BRIDGE OF FLAVOR BETWEEN FOOD AND BEER. BEEF AND LAMB HAVE PLENTY OF UMAMI, WHICH LOVES SWEETNESS AND BITTERNESS, AND NATURALLY WORK WELL WITH OTHER HIGH-UMAMI INGREDIENTS. AS WITH OTHER FOOD GROUPS, IT'S THE THINGS SERVED WITH THE PROTEIN THAT WILL DETERMINE THE BEST BEER MATCH.

BEEF CARBONNADE

GREAT WITH: BELGIAN DUBBEL

PERFECT PAIR: WESTMALLE DUBBEL
BREWED IN: WESTMALLE, BELGIUM
ABV: 7.0%

Belgium is the place to go if you like cuisine à la bière, which features dishes that use beer as an ingredient. There's mussels in Witbier, rabbit in Gueuze, duck in Kriek, lots of Witbier sauces, plus Kriek and Dubbel in desserts, but the most famous dish is Beef Carbonnade: beef slow-cooked in beer (normally either a Dubbel or a Sour Red). The sauce is thick and rich with beer, and the dish comes with fries on the side and sometimes mustard-topped croutons (it's easy to make for yourself and there's a recipe for it on page 173). A Belgian Dubbel, like Westmalle's, is the beer to drink with Carbonnade. It's got bread, caramel, and dried-fruit sweetness and then it ends with a dry, peppery, and almost savory finish, while the feisty carbonation helps to keep the mouthful balanced. A classic Belgian combo.

ROAST BEEF AND YORKSHIRE PUDDINGS

GREAT WITH: DARK MILD

PERFECT PAIR: BRAINS DARK
BREWED IN: CARDIFF, WALES
ABV: 4.1%

When I was growing up, almost without exception, we had roast dinners every Sunday, so I know a bit about them. A complete roast beef dinner is meat, roast potatoes, lots of vegetables (I like parsnips, cabbage, and carrots with beef), Yorkshire puddings, thick beef gravy, and some hot-sweet horseradish sauce. A Dark Mild is my first choice of beer. Brains Dark is a glass of balance and subtlety, a mix of malts that gives some simple grain flavor with a hint of cocoa-like darkness to highlight the roast beef. It also hits the horseradish with some extra sweetness. There's a licorice depth that highlights the carrots and parsnips, and a polite nod of bitterness at the end. It's a properly British combination.

LAMB WITH THYME
AND ROSEMARY CRUST

GREAT WITH: SAISON

PERFECT PAIR: STILLWATER CELLAR DOOR
BREWED IN: BALTIMORE, MARYLAND
ABV: 6.6%

Lamb contains thymol, the phenolic compound that gives thyme its woody, floral fragrance. Rosemary is high in terpenes, such as myrcene, pinene, linalool, geraniol, and limonene, which give the herb its woody citrus, and spicy aromas. Those terpenes are also found in hops, so lamb that has a thyme and rosemary crust and is served with beer has many cross-over compounds. Cellar Door uses floral, citrusy Sterling and Citra hops, with Citra being notably high in terpenes. A lemony depth in the beer is a brilliant booster to the inherent citrus in the herbs, a honey-like sweetness gives balance and enhances the meat, while phenols from the yeast tease out the thymol. The beer is also brewed with white sage to give a savory boost and peppery pick-up to the herbs. Most aromatic Saisons are a great match for this dish, but (scientifically) Cellar Door is the best.

LAMB KOFTA AND TZATZIKI

GREAT WITH: SAISON OR WILD ALE

PERFECT PAIR: PRAIRIE ARTISAN ALES
PRAIRIE ALE
BREWED IN: KREBS, OKLAHOMA
ABV: 8.2%

Kofta is ground (minced) lamb mixed with garlic, ground coriander, cumin, cinnamon, pepper, and parsley, and then squeezed around a stick before going onto a charcoal grill. Kofta is popular in Turkey and around the Middle East, and it tastes best when taken straight from the grill and put into a pitta where it's topped with tzatziki (a delicious mix of yogurt and cucumber with lemon and mint). Any beer that can play with the spiciness is going to work well, especially if it can add a little fruity sweetness of its own. Prairie Ale is a wonderful Saison with a tantalizing mix of stone and citrus fruit in the aroma, as well as a lively Champagne-like body with a gripping richness of malt. The subtle lemony tartness and pepper at the end pokes at both the lamb spices and the tzatzki.

STEAK AND FRIES

GREAT WITH: AMBER ALE OR AMBER LAGER

PERFECT PAIR: GREAT LAKES ELIOT NESS
BREWED IN: CLEVELAND, OHIO
ABV: 6.2%

I think most beers in this book would taste great with steak and fries, but what is the single best beer you can pour to go with a well-seasoned, medium-rare piece of well-hung beef with a thick edge of fat? Many would pick a Porter, which has a dark malt flavor to match the Maillard coloration on the meat and fries, but that's too dominant a flavor unless your steak is burnt. It's an Amber that I want, and Eliot Ness has toast and some toffee. It's clean, yet has good body and depth, and then the hops kick out and grab onto the seasoning and give some floral and citrus freshness. It's interesting to know that beef contains esters and aldehydes, which give out fruity, floral, and nutty flavors during cooking, providing another bridge to hoppy Amber beers.

BEEF CHILI

GREAT WITH: SWEET STOUT OR DARK LAGER

PERFECT PAIR: ROGUE SHAKESPEARE
OATMEAL STOUT
BREWED IN: NEWPORT, OREGON
ABV: 6.1%

Everyone has his or her own special chili recipe, right? I like Imperial Stout in mine, as it gives the kind of depth and richness you'd need a jar of chocolate-covered anchovies to recreate. Whatever the recipe, chili is one of the American southwest's greatest gifts to the culinary world and my favorite beer to drink with it is a Milk or Oatmeal Stout, such as Rogue's Shakespeare. The creamy and smooth body calms the spiciness, as if it's cooing lullabies, and then it gives its own flavor-boosting depth of chocolate and roast, while also being really generous with a full mouthfeel, which is the real key to this match. It's one of the best combinations I know of.

PIZZA AND PASTA

DOUGH GOES WITH BEER. THE CROSS-OVER FLAVORS BETWEEN PIZZA AND PASTA DOUGH AND BEER'S MALTINESS ARE EASY TO MATCH, ESPECIALLY IF YOU OPT FOR PALE BEERS WITH THEIR INHERENTLY BREADY, DOUGHY FLAVORS. WITH PIZZA, WHICH GETS A TOASTY OR CHARRED QUALITY FROM THE OVEN, DARKER MALTS EASILY MATCH THEIR ROASTED QUALITIES; WITH PASTA, THERE'S A BIG DIFFERENCE BETWEEN A TOMATO SAUCE AND, SAY, A CHEESE SAUCE, SO THAT WILL INFLUENCE YOUR BEER CHOICE. IN GENERAL, YOU WANT LIGHT PAIRINGS, SO OPT FOR A BEER WITH A LIVELY CARBONATION TO STOP IT CREATING A DOUBLE-DOUGH EFFECT THAT'S THE EQUIVALENT OF A PASTA SANDWICH.

SPAGHETTI CARBONARA

GREAT WITH: BELGIAN BLONDE, PILSNER, OR SMOKED BEER

PERFECT PAIR: SCHLENKERLA LAGERBIER
BREWED IN: BAMBERG, GERMANY
ABV: 4.3%

During my training to run a marathon, I became obsessed with cooking the perfect carbonara. I love the smoky meatiness of pancetta, the silky combo of egg yolk and Parmesan cheese, and the brashness of black pepper, plus the mix of protein, fat, and carbs make it a great post-run meal. It took me too many attempts to nail the recipe and even longer to find the perfect beer to go with it. Then I tried Schlenkerla's Lagerbier. It's pale blonde with a soft, pillowy body; there's a refreshing bite of bitterness at the back, but it's the subtle, flavor-boosting waft of bacon-like smoke that makes it amazing to drink with carbonara, bridging the pancetta before the lemony hops balance the richness—interestingly, it's not a smoked beer, but it picks up smokiness from the brewhouse. The thought of this combo made it worth running a few extra miles.

SPAGHETTI BOLOGNESE

GREAT WITH: BELGIAN DUBBEL

PERFECT PAIR: ROCHEFORT 8
BREWED IN: ROCHEFORT, BELGIUM
ABV: 9.2% ABV

At university, my mate Pez came over once a week to cook his dinner. He'd bring family-sized packs of spaghetti, ground (minced) beef, Bolognese sauce, and a loaf of bread, which, for him, was enough for one person. Pez would choose two cans of lager to go with this meal, but I prefer the chocolatey, raisiny, nutty, and spicy sweetness of a Belgian Dubbel, such as Rochefort 8. The yeast spice bridges to the basil (think of sweet anise) and pepper, while the tomato and meat are matched by the caramelized flavors in the brew. There's also a slight creaminess in the beer that loves the starchy pasta. Dubbels work with similar dishes, such as spaghetti with meatballs, and lasagne. Go meat-free if you wish with spaghetti alla Norma and drink Birra del Borgo's DucAle (also a Dark Belgian-style ale) if you can—the eggplant (aubergine) and beer share a creamy nuttiness.

MARGHERITA PIZZA

GREAT WITH: AMBER ALE OR AMBER LAGER

PERFECT PAIR: FLYING DOG OLD SCRATCH
BREWED IN: FREDERICK, MARYLAND
ABV: 5.5%

There's an elemental simplicity and greatness to holding a slice of pizza in one hand and a beer in the other. That simplicity defines the brilliance of pizza and beer, so this match is something you want to keep easy-going. Boost it with an American Amber, such as Flying Dog Old Scratch or Brooklyn Brewery's Lager—bready malt, plus some caramel, which bridges the pizza base, and then citrusy hops that love the cheese and basil. I think margherita pizza is only bettered with the additional umami-wallop of anchovies, which, in turn, makes Amber beers taste even better. Add other toppings to the pizza and the pairing can be changed to suit them, although in truth almost any beer works with almost any pizza, as you probably already know.

PESTO PASTA

GREAT WITH: BELGIAN TRIPEL OR PILSNER

PERFECT PAIR: TRIPEL KARMELIET
BREWED IN: BUGGENHOUT, BELGIUM
ABV: 8.4%

Basil is my favorite herb (apart from maybe thyme...) and I always have some growing in the kitchen or garden—I love its warm, sweet aniseed, minty, grassy fragrance. Blitz basil with toasted pine nuts, garlic (I prefer this poached or roasted for added sweetness and nuttiness), olive oil, sweet-salty Parmesan cheese, and just a little lemon juice for a simple pasta sauce. Not an easy one for a beer, with its pungent flavors, but a Belgian-style Tripel is great for its ability to balance sulfurous garlic and bridge to the lemony, peppery, spiciness of the oil and basil. The malt body brings a hint of honey and vanilla sweetness, while the hops have an apricot-like flavor and this makes it great with the cheese. A hoppy Pilsner also works well here.

LINGUINE ALLE VONGOLE

GREAT WITH: PILSNER OR WHEAT ALE

PERFECT PAIR: BIRRIFICIO ITALIANO
TIPOPILS
BREWED IN: LURAGO MARINONE, ITALY
ABV: 5.2%

Shortly before my ex-girlfriend's Grandad died, he gave me his recipe for linguine alle vongole. He loved this dish, but rarely cooked it because his wife, Lilian, didn't like it. I now think of Michael every time I see it and this entry is dedicated to him, because I always loved talking about food and wine with him and I inherited a lot of his favorite books. Like the best Italian dishes, this is simple and yet so tasty, transforming linguine, clams, white wine, garlic, parsley, and dried chili flakes into a magnificent meal. Birrificio Italiano's Tipopils is a glorious, flavor-boosting match because it's so good with the seaside saltiness in the dish, where it adds an elegance of creamy lemon, plus herbs and pepper.

WHITE PIZZA

GREAT WITH: BROWN ALE OR FLEMISH BROWN

PERFECT PAIR: SIXPOINT BROWNSTONE
BREWED IN: BROOKLYN, NEW YORK
ABV: 6.0%

Artichoke Pizza in New York is one of my "Top Five Pizzas in the World"—a thick-sliced pizza topped with a creamy white sauce, melted mozzarella, Pecorino Romano, artichokes, and spinach. It's amazing. The pizza's richness calls for a potent beer match. If you've got an Artichoke Pizza, I think you'll want to drink something local, so take a can of Sixpoint Brownstone with you for its nutty, toffee-like malt and bold hops. You can enjoy the beer and pizza together while sitting on the sidewalk outside the shop. Non-New-York specific, or if you're making your own pizza, then a good alternative is a sour Belgian Brown, which will lift the pizza's richness, as if you've dipped the dough in ketchup.

SANDWICHES AND BURGERS

THIS IS POSSIBLY MY FAVORITE FOOD GROUP AND ONE OF THE BEST FOR BEER, BECAUSE THE SIMPLICITY OF A SANDWICH IN ONE HAND AND A BEER IN THE OTHER CREATES A PERFECT BALANCE. SOME OF THE GREATEST SANDWICHES ARE DELIBERATELY OVERLOOKED—BACON, PHILADELPHIA CHEESESTEAK, CHIP BUTTY—BECAUSE THEY ARE JUST TOO DELICIOUS AND, ONCE YOU START EATING ONE, YOU DON'T WANT TO THINK ABOUT ANYTHING OTHER THAN TAKING YOUR NEXT BITE OF SANDWICH. IN MANY WAYS, A SANDWICH IS A VERY PERSONAL THING, DETERMINED BY INDIVIDUAL PREFERENCES (TYPE OF BREAD, CONDIMENTS ADDED, AND SO ON), SO THE BEER SELECTION SHOULD REFLECT THAT: CHOOSE A BEER THAT YOU WILL LOVE WITH YOUR SANDWICH.

CHEESEBURGER

GREAT WITH: IPA

PERFECT PAIR: BALLAST POINT SCULPIN IPA
BREWED IN: SAN DIEGO, CALIFORNIA
ABV: 7.0%

"A cheeseburger is a hamburger topped with cheese." That's what Wikipedia says for anyone who is unsure. It goes on to explain that the name is a portmanteau (two words combined into one new one) of "cheese" and "hamburger." The first time I went to America, I ate seven cheeseburgers in five days. And I ate all of them with an IPA. No style of beer is better with a cheeseburger: you've got fruity hops, which match the ketchup and the cheese; you've got bubbles that get rid of the fat; the malt sweetens the char on the meat; the bitterness makes it refreshing; and there's body and booze to handle the big flavors. Choose an IPA with lots of juicy fruit aroma, some soft caramel in the body, and then a balanced bitterness: try Feral Hop Hog, Lagunitas IPA, Beavertown Gamma Ray, or Ballast Point's Sculpin IPA.

HOT DOG

GREAT WITH: AMBER ALE OR AMBER LAGER

PERFECT PAIR: TRÖEGS HOPBACK AMBER ALE
BREWED IN: HERSHEY, PENNSYLVANIA
ABV: 6.0%

Hot dogs come in lots of different styles: never get any ketchup near the sport peppers (which are bite-sized chili peppers in seasoned brine) in a Chicago-style hot dog; in Copenhagen, your hot dog will be topped with raw onions; in England, it'll likely be fried onions; Seattle-style, it's topped with cream cheese; Carolina-style, chili dogs are loaded with beef chili; and sauerkraut is slapped on in Central Europe... Whether you want onions or not, ketchup or mustard, or both, sauerkraut and whatever else, a good beer to go for is an Amber Ale, such as Tröegs Hopback. Ambers share the same approachability as the sausage in a roll, while the beer's sweet, bready caramel boosts the sausage and onion; the fruity hops bridge to whatever condiments you put on top; and a quenching, dry bitterness gives it balance. Keep this one simple.

BÁNH MÌ

GREAT WITH: BROWN ALE OR DARK LAGER

PERFECT PAIR: ANCHOR BREKLE'S BROWN
BREWED IN: SAN FRANCISCO, CALIFORNIA
ABV: 6.0%

This is a Vietnamese sandwich. A French-style baguette is stuffed with a range of different fillings, such as roast pork, grilled chicken, or pâté, plus cucumber, carrot, daikon (a white radish), peppers, and cilantro (fresh coriander). It's traveled widely, and can now be found from Saigon to San Francisco, which is where I had my first Bánh mì: in a little place in the Tenderloin area. Unlike others nearby, I didn't want to drink in the street in that part of town, so I walked and ate. With the sweet meat and the fresh crunchy veg, the Bánh mì is made for a Brown Ale, especially one like Anchor Brekle's Brown with its toffee, semi-sweet (dark) chocolate, and bready body juiced up with Citra hops, which give a lime-like lift to echo the cilantro and vegetables.

FISH FINGER SANDWICH

GREAT WITH: AMERICAN WHEAT OR PALE ALE

PERFECT PAIR: THREE FLOYDS GUMBALLHEAD
BREWED IN: MUNSTER, INDIANA
ABV: 5.6%

I think that fish finger (or fish stick) sandwiches are the best sandwiches in the world. I don't want fancy fried fillets of fish and freshly baked bread; I want four fish fingers from the freezer, grilled, and put between two slices of buttered, store-bought bread. And ketchup is essential. I've probably had better individual sandwiches than this, but fish finger is my favorite. And my favorite sandwich in the whole world deserves one of my favorite beers in the world. Three Floyds Gumballhead is an American Wheat Ale. It's got an incredible peach, mango, lemon, and apricot aroma, a hint of sweetness, a smooth and full body, and then a lasting, balanced bitterness. I love it. This is a perfect pairing for me, because I get the unmatchable brilliance of putting two of my favorite things together.

CROQUE MONSIEUR

GREAT WITH: BIÈRE DE GARDE OR AMBER ALE

PERFECT PAIR: BRASSEURS GAYANT
LA GOUDALE
BREWED IN: DOUAI, FRANCE
ABV: 7.2%

This is a very fine French sandwich in the family of other very fine bread-and-cheese-based grilled snacks. The Croque Monsieur is a grilled ham, cheese, and mustard sandwich that gets an extra layer of toasted cheese on top (plus a fried egg on top of that for a Croque Madame). La Goudale is a Bière de Garde with a honey-like sweetness and some orangey, peppery hop aromas; the malt middle is like toast; and it finishes with herbs and a subtle tartness, which gives all the balance you want against the cheese stack. For worldly alternatives: grilled cheese goes well with American Amber; with cheese on toast, you want an ESB; and you should have an Italian Pale Ale with a ham and cheese panini.

FALAFEL WRAP

GREAT WITH: WITBIER OR SAISON

PERFECT PAIR: HOEGAARDEN
BREWED IN: HOEGAARDEN, BELGIUM
ABV: 4.9%

Hoegaarden is the classic Witbier. It's a style with hundreds of years of history, although it was essentially extinct by the 1950s until the late Pierre Celis brought the brew back to life in 1966. The spicing—coriander seeds and curacao bitter orange peel—has some history in Belgium's tie with the Netherlands, which had links to exotic spices, and may also be a hangover from the days when hops weren't the main ingredient used to flavor beer. Hoegaarden has a smooth body, a swathe of delicate floral citrus from the coriander, and a clove-like spiciness at the end. With the falafel, a Middle East mix of chick peas, fava (broad) beans, garlic, herbs, and spices, wrapped in pitta bread, the citrus, nuttiness, and spice in the food mirror those in the beer, with coriander being the cross-over flavor in the middle.

BARBECUE

I THINK THAT THE WORLD'S CARNIVORES OWE A BIG HIGH-FIVE OF THANKS TO "MAN V. FOOD," THE TV PROGRAM THAT TRAVELED AMERICA SHOWING OFF SOME OF THE TASTIEST THINGS AROUND BEFORE TAKING ON ENORMOUS EATING CHALLENGES. IT WAS IN THIS SHOW THAT WE GOT TO SEE HOW INCREDIBLE BARBECUED FOOD COULD BE, WITH HUGE SMOKE PITS, GREAT TRAYS OF SLOW-COOKED RIBS, GRILLS THE SIZE OF GRAND PIANOS, BITS OF PIG SOAKING IN ALL KINDS OF MARINADES AND RUBS, AND A HUNGRY HOST HOLLERING "HELL, YEAH" ABOUT HOW GOOD IT ALL TASTED. NOW THE REST OF THE WORLD IS TRYING TO MAKE THEIR OWN, MEANING THAT A BARBECUE IS NOW, THANKFULLY, A LOT MORE DELICIOUS THAN THE UNDER-COOKED SAUSAGE AND BURNT BURGERS THAT I GREW UP EATING.

BEEF RIBS

GREAT WITH: RED IPA OR AMBER ALE

PERFECT PAIR: OSKAR BLUES G'KNIGHT
BREWED IN: LONGMONT, COLORADO
ABV: 8.7%

Let your inner cannibal out for the night as you rip the soft meat from a rib bone. Beef ribs are bigger and meatier than baby-back pork ribs, although when cooked they both have a familiar, smoky-sweet flavor with char, caramel, and seasonings, plus the richness of meat. Oskar Blues G'Knight is an Imperial Red that's got loads of toffee-malt depth and then citrus and peppery hops, which combine to boost the flavor in those big beef ribs by mimicking the sweetness in the barbecue sauce, adding a savory-like spiciness, and then freshening it up with the fragrant hops. It works especially well with some creamy coleslaw on the side.

BEEF BRISKET

GREAT WITH: BLACK IPA

PERFECT PAIR: BEAVERTOWN BLACK BETTY
BREWED IN: LONDON, ENGLAND
ABV: 7.4%

Brisket is beef's breast and, given the way bovines move, it supports a lot of the animal's body weight. Because of this, brisket has a lot of connective tissues, so it needs to be cooked for a long time in order to break down the collagen fibers and give a tender cut. This makes brisket good for corned beef and also for barbecue, especially if you cook it over wood to get some smoke flavor in there. Beavertown's Black Betty is a Black Ale with a full, smooth body, just a hint of dark malt (a hint is enough to highlight the meat's barbecued richness), and then loads of juicy citrus from the American hops, which highlights the spice in the rub. Beavertown Brewery started up in a barbecue restaurant before out-growing its cellar; this happily reunites them.

PULLED PORK ROLLS

GREAT WITH: BELGIAN DUBBEL
OR SWEET STOUT

PERFECT PAIR: OMMEGANG ABBEY ALE
BREWED IN: COOPERSTOWN, NEW YORK
ABV: 8.2%

British barbecue gets as much fire burning as quickly as possible, then cooks pallid, pink pieces of pork until they turn black. Pulled pork is the epitome of American barbecue's patient, thought-out approach to really great meat. The pork gets a sugar-and-salt rub and is then slow-cooked for six to eight hours before being pulled apart. It's best served in a bun with some hot-sweet barbecue sauce. Big flavor can cope with a big beer, and there's a great bridge of flavor between the spices in barbecue sauce and those in Belgian Dark Ales, such as Ommegang Abbey Ale. This is brewed with licorice root, star anise, orange peel, coriander, and cumin. It has a cola-like quality, lots of spiciness, and dried fruit, and the orange really bursts through to keep it light and fruity. It's a big, bold, and brilliant combo.

SMOKED WINGS AND COLESLAW

GREAT WITH: PALE ALE OR DARK LAGER

PERFECT PAIR: OSKAR BLUES DALE'S
PALE ALE
BREWED IN: LONGMONT, COLORADO
ABV: 6.5%

Dale's Pale Ale was the first canned craft beer. It has a smooth body of malt, a little sweetness, a bold citrusy aroma, and a great balance, which makes it a mighty match for smoked wings and 'slaw. Being cooked over wood gives the wings their smokiness, plus you get the skin-puckering char from the grill, which adds infinitely to the chicken's flavor and depth. With a spicy dry rub and then a marinade of honey, Worcestershire sauce, ketchup, and chili powder, you get wicked wings. The coleslaw adds a cooling quality to give balance and that opens up the pairing for a Pale Ale's fruitiness to jump right in. Being in a can also helps here: you'll have very messy fingers by the time you're done eating, so you can finish your beer and toss the can away before opening another.

BARBECUED BANANA AND CHOCOLATE SAUCE

GREAT WITH: OATMEAL STOUT

PERFECT PAIR: FOUNDER'S BREAKFAST STOUT
BREWED IN: GRAND RAPIDS, MICHIGAN
ABV: 8.3%

Once the meat has left the grill, there's still a lot of heat on the barbecue and that can do brilliant things to bananas. Just throw the bananas on the grill, unpeeled, and leave them while you eat. When it's time for dessert, take the bananas, cut them open, and scoop out the hot, soft, caramel-like flesh, pour over some melted semi-sweet (dark) chocolate, and add a scoop of vanilla ice cream. Founder's Breakfast Stout is brewed with chocolate, coffee, and oats. The dark malt and chocolate hit the sweet fruit and chocolate sauce, and the oats give a smooth, full body. The coffee and banana are also amazing together. Once you've done this once, you'll always have bananas ready to go on that grill.

BARBECUE BEANS

GREAT WITH: STOUT OR PORTER

PERFECT PAIR: BIRRIFICO DEL DUCATO VERDI
IMPERIAL STOUT
BREWED IN: SORAGNA, ITALY
ABV: 8.2%

These beans make a perfect side dish for meat owing to their rich, creamy, meaty depth. The beans are slow-cooked with molasses and smoked pork, plus a few other ingredients, such as Worcestershire sauce, cinnamon, tomato paste (purée), and brown sugar. The sweetness and deep savoriness require a hulk-like brew to handle them, but also one that is as elegant as a ballerina. This is a tough ask, but Verdi Imperial Stout is up to it. Expect chocolate, a little sweet smoke, and a pleasing, molasses-like sweetness. The beer also contains chili, which, although not hot, does add a peppery depth. Any rich, dark Porter or Stout that's low in roast bitterness is good here; just avoid too much alcohol, as it can overpower and end up tasting like nail polish.

BEER SNACKS

Two pints and a packet of crisps, cheers. Zwei helles und ein brezel, bitte. Dos cervezas y aceitunas, por favor. Two IPAs and some fries, please. Little salty mouthfuls between gulps of beer keep us going when we're out drinking. Everywhere has their own beer snack and, while most work with literally any kind of beer, I think it's possible to find some stellar pairings, where typically you'll find that bitterness and acidity are the best matches to balance the savory saltiness.

PRETZELS

GREAT WITH: PALE LAGER OR DARK LAGER

PERFECT PAIR: KEESMANN HERREN PILS
BREWED IN: BAMBERG, GERMANY
ABV: 5.0%

At the Great American Beer Festival held every year in Denver, Colorado, a significant number of drinkers walk around with pretzel necklaces. I spent three days trying to find the stand selling them at the festival (just to see such a thing, not to buy one!), but it didn't exist, which made me realize something: these people had made them at home and brought them along like the world's least-cool but most-delicious fashion accessory. I prefer the fresh pretzels in Germany: chewy and warm, a little sweet, and then dangerously salty—don't even try to eat one without a beer because it's impossible. I want lager with mine, but the most important quality is a beer that you drink in big gulps. Herren Pils is a favorite, with its stone-fruit and pepper fragrance, as well as its long, dry bitterness.

SCOTCH EGG

GREAT WITH: BEST BITTER OR PALE ALE

PERFECT PAIR: SALOPIAN DARWIN'S ORIGIN
BREWED IN: SHREWSBURY, ENGLAND
ABV: 4.3%

"A pint of Darwin's Origin, please," I say. The landlord grabs a glass and places it beneath the tap. One long, deliberate drag on the handle and copper-colored ale pours out, frothing with white foam. Another drag, long and slow, pushes more beer as the glass fills, then one final small pull and the pint is topped up and placed on the bright bar towel. "And a Scotch egg." He cuts it in half and spoons a dollop of English mustard on the side. I sit across the bar. The beer is singing citrus fruits and a soft pale malt body quickly gives way to a dry and quenching finish, which cuts through the fatty Scotch egg's richness and teases out the sweetness in the herbs, all while trying to tame the ferocious mustard. When I'm done, the landlord calls over: "Another Salopian?" I just smile and nod.

FRENCH FRIES

GREAT WITH: PALE ALE

PERFECT PAIR: ANY FRESH AMERICAN-STYLE PALE ALE
BREWED IN: WHEREVER YOU ARE

French fries are probably the most beer-friendly food in the whole galaxy and I can't think of anything so universally unbeatable with a brew, but what's the perfect beer for a plate of seasoned fries? For me, it's an American-style Pale Ale, a craft-beer style with a similar bar ubiquity to fries. Citrusy, floral, fragrant, a juicy body of malt, which gives some sweetness, and then a bitterness that balances the salt—it's got everything you need for a good match and these attributes have the ability to make each other taste better together. Fresh is always best with Pale Ale, so drink whatever is local and freshest. Cheese-topped fries want IPA, garlic fries want Double IPA, chili fries want Black IPA.

CRISPS/POTATO CHIPS/PEANUTS

GREAT WITH: EVERY BEER IN THE WORLD

PERFECT PAIR: SIERRA NEVADA
TORPEDO EXTRA IPA
BREWED IN: CHICO, CALIFORNIA
ABV: 7.2%

Potato chips or crisps are the best-selling snack in the world. Together with peanuts, they are also great with beer, thanks to their saltiness, which has the ability to make bitter beer taste sweeter and also make you thirstier. In the United Kingdom, some pubs offer more crisp flavors than beer varieties, although this isn't a compliment. But the best pairings? The nuttiness in a Red IPA, such as Half Acre Ginger Twin, rocks with peanuts; with potato chips (crisps), I want salt and vinegar flavor with a classic Best Bitter, such as Harvey's Best; sour cream and onion calls for Saison Dupont; paprika or barbecue flavor needs a Porter such as Renaissance Brewing's Elemental; and simple salted crisps require a Sour Beer, such as Boon Geuze or Kriek. But the ultimate crisp and beer match is hand-fried cheddar and onion with Sierra Nevada Torpedo IPA.

PORK SCRATCHINGS

GREAT WITH: SOUR BEER OR
HOPPY SESSION BEER

PERFECT PAIR: TILQUIN GUEUZE
BREWED IN: REBECQ, BELGIUM
ABV: 4.8% (6.0% IN BOTTLE)

Next to boxes of crisps in British pubs will be packets of pork scratchings. These are fried pieces of pork fat: tooth-shatteringly crunchy, artery-alarming in their fat content, doctor-scaring in their salt content, but oh-so-wonderfully good to eat. The best I've ever had are the ones you can buy at the Great British Beer Festival. They are stacked up like a mountain, profoundly porky, gnarly, and salty, and have the most intensely savory taste you could ever find. The extreme saltiness of pork scratchings means they work with every beer in the world, but the single best thing to drink with them is Gueuze. Tilquin Gueuze has an apple-like tartness, a clean and lemony acidity, a savory note, and a bright, tongue-teasing carbonation. Simple, but sensational.

OLIVES AND IBERICO HAM

GREAT WITH: SOUR FRUIT BEER
OR DRY CIDER

PERFECT PAIR: 3 FONTEINEN OUDE KRIEK
BREWED IN: BEERSEL, BELGIUM
ABV: 6.0%

We live in a modern world in which a plate of olives and some finely sliced aged ham can genuinely be considered a beer snack. I used to hate olives because of their intense flavor, plus the texture, which I imagined to be like biting into a tiny whale, but I persevered and now I love them. As for Iberico ham, I feel as if eating a whole leg wouldn't be beyond me. It's deeply savory, yet slightly sweet, and the texture almost melts, but demands that you chew it. A glass of dry cider is very good, but cold Kriek is the best. With a background of almond and cherry flavor, it really enhances the nuttiness in the ham and balances the olives' intensity before a lemon-like sharpness keeps it fresh. A dry oak tannin finds a distant link to the pigs fed on acorns.

FAST FOOD

No snobbery here! I sometimes love a McDonald's cheeseburger in the same way that I sometimes really want a bottle of Bud. And don't you want to know what the very best beers are to go with foods we see every day? The whole purpose of this book is to think differently about beer and food, but also to make it fun. The main consideration here is balance: these foods are popular because their flavors are balanced to appeal very broadly, so you'll typically want a beer that can do the same.

MCDONALD'S BIG MAC

GREAT WITH: BROWN ALE

PERFECT PAIR: BIG SKY MOOSE DROOL BROWN ALE
BREWED IN: MISSOULA, MONTANA
ABV: 5.1%

The bun is sweet and chewy, the patties don't give a whole lot more than a little general meatiness, the cheese is like salty caramel, there are dill pickles and the special sauce with a mix of mayo, mustard, sweet relish, and onion. It's a lot of bread to match and also a lot of sweetness, which is what you need to balance. Big Sky's Moose Drool is a great choice. A Brown Ale that has a toasty, caramel, and nutty sweetness, plus a little vanilla, before leading into a dryish finish with a hint of herbal hops (it's kind of cola-like). It's the sweet flavors we need, but crucially it's also light bodied so doesn't overpower the pairing. It's a fun match and most easy-drinking Ambers (lager or ale) and Brown Ales work well with a Big Mac.

KFC BUCKET

GREAT WITH: PALE LAGER

PERFECT PAIR: BUDVAR ORIGINAL
BREWED IN: ČESKÉ BUDĚJOVICE,
CZECH REPUBLIC
ABV: 5.0%

KFC is my first choice for fast food. I can't walk past one without wanting to go in for a piece of chicken, especially if I've had a few beers. With it you want a beer that you can drink from the bottle, something simple and clean, which will balance the fat and salt in the food, but also something that's still tasty. Budvar Original has a richness of malt that gives some bready, chewy caramel, but low sweetness. This lager has a lovely little hop fragrance from the Czech Saaz, which give a floral and citrus aroma that is excellent with the secret blend of herbs and spices, while it's bitterness is dry and long, making it very refreshing. Together, they make a marvellous match.

SUBWAY SUB

GREAT WITH: GOLDEN ALE OR PALE ALE

PERFECT PAIR: CROUCH VALE BREWERS GOLD
BREWED IN: SOUTH WOODHAM FERRERS,
ENGLAND
ABV: 4.0%

You can get a Subway sandwich in over 100 countries and it's the largest restaurant chain in the world. If I get a Subway, then I go for a simple one, such as ham and turkey, and then load it with as much salad stuff as I dare ask for. Like the Big Mac, the dominant taste is toasty sweetness from the bread and then the bitter-sweet crunch of vegetables, so think toasty malt followed by fruity hops. Crouch Vale Brewers Gold is a great Golden Ale with a chewy, honey-like malt sweetness, hops that give grapefruit and orange, and then a lasting, dry, quenching bitterness. It's a very good and well-balanced beer, which enhances everything in the sub, but doesn't dominate it. Other Golden Ales work, as do Pale Ales, but subtle works best here.

BURGER KING WHOPPER

GREAT WITH: AMBER ALE OR PORTER

PERFECT PAIR: LAGUNITAS CENSORED ALE
BREWED IN: PETALUMA, CALIFORNIA
ABV: 6.7%

It's the flame-grilled patty that gives the Whopper its distinctive charcoal taste. Around it you get tomato, lettuce, pickles, onion, ketchup, and mayo. You should always get some fries with a Whopper because their golden, salty, savory crunch begs for beer. A bold Amber Ale such as Lagunitas Censored Ale has lots of malt and a deep copper-colored body, which brings bready, caramel sweetness. There's even a little roast or smoke from the crystal malt that bridges to the grilled burger. Citrus and floral hops carry the condiments and add an extra fruitiness. With a Whopper you want big body, some sweetness, and aromatic American hops, but still a beer with balance.

GYROS

GREAT WITH: DARK LAGER OR PALE LAGER

PERFECT PAIR: FIX DARK
BREWED IN: ATTICA, GREECE
ABV: 5.2%

Only order gyros in Greece or Turkey. Don't bother anywhere else, okay. The best cost around 2€ and fill a hot, chewy pitta with charred, fatty pork carved from a giant spit. The meat is then topped with tzatziki (yogurt and cucumber), a few fries (in the pitta!), and a slice of tomato. It's salty and satisfying, the pork is outrageously good, and they are nothing like the crappy kebabs you get elsewhere in the world. Fix Dark is a Greek Schwarzbier that has subtle caramel, cocoa, and roasted nuts, which bridge, balance, and boost everything in the gyros. The carbonation is strong enough to lift the fatty richness, while the hops find a friend with the zealous seasoning. It's a simple, unimposing pairing that you'll end up repeating as often as you can.

CURRYWURST

GREAT WITH: DARK LAGER OR IPA

PERFECT PAIR: BREWBAKER DOPPEL IPA
BREWED IN: BERLIN, GERMANY
ABV: 9.0%

Around 800,000,000 currywurst are eaten in Germany each year, with almost 10 percent of this consumption taking place in Berlin. Currywurst is a curious thing: it's a chopped-up wurst that is covered in curry ketchup and sprinkled with curry powder. What makes it hard to match is that the curry ketchup is really sweet, meaning that you need a powerful beer, such as a Black Ale or Double IPA. BrewBaker's Doppel IPA delivers a whack of intense citrusy hops, big bitterness, and juicy malt, and yet somehow it manages to control the currywurst. Herter Heuwer is credited with creating currywurst in 1949. On 30 June 2013, on what would've been Heuwer's 100th birthday, she got the ultimate modern honor: a Google Doodle.

PUB GRUB

THE BEST THING ABOUT A PROPER PUB IS THAT IT'S LIKE AN EXTENSION OF YOUR LIVING ROOM. IT SHOULD BE COMFORTABLE AND HOMEY, WITH THE BONUS OF DRAFT BEER AND NO WASHING UP TO DO AFTER DINNER. PUB GRUB IS RELAXED FOOD IN A RELAXED ENVIRONMENT AND THE KIND OF COMFORTING, UNPRETENTIOUS, SIMPLE, STOMACH-LINING FOOD THAT SHOULD ALWAYS BE SERVED WITH BEER. BAR FOOD IS ALSO INCLUDED HERE, WHERE IT'S THE AMERICAN VERSION OF PUB GRUB: IT'S FASTER, FATTIER, AND MESSIER, BUT JUST AS BRILLIANT WITH BEER.

FISH AND CHIPS

GREAT WITH: PILSNER

PERFECT PAIR: CURIOUS BREW
BREWED IN: TENTERDEN, ENGLAND
ABV: 4.7%

I like to eat fish and chips outside on cold days, with the food wrapped in paper from the chip shop, and I want to be sitting on the beach with a bottle of beer buried in the sand beside me. I think there's something incongruous about fish and chips in a pub, to be honest, rather like having tea and cake on a deckchair in the sun, but I do love seeing pieces of golden-battered fish the size of my arm carried from pub kitchens. And I also love fish and chips with beer. A simple, sharp Pilsner is the best. Curious Brew, made by Chapel Down Winery, is brewed with Saaz, Cascade, and Nelson Sauvin hops and re-fermented with Champagne yeast. It has brisk bubbles to see away the fried heaviness, it's elegant, and it has a lovely, fruity freshness that zings with the vinegar (because you have to put vinegar on your chips). The beer is also good on the beach.

PLOUGHMAN'S LUNCH

GREAT WITH: BEST BITTER

PERFECT PAIR: TIMOTHY TAYLOR'S LANDLORD
BREWED IN: KEIGHLEY, ENGLAND
ABV: 4.3%

A ploughman's is a pub lunch consisting of cheese (Cheddar, stilton), chutney (fruit-based), and bread (farmhouse loaf), plus you'll often get a slice of carved ham, perhaps some pickled onions or piccalilli, and maybe a piece of pork pie or a Scotch egg, if you're lucky. Order a pint with your ploughman's, preferably a well-kept cask Bitter or Pale Ale. Landlord is a classic beer. Amber in color, a frothing foam, the smell of fall with roast apples, spice, marmalade, earth, and wood, a clean malt depth, and a dry, bitter finish. It's capable of standing up to the cheese and balancing the pickle's sweetness or acidity before the bitterness gives it a refreshing finish.

WELSH RAREBIT

GREAT WITH: ENGLISH PALE ALE OR BEST BITTER

PERFECT PAIR: SAMUEL SMITH
ORGANIC PALE ALE
BREWED IN: TADCASTER, ENGLAND
ABV: 5.0%

Cheese on toast is one of the greatest lunches in the world. As soon as the thought of this snack gets into my head, I have to eat it as soon as possible. Use strong Cheddar cheese and loads of black pepper, and douse it in Worcestershire sauce, which I think is essential: for about 20 years I ate cheese on toast without Worcestershire sauce—and I'll never get those wasted years back. Welsh rarebit is the next level in cheese on toast: it's best when you use a thick slice of farmhouse bread topped with a cooked mix of cheese sauce, beer, mustard, and Worcestershire sauce and then grill it until it bubbles. It's excellent with an English-style Pale Ale like Samuel Smith's. Deep copper in color, there's caramel, brown sugar, baked apples, stone fruit, and a spicy hop finish—it's like having some chutney on the side.

BUFFALO WINGS

GREAT WITH: PORTER OR BLACK ALE

PERFECT PAIR: GREAT LAKES EDMUND
FITZGERALD PORTER
BREWED IN: CLEVELAND, OHIO
ABV: 5.8%

These were created in Buffalo, New York, in
the 1960s. The thing I like most about buffalo
wings is how, because they are available
almost everywhere, it's easy to compare wing
for wing in the never-ending search for the
best. Fried chicken is mixed with a vinegar-
based hot sauce and often comes with a blue
cheese dip, which is a lot of flavor to deal with.
So, the best thing for it is a Porter, with its
cayenne-cooling chocolate malt and some
sweet cocoa to soften the vinegar acidity.
Great Lakes Edmund Fitzgerald is a perfect
Porter: there's cocoa, dark chocolate milk,
vanilla, a rich malt body, and floral and citrus
hops, which zing against the spice. Your beer
glass will be etched with orange fingerprints
when the wings are done.

LOADED NACHOS

GREAT WITH: GOLDEN ALE

PERFECT PAIR: VICTORY SUMMER LOVE
BREWED IN: DOWNINGTON, PENNSYLVANIA
ABV: 5.2%

Tortilla chips topped with chili, cheese, and
salsa have become a regular on bar menus
around the world. Designed for sharing from
one plate, nachos are crispy, salty, sharp, spicy,
and often creamy, with sour cream, mild
cheese, or guacamole. This is a lot of stuff to
bombard your beer with, so keep it simple with
a Golden Ale. Fruity hops to bridge the spices,
some toasty malt to manage the saltiness, a
decent body to carry the salsa, and a dry finish
to make you want to eat and drink more.
What's key is that this isn't a pairing you want
to have to think about; you just want a good
tasty beer like Victory Summer Love, which is
a simple, quenching summer beer that's easy-
drinking, but with enough body not to be
overloaded by the nachos.

PIE AND MASH

GREAT WITH: PORTER OR DARK MILD

PERFECT PAIR: EMERSON'S LONDON PORTER
BREWED IN: DUNEDIN, NEW ZEALAND
ABV: 4.9%

The ultimate belly-filler, pie and mash is
hearty and heart-warming, and best when
home-cooked. You can expect meat and gravy
wrapped in pastry, served with mashed
potatoes, overboiled vegetables, and more
gravy. The pie filling will sway the beer choice,
but, if you're in the pub, then it's likely to be
a beef and ale pie. Given the rich meat gravy,
the best brew is a Dark Ale, such as Emerson's
London Porter. With toasty malt (and a hint of
salty pie-crust), a little sweetness, and some
dried fruit, it's dark in color, but low in roast
bitterness, and it's just the right beer to
balance the flavors in the pie. Just avoid roast-
barley bitterness, as it's the taste equivalent of
a burnt pie dipped in crap coffee.

INDIAN

The food of the Indian subcontinent is enormously varied, with each region having its own cuisine, although most share the spices for which the dishes are known. When choosing beers to drink with Indian food, the best approach is to look for balance and refreshment, which is why the clichéd classic of curry and lager seems to work unequivocally. Don't be tempted to put big hops against a fierce chili heat because it doesn't work; instead, look to Hefeweizen, Sweet Stouts, and Lagers for good matches.

JALFREZI BEEF

GREAT WITH: HEFEWEIZEN OR DUNKEL

PERFECT PAIR: SCHNEIDER WEISSE TAP 4 MEIN GRÜNES
BREWED IN: KELHEIM, GERMANY
ABV: 6.2%

The British Curry Club, which publishes the magazine *Chaat!*, took a poll in 2011 to see what was "Top of the Poppadoms" in United Kingdom curry houses. They found that the long-time favorite chicken tikka masala had been replaced by jalfrezi as the number-one curry. Jalfrezi marinates meat and then cooks it with chili peppers, bell (sweet) peppers, onions, and tomato, giving a thick, spicy sauce with the bitter, green crunch of fresh vegetables. I like Schneider Weisse with jalfrezi, and many of the range work well: Tap 7 Original has a creamy sweetness and adds a balancing softness; Tap 5 Hopfenweisse is a huge hop explosion, which mirrors the peppers and chili; and Tap 4 Mein Grünes, a hoppy Hefeweizen, is grassy, fresh, and floral (like the chili and bell peppers), with a creamy body that works like yogurt on the side.

TANDOORI CHICKEN AND NAAN BREAD

GREAT WITH: SWEET STOUT

PERFECT PAIR: MIKKELLER MILK STOUT
BREWED IN: COPENHAGEN, DENMARK
ABV: 6.0%

Tandoori chicken takes chunks of meat and marinates them in a yogurt and spice mix, which includes lots of cayenne pepper and chili powder to produce the distinctive red color. The name tandoori comes from the tandoor oven in which the dish is cooked. This traditional wood- or charcoal-fired clay pot can reach very high temperatures, meaning that the meat cooked inside gets seared and smoky. Chefs can also slam doughs into the side of the tandoor in order to make light, chewy naan breads. Mikkeller's Milk Stout gives you cocoa, berries, and a little lactic sweetness, which bridges to the yogurt coating on the bird. The food brings out more sweetness in the beer, an aniseed depth pokes at the spice mix, and the roast grain enhances the char on the chicken.

SEABASS WITH COCONUT CURRY SAUCE

GREAT WITH: AMERICAN IPA

PERFECT PAIR: THORNBRIDGE JAIPUR IPA
BREWED IN: BAKEWELL, ENGLAND
ABV: 5.9%

Jaipur IPA is named after the honeymoon destination of the owners of the Thornbridge Brewery, and this match is indeed marriage material. One of the very best Indian dishes I've ever eaten was a fresh fillet of seabass grilled and served with a phenomenal coconut curry sauce. It showed a modern approach to Indian food and how it could be delicate, vibrant, and deeply flavored without tasting like an old spice rack. Jaipur IPA is golden in color, there's a richness of malt in the body, and then a lovely freshness of hops that gives lime, tangerine, and blossom. Those citrusy hops and curry leaves are very good together, while the coconut adds a tropical sweetness. Thornbridge's Kipling, brewed with New Zealand hops, also works well.

ONION BHAJIS WITH MINT RAITA

GREAT WITH: SAISON OR PILSNER

PERFECT PAIR: BURNING SKY SAISON
À LA PROVISION
BREWED IN: WEST FIRLE, ENGLAND
ABV: 6.5%

Opened at the end of 2013, Burning Sky splits production between American-style hoppy ales and Belgian-style Saisons and wild beers. All are made in a barn in the English countryside where they have four wooden foudres (huge oak barrels), the first of their kind to be used in British craft breweries. Saison à la Provision is a year-round non-foudred Farmhouse ale that gets a little wild yeast right at the end of fermentation and this throws out a delicate fruitiness to combine with American hops. Sorachi Ace is used and this pushes a little lemon forward, making a mighty match for bhajis and raita. The fried onions are cooled with the yogurt, cucumber, and mint raita, and the combination of fruity hops and a slight tartness from the yeast is very pleasant.

DAL AND ROTI

GREAT WITH: HEFEWEIZEN OR DUNKELWEIZEN

PERFECT PAIR: EMERSON'S WEISSBIER
BREWED IN: DUNEDIN, NEW ZEALAND
ABV: 5.0%

A classic meat-free and nutritious staple of the Indian subcontinent, dal (or dhal, daal) is a thick stew-soup made with dried lentils, peas, or beans. It's easy to make: simmer the dried pulses with some spices (garlic, ginger, turmeric, chili powder, and maybe something sour, such as tamarind) for an hour or two until you have a mix that might be soup-thin or porridge-thick. At the end some tarka is added, which is a mix of fried shallots and spices. Served with roti, a thin Indian bread, it's a filling, healthy, and cheap comfort food. Emerson's Weissbier is classically German in style. There's creamy banana and a full body that is similar to the dal; there's a little bridge of fragrant spice; and then the beer ends with a light and refreshing lemony dryness.

LAMB KORMA

GREAT WITH: BROWN ALE OR DUNKEL

PERFECT PAIR: ALESMITH NUT BROWN ALE
BREWED IN: SAN DIEGO, CALIFORNIA
ABV: 5.0%

If phal is at the fearsomely hot end of the curry-house spectrum, then korma is at the opposite, wussy, mild end. Korma is a creamy curry cooked with yogurt, spices, and nuts (normally coconut and cashew), which is excellent for its approachability and a sweet richness of flavor that won't burn a hole in your tongue. It uses fragrant spices such as cardamom, cinnamon, cloves, and ginger, which all share an earthy spiciness with hops. Bridge that and the curry's nuttiness to AleSmith's Nut Brown Ale. Crucially low in bitterness and big in body, it can wrap around the dish's sweetness, while giving its own roasted nuttiness (which is great with lamb or other red meats), toasty malt sweetness, and a dry, balancing finish of hops.

JAPANESE

THERE ARE SOME REALLY EXCELLENT
BEERS BEING BREWED IN JAPAN,
ALTHOUGH NOT MANY ARE WIDELY
AVAILABLE YET. PALE LAGERS STILL
DOMINATE, WHILE WHEAT BEERS,
SCHWARZBIERS, STOUTS, AND IPAS ARE
ALSO POPULAR. TOGETHER, THESE
STYLES SHOULD BE A HINT TOWARD WHICH
BEERS WORK BEST WITH JAPANESE FOOD.
THE DISHES ARE LESS FRAGRANT AND ZINGY
THAN THE FOOD OF SOUTHEAST ASIA, WITH
RICE AND MISO SOUP FORMING THE BASE OF MANY
MEALS IN WHICH FISH AND POULTRY ARE MORE POPULAR THAN
FOUR-LEGGED ANIMALS. IF IN DOUBT, HAVE A DARK LAGER—
IT SEEMS TO WORK WITH EVERYTHING.

SASHIMI AND SUSHI

GREAT WITH: GINGER ALE, SAISON,
OR PILSNER

PERFECT PAIR: OMMEGANG HENNEPIN
BREWED IN: COOPERSTOWN, NEW YORK
ABV: 7.7%

Sashimi is thinly sliced raw fish (or meat),
which can be served on its own or with some
rice and miso soup. Sushi is food based
around vinegared rice combined with other
ingredients, which may include raw fish or
cooked proteins. Both are often served with
soy sauce and sinus-clearing wasabi. With
sushi, pickled ginger is often used as a palate-
cleanser between bites, so that's the inspiration
for this match. Hennepin is a Saison brewed
with ginger, grains of paradise (a type of
spice), coriander, and sweet orange peel, but
it's the ginger that really pops with the
fish, being zesty and refreshing. It's brisk,
invigorating, and frisky with a fizzing
carbonation, but also has a soft creaminess,
and this all combines to be fresh and clean.
It's wicked with the wasabi, too.

RAMEN

GREAT WITH: SMOKED BEER
OR DARK LAGER

PERFECT PAIR: SPEZIAL RAUCHBIER
MÄRZEN
BREWED IN: BAMBERG, GERMANY
ABV: 5.3%

Ramen is a big bowl of broth, noodles,
vegetables, meat, and egg, providing a belly-
filling combo of carbs and umami. There's
enormous variety in ramen, whether it's the
choice of noodles (thick or thin); the selection
of toppings (pork, seaweed, scallions/spring
onions, beansprouts, boiled egg, beef, chicken,
or seafood); or the broth (salt-based, soy-
based, pork-bone-based, or miso-based).
Ultimately, you are getting a deeply savory
bowl of food that you greedily slurp and
spill down your chin and shirt. I like to
enhance the meatiness, so I love this dish
with Rauchbier. Spezial's is sweetly smoky,
like maple-cured bacon, and has a bready
sweetness before a dry finish—it works like
a splash of smoked soy in the broth. Japan's
Fujizakura Brewery makes a great Rauchbier
if you want a local match.

YAKITORI

GREAT WITH: DARK LAGER
OR DUNKELWEIZEN

PERFECT PAIR: COEDO SHIKKOKU
BREWED IN: SAITAMA, JAPAN
ABV: 5.0%

Yakitori translates as "grilled chicken," but it's not limited to poultry—other skewers of meat and veg are also brushed with a "tare" sauce of soy, mirin (a type of rice wine), and sugar, then cooked over a charcoal grill. It's an early evening snack, and you buy a couple of skewers and wash them down with a cold beer. At Toritama, in Tokyo, they grill 33 different cuts of chicken, including the heart, tail, and liver, as well as far gorier cuts. Thigh meat, plus crispy skin, works for me. Coedo Shikkoku is a Japanese Schwarzbier. It's cola-colored, with a light texture and hints of caramel, roast barley, and barbecue smoke before a dry finish. The dark malt flavors enhance the char on the chicken and give it a great depth of flavor. Any easy-going, light-bodied Schwarzbier works very well, as do Dunkelweizen.

SEAFOOD TEMPURA

GREAT WITH: SOUR FRUIT BEER

PERFECT PAIR: BOON OUDE KRIEK
BREWED IN: LAMBEEK, BELGIUM
ABV: 6.5%

The crisp crunch and oiliness of fried food calls for something cold and carbonated to lift the flavors and lighten the way in which they hang around in the mouth. The easy choice is a Pale Lager such as Asahi Super Dry, which will grab the grease and see it away in a second. But there are better choices, especially when you consider the sweet and salty dipping sauce on the side (rice wine vinegar, soy, and sugar). In my head I'm thinking Champagne: big bubbles, acidity, freshness, and lightness. Boon's Oude Kriek is like a tart, cherry-infused Champagne. It's very dry and the fruit gives a distant subtlety of sour-cherry pips and cherry pie, but no sweetness. The bubbles burst and lift the crisp batter, while the beer also makes the dipping sauce taste fruitier—and it all works to allow the seafood flavor through.

KATSU SANDO

GREAT WITH: PALE ALE

PERFECT PAIR: YO-HO YONA YONA ALE
BREWED IN: NAGANO, JAPAN
ABV: 5.5%

Katsu is breaded and deep-fried chicken. It can be served with shredded cabbage, in a similar way to schnitzel; it can come with a curry sauce; or it can be one of the world's best sandwich fillings in katsu sando. An extension of this is Japanese fried chicken (kara-age) burgers. Both are the type of dishes that could take over the world and become fashionable must-eats. In Japan, katsu sando is often served cold between crappy white bread; new versions will probably come hot between slices of good bread and fruity, spicy tonkatsu sauce. If it does catch on, then a Pale Ale is a good choice to drink with it. Yona Yona has a little bready malt, as well as some orange pith and floral fragrance to match the sauce, before a clean bitterness to balance the buttery crumb. Sierra Nevada Pale Ale and Beavertown Gamma Ray are both good alternatives.

TERIYAKI MACKEREL

GREAT WITH: SWEET STOUT

PERFECT PAIR: BRASSERIE MCAUSLAN
ST AMBROISE OATMEAL STOUT
BREWED IN: MONTREAL, CANADA
ABV: 5.0%

Teriyaki sauce is traditionally made with a mix of soy sauce, mirin, and sugar. When cooked, the teriyaki marinade gives a sweet and salty glaze to whatever it's basted onto, which is typically fish and white meat. I like it most on oily fish, where it adds sweetness to balance the richness. St Ambroise Oatmeal Stout pours black with a dark foam, the body is creamy from oats and bitter-sweet with dark malts, and that mix matches the oily fish and the salty-sweet marinade. A bitter chocolate finish adds roast flavor to give it an extra boost. In McDonald's, in Japan, you can buy a Teriyaki McBurger, which is a pork patty topped with teriyaki sauce. Good with cola, but weird with the green-tea milkshakes.

CHINESE

Most Chinese restaurants have a terrible selection of beers, so, if you want to drink great beer with Chinese food, then you either need to have take-out, cook for yourself, or find a "bring-your-own-bottle" place. It's definitely worth the effort to get a good beer to go with Chinese food, though, as there are some remarkably good matches to be had. Three beer styles work particularly well with most dishes: Dark Lager, Saison, and, surprisingly, Belgian Dubbel. These all tend to have crisp carbonation and dry finishes to lift and balance flavor.

KUNG PAO CHICKEN

GREAT WITH: HEFEWEIZEN
OR DUNKELWEIZEN

PERFECT PAIR: AYINGER UR-WEISSE
BREWED IN: AYING, GERMANY
ABV: 5.8%

Kung pao is a Sichuan (or Szechuan) dish with a base of chili, garlic, ginger, peanuts or cashew nuts, and Sichuan pepper. It's from the Sichuan province of southwest China and the eponymous peppercorns are fruitier than black pepper, have an aniseed spiciness, and are unique in that they make the tongue go tingly and numb. Ayinger Ur-Weisse, a Dunkelweizen, is a good choice of beer: it bridges to the pepper with an aniseed-like yeast depth and then adds a caramel and roasted-nut sweetness, plus the hops share a floral quality with the pepper. If the tongue is going to be numbed by pepper, then a sharp carbonation will only irritate it, but this beer is full, creamy and smooth, which pleases rather than pokes.

DIM SUM

GREAT WITH: SAISON OR
NEW WORLD LAGER

PERFECT PAIR: SAISON CAZEAU
BREWED IN: TEMPLEUVE, BELGIUM
ABV: 5.0%

Dim sum, which means "touch the heart," are small, stuffed dumplings eaten as a snack; hence they touch the heart but don't fill the stomach. Some are thick, bread-like buns, while others are wrapped in almost-translucent rice flour with classic fillings, including pork, shrimp (prawns), and vegetables. Dim sum are traditionally eaten with tea as an accompaniment, so Beijing's Great Leap Brewery's Danshan Wheat, brewed with black tea, would be a very nice choice. The trouble with matching Chinese craft beer to Chinese food, though, is that the beer is difficult to find unless you are in Beijing or Shanghai, and even Snow, the world's best-selling brew, is hard to get outside of China. So, it has to be something else. Saison Cazeau is brewed with elderflowers and mixes a fragrant, tea-like, floral freshness with a clean, dry spiciness that is light enough to let the dim-sum flavor through, while also announcing any alliums inside.

BEEF AND BLACK BEAN SAUCE

GREAT WITH: BELGIAN DUBBEL

PERFECT PAIR: CHIMAY RED
BREWED IN: CHIMAY, BELGIUM
ABV: 7.0%

Black bean sauce is made with fermented and salted soy (soya) beans, which are then mixed with garlic, soy sauce, and sugar. During a big beer and Asian/spicy food tasting with some friends, one of the best combos we found was beef in black bean sauce with an Israeli Dubbel—Negev Chariton Abbey Ale, which is excellent. The raisin-like sweetness, plus cocoa, toasted nuts, and some delicate fruity esters boosted the dish in a remarkable way, balancing the umami richness and making it fruitier, while lightening the pungency of garlic and soy. Chimay Red is a more available brew and is just as excellent with its brown sugar, tea leaves, dried fruit, cinnamon, and apple depth, all of which work wonderfully (if surprisingly) well with black bean sauce.

SWEET AND SOUR PORK

GREAT WITH: SMOKED BEER

PERFECT PAIR: STONE SMOKED PORTER
BREWED IN: SAN DIEGO, CALIFORNIA
ABV: 5.9%

Smoked beer is a hero of beer and food pairing. It's gymnastically versatile in that it can balance sharpness and dull sweetness, but also enhance meatiness. Smoked malt isn't dark in color, but the beers are often brewed with dark malt, so you get the fiery smoke notes, plus semi-sweet (dark) chocolate and coffee, which combine like a liquid barbecue. Put that with sweet and sour pork, and what could be an overpoweringly sweet dish turns into something surprising and exciting, especially with the boost of faux-charred meat. The reason Stone works so well is that the smokiness is subtle and yet lends something reminiscent of umami to balance all the flavors before finishing dry and quenching. Just make sure you avoid hops and sweetness with this dish—they crash horribly.

DUCK PANCAKES

GREAT WITH: FRUIT BEER OR SAISON

PERFECT PAIR: FOUNDER'S RÜBÆUS
BREWED IN: GRAND RAPIDS, MICHIGAN
ABV: 5.7%

How good are duck pancakes? Little wraps of juicy dark meat and crispy skin, topped with the green freshness of cucumber and scallions (spring onions), and then covered in a sweet hoisin sauce—chewy, crunchy, and fresh, and yet also rich and meaty. Saison is superb with these pancakes, as the dry, fruity beer somehow manages to glide between all the elements of the roll. Hoppy Session beers also work very well, giving the balance of bitterness and additional fruitiness for the hoisin. But Fruit Beer is my first choice. In Founder's Rübæus, a raspberry Wheat Beer, the fruit encourages all the sweeter notes of the hoisin to come out to play, while the raspberry-pip and wheat tartness cuts off the duck fat—they are superb together.

CHAR SUI PORK

GREAT WITH: STOUT OR BROWN ALE

PERFECT PAIR: DUGGES KALS STOUT
BREWED IN: LANDVETTER, SWEDEN
ABV: 5.0%

This is Cantonese barbecued pork seasoned with five spice powder, honey, rice wine, yellow bean curd, soy, and hoisin, giving a fragrant and sweetly charred coating to the meat. Sometimes you'll get it served in bao, or buns, but it's also great with some simple steamed Asian greens and white rice. Light-bodied Brown Ale, or even a fruity British Bitter, are good, but it's the five spice that is the interesting thing to hook the pairing onto and the smooth, roasty Stout loves the anise, which is mirrored by a licorice depth in the brew. Dugges Kals Stout has a lush body from the use of oatmeal; there's cocoa and roast, some citrus juice and berries in the background, and a dry bitterness, all boosting the pork's sweet-salty flavor.

SOUTHEAST ASIAN

THIS COMBINES THE CUISINES OF
THAILAND, VIETNAM, AND SINGAPORE,
AS WELL AS OTHER COUNTRIES AROUND
SOUTHEAST ASIA. WHAT THEY HAVE IN
COMMON IS A LIGHTNESS OF SPICING AND
A FRAGRANCE OF FRESH INGREDIENTS,
WHERE HERBS SUCH AS THAI BASIL,
CILANTRO (FRESH CORIANDER), AND
MINT GIVE A BRIGHT FLAVOR TO THE
DISHES; FISH SAUCE IS USED MORE
WIDELY THAN SOY SAUCE; AND YOU'LL
FIND MORE LIME, TAMARIND, GALANGAL,
AND LEMONGRASS THAN IN OTHER ASIAN
COOKING. NONE OF THESE COUNTRIES
ARE KNOWN FOR MAKING BEER, BUT THE
DISHES ARE VERY GOOD WITH VARIOUS
BEERS, ESPECIALLY THOSE THAT HAVE A
LIGHT, BRIGHT HOP FRUITINESS TO ECHO
THE HERBS AND CITRUS.

PAD THAI

GREAT WITH: KÖLSCH OR PACIFIC PALE ALE

PERFECT PAIR: 4 PINES KOLSCH
BREWED IN: MANLY, AUSTRALIA
ABV: 4.6%

Pad Thai is a dish with a great mix of textures and
tastes: there's satisfying umami richness from the
fish sauce, shrimp (prawns), and egg; crunch from
beansprouts and peanuts; the freshness of lime and
cilantro (fresh coriander); chewy, light noodles;
and four of the five tastes mix together with a chili
heat. Beer becomes the missing fifth taste and, when
its bitterness combines with everything else, it gives
an additional lift to the dish. You want a Kölsch or
a Pale Lager with Pad Thai, something that's simple,
clean, and quenching. 4 Pines Kolsch is brewed
with Southern Hemisphere hops and they give a
dish-bridging, lime-like fruitiness above the smooth,
creamy, classic Kölsch body. Pad Thai also works very
well with Chang, a sweetish, but refreshing, Thai lager.

MASSAMAN CURRY

GREAT WITH: HEFEWEIZEN

PERFECT PAIR: HOPF HELLE WEISSE
BREWED IN: MIESBACH, GERMANY
ABV: 5.3%

I really like Weissbierbrauerei's Helle Weisse because
it's just about the smoothest, creamiest Weissbier I've
tasted. With massaman curry, a Thai dish rich with
coconut milk and containing peanuts (or cashew nuts)
and potatoes, the beer works like a clove-infused
banana lassi (a traditional, yoghurt-based drink) on
the side. The massaman spice paste uses cumin,
cilantro (fresh coriander), lemongrass, cloves, star
anise, cinnamon, cardamom, galangal, and chili, so it's
deeply flavored with an earthy, citrusy, aniseed spice.
The banana creaminess of Hopf balances the chili heat,
while the hints of spice and citrus in the Weissbier
yeast are like an echo of the curry paste, all while a
little toasted nut duo of malt and peanut play in the
background. Other Hefeweizen are good, but try to
get the smooth, creamy ones such as Franziskaner
or Weihenstephan.

THAI GREEN CURRY

GREAT WITH: NEW WORLD LAGER OR PACIFIC PALE ALE

PERFECT PAIR: THE TWISTED HOP SAUVIN PILSNER
BREWED IN: CHRISTCHURCH, NEW ZEALAND
ABV: 5.0%

The green part of a green curry (as opposed to a red or yellow curry) comes from green chili peppers, plus the usual paste of shallots, garlic, galangal, and cilantro (fresh coriander); coconut milk makes the curry smooth and creamy; palm sugar gives sweetness; fish sauce gives salt; and lime, cilantro, and Thai basil give it a zingy freshness. The beer accompaniment needs clean malt and zesty hops, which work like a wedge of lime on the side. Look for a New Zealand Pilsner, such as Mac's Hop Rocker, Emerson's Pilsner, or The Twisted Hop Sauvin Pilsner, which is floral, zesty, and a little like a sparkling Sauvignon Blanc that adds a burst of juicy tropical fruit to the curry. Just keep it light and avoid too much bitterness to aggravate the chili.

SEAFOOD LAKSA

GREAT WITH: WITBIER OR NEW WORLD LAGER

PERFECT PAIR: CAMDEN TOWN GENTLEMAN'S WIT
BREWED IN: LONDON, ENGLAND
ABV: 4.3%

Laksa takes a curry paste—the typical ginger, galangal, lemongrass, and chili, plus curry spices and sugar—and cooks it into a rich noodle soup with stock, coconut milk, thick rice noodles, beansprouts, shrimp, and crab meat, as well as fish sauce, lime, Thai basil, and cilantro (coriander). It has the power to be restoratively fresh, but also comforting and rich. Gentleman's Wit is brewed with lemon and bergamot, and both of these are naturally very good with ginger, lemongrass, and lime, sharing the same aromatic compounds, so drink the beer with the dish and all those spiky citrus flavors will be enhanced. The beer's body is creamy with a vanilla background, sweetening the chili heat and being very good with the fish.

VIETNAMESE SUMMER ROLLS

GREAT WITH: SAISON OR BELGIAN BLONDE

PERFECT PAIR: JESTER KING LE PETIT PRINCE
BREWED IN: AUSTIN, TEXAS
ABV: 2.9%

Summer rolls are fresh and crunchy bundles of vegetables (finely diced carrots, lettuce, beansprouts), rice noodles, cilantro (fresh coriander), and mint leaves, as well as some shrimp (prawns) or pork, wrapped in almost-transparent rice paper. It gets interesting for beer when you choose the dipping sauce, which will typically be either sweet chili, peanut, hoisin, or nuoc cham (fish sauce, sugar, lime, chili, garlic). Keeping with the classic salty-sweet-sour-hot mix of nuoc cham, I want a beer that is elegant, effervescent, and fresh. Le Petit Prince, at only 2.9% ABV, is light, has a lemon-pith bitterness, and a breezy, herbal spiciness that hits the herbs in the rolls to create a fantastic, fresh, feel-good combo.

NASI GORENG

GREAT WITH: BROWN ALE, BELGIAN DUBBEL, OR AMBER ALE

PERFECT PAIR: GOLDEN ROAD GET UP OFFA THAT BROWN
BREWED IN: LOS ANGELES, CALIFORNIA
ABV: 5.5%

Nasi goreng, an Indonesian fried rice, is a leftover dish that can be eaten at any time of day. The dish uses sweet soy, garlic, shallots, and chili as a sauce base and it can then be built up with many other ingredients, such as egg, seafood, chicken, and vegetables. Salty, sweet, spiced, and packed with protein richness, I think there's a central flavor that pulls the food/beer pairing together: nuts. You want a nuttiness in the brew to give a sweet and savory roundness of flavor. Golden Road's Get Up Offa That Brown is nutty, has a little caramel, an appetizing saltiness from the smoked malt, and a dry, woody bitterness. It rounds up the flavors into a big group hug.

AFRICAN

AFRICA HAS OVER **20** PERCENT OF THE
WORLD'S LANDMASS AND **15** PERCENT OF
THE WORLD'S POPULATION. SUCH A VAST SIZE
RESULTS IN ENORMOUS DIVERSITY AND A
CUISINE THAT VARIES GREATLY THROUGHOUT
THE CONTINENT, BEING DEFINED BY LOCAL
INGREDIENTS, CULTURES, AND CUSTOMS.
NORTH AFRICAN DISHES, INCLUDING KEBABS,
TAGINES, FALAFEL, AND COUSCOUS, ARE THE
MOST FAMILIAR TO WESTERN PALATES.
THERE'S NOT MUCH CRAFT BEER IN AFRICA
AND MOST OF THE STUFF BREWED THERE IS
BLONDE AND DELICATE IN TASTE, WHICH
IS A SHAME, AS MOST OF THESE DISHES WORK
REALLY WELL WITH BOLD BEERS.

BILTONG

GREAT WITH: IPA (AND ALL OTHER BEERS)

PERFECT PAIR: DEVIL PEAK'S THE KING'S
BLOCKHOUSE IPA
BREWED IN: CAPE TOWN, SOUTH AFRICA
ABV: 6.0%

Biltong is a South African snack, similar to jerky,
which is made by cutting raw fillets of meat
(typically beef, but it could also be African game,
such as ostrich or springbok) and marinating
them in a solution of vinegar, sugar, salt, pepper,
and coriander. They are then allowed to dry,
leaving the meat chewy and salty. It works with
every type of beer, but I particularly love how
the mix of salt, sugar, and pepper pairs with the
punchy hops in IPA. Devil Peak's The King's
Blockhouse IPA is an American-style brew,
copper-colored, bright with citrusy and floral
hops, and with a surprising dry bitterness.
The brewery, which is named after one of the
mountains that provides the stunning backdrop
to Cape Town, has a taproom, so you can drink
it fresh if you're nearby.

LAMB AND APRICOT TAGINE

GREAT WITH: BLACK ALE

PERFECT PAIR: MOOR ILLUSION
BREWED IN: PITNEY, ENGLAND
ABV: 4.7%

Tagine is the name for an earthenware pot, as
well as the food that's cooked in it. The pot has
a deep, flat base and a tall, tepee-like top that
catches all the steam from the cooking process
and returns it to the dish. Lamb and apricot
is a popular combination, cooked with tomato,
ginger, garlic, and ras-el-hanout, a North
African spice mix that includes cardamom,
cloves, ground coriander, turmeric, paprika,
chili, fenugreek, and cumin. It's big enough to
handle strong flavors, so a Black Ale works
well. Moor's Illusion is a stellar example of the
style: a full body of malt, some cocoa and toast,
with the hops adding orange, lemon, mango,
and some mint. That hoppy freshness is super
with the spices and the apricot, while the
darker malt is lovely with the lamb and tomato.

BOBOTIE

GREAT WITH: BRITISH ALE OR SWEET STOUT

PERFECT PAIR: BIERWERK VLAKVARK
BREWED IN: CAPE TOWN, SOUTH AFRICA
ABV: 3.8%

Bobotie is a classic South African dish. It's made with curried and spiced ground (minced) beef with ginger, garlic, raisins, and apricot jam, and this is topped with a thick, savory egg custard and then baked—a bit like a moussaka with an African accent. With a national dish, you want a local beer. Trigger Fish Brewing Empowered Stout is sweetly chocolatey and balances the spice; Darling Brew's Native is an amber color, with a full body and a fruity hop aroma; African-brewed Guinness Foreign Extra Stout gives semi-sweet (dark) chocolate and a plum-like fruitiness; or Bierwerk's Vlakvark, a British-style ale made with local barley and South African Southern Promise hops, is toasty, has a little caramel sweetness to match the meal, and then a woody and citrusy hop profile.

FISH TAGINE AND CILANTRO COUSCOUS

GREAT WITH: WITBIER

PERFECT PAIR: BRASSERIE THIRIEZ LES QUÉBECOISES
BREWED IN: ESQUELBECQ, FRANCE
ABV: 5.5%

There's a natural harmony between Wit and Moroccan dishes, where the coriander and orange peel in the beer bridges to the spices in the food. A fish tagine, served with couscous that's mixed with lots of cilantro (fresh coriander) and lemon juice, is ideal with Witbier. Les Québecoises is a French Bière Blanche, made near the Belgian border. It has plenty of earthy, orangey coriander, some aniseed and mint, and the sort of carbonation that is lively and refreshing, and able to allow the fruity flavors to play together, while balancing all the spices in a wonderful way without ever overpowering. Brasserie Thiriez also makes a Double IPA called Dalva; it's brashly bitter, pleasingly sweet, and like a glass of liquidized citrus pith.

SHAWARMA

GREAT WITH: BROWN ALE

PERFECT PAIR: BROOKLYN BROWN ALE
BREWED IN: BROOKLYN, NEW YORK
ABV: 5.6%

"Have you ever tried shawarma?" asks Ironman near the end of the 2012 film "The Avengers." "There's a shawarma joint about two blocks from here. I don't know what it is, but I want to try it." Not finished with the ongoing attack, they have to forget the food and get back to work, meaning Tony Stark will have to wait a little longer to discover shawarma is meat (lamb, chicken, or beef) carved from a large turning spit, stuffed into a flatbread or pitta with some tomato, cucumber, pickled turnips, and hummus. After the epic battle has been won in "The Avengers," there's a post-credit scene with the heroes eating shawarma in tired silence. Job well done, you deserve a beer. Try Brooklyn Brown Ale in which toasty malt matches the meat, while the use of late hops gives a fruity, floral aroma to pick out the kebab spices and condiment.

MOROCCAN MEATBALLS WITH SAFFRON RICE

GREAT WITH: PORTER

PERFECT PAIR: NØGNE Ø PORTER
BREWED IN: GRIMSTAD, NORWAY
ABV: 7.0%

Make lamb meatballs with Moroccan spices and herbs, including cumin, cinnamon, coriander, parsley, garlic, and mint, then serve in a tomato-based sauce spiked with harissa—this is a spicy spin on Italian or Scandinavian recipes. Given the sweet-sharp-spiciness of the sauce, plus the full-on flavor from all the herbs, you need a beer that can handle it all. Nøgne Ø Porter is robust and full-bodied; it's got a little spicy-citrusy aroma; there's tomato-balancing, dark, smoky malt, an earthy and herbal bitterness which bridges to the meatballs, and a sweetness to go with the spice; and it also gives an umami-like boost of flavor. Dark beers are good with tomato-based sauces—just avoid too much earthy hop bitterness or it tastes weird, like burnt tomatoes with crap coffee.

EUROPEAN

Including a broad mix of different cuisines, this section pulls together some popular plates from Central and Southern Europe and Scandinavia. These are the kinds of dishes that are best enjoyed locally with local beers where possible, although they can easily be made at home and eaten with beers more local to wherever you may be.

SPANAKOPITA

GREAT WITH: **RED IPA OR DARK LAGER**

PERFECT PAIR: SANTORINI BREWING RED DONKEY
BREWED IN: SANTORINI, GREECE
ABV: 5.5%

Santorini Brewing's Red Donkey is impossible to categorize according to the beer style guides: it's a reddish color, made with Slovenian, American, and New Zealand hops, and fermented with a Belgian yeast. It's a bit like strawberries, honey, banana, cloves, orange, pineapple, mango, and pepper, which might sound odd, but it's actually as mesmerizing and memorable as the sunsets on the island where it's brewed. Spanakopita is a filo pastry pie made with spinach and feta cheese, and a bakery favorite in Greece. Red Donkey's round sweetness is great with the cheese and saltiness; the hops make it taste fruitier; there's shared dill and parsley between the hops and herbs; and then there's a soft balancing bitterness. If you want to holiday in Greece, get some sunshine, and drink good beer, then go to Santorini.

APPLE STRUDEL

GREAT WITH: **DOPPELBOCK**

PERFECT PAIR: SCHLOSS EGGENBERG SAMICHLAUS CLASSIC
BREWED IN: VORCHDORF, AUSTRIA
ABV: 14.0%

Samichlaus Classic is the only beer to drink with strudel, the classic dessert of pastry wrapped around apples, sugar, cinnamon, and raisins. At one point, it was the strongest beer in the world at 14.0% ABV. It's brewed just once a year—always on December 6. It's a one-of-a-kind brew, like the man it's named after, and it's like a glass of port with chocolate, cinnamon, cherry brandy, dried fruit, caramel, molasses, and rum, so kind of like liquid strudel. The beer was originally brewed in Switzerland in 1979 by Hürlimann. In 1997 the brewery closed down and the famous beer disappeared until 2000 when it was saved from extinction by Schloss Eggenberg. The significance of December 6 is that this is St Nicholas Day and, in Switzerland, that's when Santa visits children, leaving them a bag of oranges, chocolate, gingerbread, and nuts.

TAPAS

GREAT WITH: PALE LAGER OR PALE ALE

PERFECT PAIR: NAPARBIER NAPAR PILS
BREWED IN: BARCELONA, SPAIN
ABV: 4.9%

Tapas has become a style of small-plate eating, which evolved from its origins as a free bar snack placed on top of your drinking glass. Classic dishes now include patatas bravas, tortilla, olives, Serrano ham, croquetas, and calamari—salty things that make you thirsty for another drink, where that drink is generally refreshingly cold lager. But Spain has a growing number of craft breweries making some really great beers, including Nómada, Fort, Agullons, Guineu, La Pirata, and others. Napar Pils has a clean, botanic, and citrus pith bitterness, making it quenching and demanding another nibble of something salty, setting in motion a never-ending flow of food then beer then food then beer.

SCANDINAVIAN MEATBALLS

GREAT WITH: PORTER OR STOUT

PERFECT PAIR: JÄMTLANDS OATMEAL
PORTER
BREWED IN: PILGRIMSTAD, SWEDEN
ABV: 4.8%

There are endless variations of the recipe for Scandinavian meatballs, with each country rolling them differently. All I know is that I'm happy to go furniture shopping at Ikea if it means I can get a large plate of meatballs before I have to go home and fight with the flat-pack. Most Scandinavian recipes come with potato and a scoop of sharp-sweet lingonberries, plus a creamy beef gravy might go on top. Jämtlands Oatmeal Porter is a good beer choice. Relatively modest in ABV, with a soft and creamy texture from the oats, there's a little smoke, some berries (which the lingonberries bring out), savory malt, spicy hops, and meatball-loving roastiness. Try and smuggle a bottle in when you next go furniture shopping.

GOULASH

GREAT WITH: DARK LAGER

PERFECT PAIR: SVATÝ NORBERT DARK LAGER
BREWED IN: PRAGUE, CZECH REPUBLIC
ABV: 5.5%

Goulash is Hungarian in origin and has spread to surrounding countries where it's a warming, filling dish, earthy and peppery with paprika. Any full-bodied Dark Lager is great with goulash. The dark malt smothers the smoky pepper and softens the sharper flavors, while also working with the potatoes or dumplings that are typically served on the side. If you're in Prague, then go to U Fleku, the famous 500-year-old brewpub, or visit Klášterní Pivovar Strahov—their IPA is as good as anything America makes, while their Dark Lager is a glass of toast, cocoa, roasted nuts, and earthy bitterness. They serve goulash and goulash soup at the brewery, so order either.

KIELBASA AND SAUERKRAUT

GREAT WITH: DARK LAGER

PERFECT PAIR: BROWAR PINTA
CZARNA DZIURA
BREWED IN: ZAWIERCIE, POLAND
ABV: 4.5%

The good thing about Germany and Poland is that you can always find sausages. One day in Munich, I had ten sausages for lunch and then five more in the evening. I felt like a hero. Polish kielbasa is a generic name for sausage, and could be smoked or not, made with a variety of different meats (although pork is most common), and often spiced with garlic, paprika, and other nice things. Served with fried onions and sauerkraut, and either potatoes or bread, it's a classic feast. Look for Browar Pinta, as they make an impressively vast range of styles, from a Double IPA to a rarely seen Grodziskie (a light, sour-smoky Wheat Beer). Czarna Dziura, or Black Hole, is an unfiltered Schwarzbier. Dark, creamy, roasty, and bitter, it's got substance and some sweetness to stand up to the sauerkraut and sausage.

MEXICAN

A MIX OF CREAMINESS, HEAT, AND FRESH
ACIDITY DEFINES MEXICAN FOOD, AND A
SUCCESSFUL BEER MATCH MUST HAVE
THE ABILITY TO BALANCE ALL THOSE
QUALITIES, WHILE ALSO BOOSTING THEM
WITH EXTRA FLAVOR. DARK BEERS TEND
TO WORK VERY WELL, GIVING A
SUGGESTION OF SWEETNESS, AS WELL
AS A CARAMELIZED DEPTH TO GO WITH
THE SPICE. THE DISHES INCLUDED HERE
ARE A MIX OF CLASSIC MEXICAN ONES
AND THOSE THAT HAVE AN AMERICAN
INFLUENCE.

GUACAMOLE AND TORTILLA CHIPS

GREAT WITH: PALE ALE OR
HOPPY SESSION BEER

PERFECT PAIR: FYNE ALES JARL
BREWED IN: ARGYLL, SCOTLAND
ABV: 3.8%

Jarl is a Citra single-hop Blonde Beer. Fyne Ales
should probably call it Golden Ale, not because
of its color, but because of the luminous shine
of medals that hangs from its neck. It deserves
every award it's won because it's excellent:
mango, tropical fruit, grapefruit, and lime,
really fruity and fresh. It's soft-bodied, with the
malt hanging in the background and holding up
all the hop flavor. Serve with a bar snack of
fresh guacamole and salty tortilla chips, and
you get a great match. The lime in the hops
goes straight for the citrus in the dip, while the
avocado balances out the bitterness. Guacamole
gets into most refrigerators and bar menus, and
Pale Ale is always a good match.

BEEF TACOS

GREAT WITH: PALE ALE OR BROWN ALE

PERFECT PAIR: CUCAPÁ OBSCURA
BREWED IN: BAJA CALIFORNIA, MEXICO
ABV: 4.8%

Tacos are small tortillas filled and rolled with
different ingredients. They've moved beyond
Mexican streets and are frequently found on
bar menus. Carne asada (seasoned and grilled
beefsteak) goes into a tortilla and is topped
with guacamole, beans, and salsa in a classic
taco. The simplicity belies the satisfaction that
is derived from eating them: chewy, grill-
charred tacos, deeply savory meat and beans,
refreshing salsa, and cooling avocado. The
toast and semi-sweet (dark) chocolate depth of
Cucapá Obscura, a Brown Ale from one of
Mexico's premier craft breweries, pulls
everything together, and then the earthy,
lightly citrusy hops add some freshness. Also
look out for Chupacabras, Cucapá's Pale Ale.

BURRITOS

GREAT WITH: DARK LAGER

PERFECT PAIR: NEGRA MODELO
BREWED IN: MEXICO CITY, MEXICO
ABV: 5.4%

Burritos have become a fast-food favorite,
whether it's from a taqueria or food truck.
Some can be like bricks to eat: enormous
wraps stuffed with meat, beans, rice, cheese,
guacamole, salsa, and whatever else can be
packed into them. Now the burrito has become
well traveled and it suits a beer that's followed
it. Negra Modelo is a very good Dark Lager,
especially with Mexican food. Amber-brown
in color, it's subtle, smooth, and clean, with a
fruity sweetness like apple and vanilla before
a dry bitterness. It's delicate, yet powerful
enough to deal with a burrito's bulk. A good
Porter also works well with a burrito.

TOSTADA

GREAT WITH: SWEET STOUT

PERFECT PAIR: TALLGRASS BUFFALO SWEAT
BREWED IN: MANHATTAN, KANSAS
ABV: 5.0%

A disheveled taco walks into a bar. Upset at how the taco's falling apart, how his lettuce is limp, and his beans are cold, how he looks saddened by staleness and sorry for himself and his unraveling state, the bar's chef does the food equivalent of a ten-minute makeover to give new life to the troubled taco. First, he's stripped and all of the old toppings are chucked out. Next, his shell is deep-fried and becomes golden and crisp. And then he gets a new coat of fresh ingredients: refried beans, grilled chicken, salsa, hot sauce, lettuce, sour cream, and cheese. He returns to the bar a new man: hot, spicy, and cool with cream. He stops in front of a drinker who raises a toast before eating our friend in a few big bites, washed down with Tallgrass Buffalo Sweat, which is an Oatmeal Cream Stout that's as slick and smooth as our made-over tostada.

MOLE POBLANO

GREAT WITH: STOUT OR SWEET STOUT

PERFECT PAIR: MARBLE CHOCOLATE
BREWED IN: MANCHESTER, ENGLAND
ABV: 5.5%

The legend of this dish's creation says that the nuns at the Convent of Santa Rosa in Puebla, Mexico, panicked when they discovered that the archbishop was coming to visit. They prayed and then gathered together all the ingredients they had, including chili, spices, stale bread, nuts, and cocoa, and cooked it all together with an old turkey. The archbishop loved it and the dish eventually became a national favorite. Expect a thick sauce—made with chocolate, it's chili-hot, fruity, nutty, and with a depth of spice and smoke—poured over meat (there's a recipe for mole on page 176 which uses Milk Stout). Marble Chocolate is creamy and chocolatey; there's vanilla, licorice, smoke, coffee, and a roasty-bitter, dry finish that is marvelous with mole as it bridges to the cocoa and cools the chili.

BREAKFAST-STYLE QUESADILLA

GREAT WITH: PALE ALE OR DARK LAGER

PERFECT PAIR: EPIC PALE ALE
BREWED IN: AUCKLAND, NEW ZEALAND
ABV: 5.4%

A portmanteau of queso (the Mexican word for cheese) and tortilla, a classic quesadilla takes a tortilla, grills it, puts stuff on top (usually lots of cheese), and adds another tortilla to create a giant pizza-like sandwich, which is then cooked until the cheese inside melts. It's evolved to include different ingredients and fits on many bar menus due to its finger-food friendliness. I like a breakfast tortilla filled with chorizo, potato, egg, and cheese. With a Pale Ale, the beer's fruitiness bridges to the cheese and then the bitterness balances the fat. It also works like a glass of blended orange and grapefruit juice on the side, which is exactly what you get from Epic's Pale Ale: juicy fruit, bitter citrus pith, some caramel sweetness, and then a dry, quenching bitterness.

CARIBBEAN AND SOUTH AMERICAN

CARIBBEAN FOOD IS FOCUSED LOCALLY, WITH EACH ISLAND HAVING DIFFERENT DISHES AND INFLUENCES COMING FROM ALL CORNERS OF THE GLOBE. COMMON INGREDIENTS INCLUDE PEPPERS, SWEET POTATOES, COCONUT, PLANTAINS, AND RICE, PLUS HERBS AND SPICES SUCH AS CINNAMON, NUTMEG, THYME, GINGER, BAY LEAVES, AND ALLSPICE. IN SOUTH AMERICA, EACH COUNTRY'S FOOD IS SHAPED BY ITS HISTORY, BUT CORN, POTATOES, PEPPERS, AND CASSAVA ROOT ARE ALL IMPORTANT INGREDIENTS. THERE'S LITTLE CRAFT BEER IN THE CARIBBEAN, BUT THE BIGGER SOUTH AMERICAN CITIES, PARTICULARLY THOSE IN BRAZIL, OFTEN HAVE A LOCAL SELECTION OF BETTER BEERS.

ACKEE AND SALTFISH

GREAT WITH: WHEAT ALE OR PALE LAGER

PERFECT PAIR: ODELL EASY STREET WHEAT
BREWED IN: FORT COLLINS, COLORADO
ABV: 4.6%

Ackee is weird. It's a fruit that doesn't taste of much and has the texture of scrambled egg. Saltfish is dried, salted cod that tastes dry and salty. Ackee and saltfish combine to become one of Jamaica's national dishes in which they're cooked with onions, peppers, tomatoes, and spices. This dish is way tastier than the sum of its parts. The salt and spice are the things to work with and for that you need sweetness and dryness. A can of Red Stripe works fine, but I like how the orange fruitiness in Easy Street Wheat can pull out the fragrant spices, while giving some sweetness to the fish and finishing with a quenching dryness.

JERK CHICKEN, RICE, AND PEAS

GREAT WITH: WHEAT ALE OR SWEET STOUT

PERFECT PAIR: GUINNESS FOREIGN EXTRA STOUT
BREWED IN: KINGSTON, JAMAICA
ABV: 6.5%

Jerk's mix of fragrant allspice and ginger with the ferocity of Scotch bonnet chili pepper, backed up with woody thyme and pungent garlic, provides a lot of flavors for beer to go with. Hoppy Wheat Ales give a juicy fruitiness, Red IPAs give a sweet nuttiness, and Pale Lagers quench against the Scotch-bonnet sear. Go for a local favorite with Dragon Stout or Guinness Foreign Extra. This Guinness is stronger than usual and brewed in a number of countries around the world, including Jamaica (the taste and ABV varies depending on where it's made). It has semi-sweet (dark) chocolate, berries, licorice, dark fruit, and sweet coffee, all with a creamy, full body that softens and sweetens the spice and adds some dark flavors to the charred chicken skin. It can also handle as much hot sauce as you dare to pour on.

ARGENTINIAN STEAK WITH CHIMICHURRI

GREAT WITH: SCHWARZBIER OR SAISON

PERFECT PAIR: CERVECARÍA DE MATEVEZA
ORGANIC BLACK LAGER
BREWED IN: SAN FRANCISCO, CALIFORNIA
ABV: 5.2%

Barbecue, or asado, is a national Argentinian dish and the best way to cook the famous steaks. Chimichurri, a sauce made from parsley, oregano, garlic, olive oil, and vinegar, is served on the side. A popular drink in South America is mate (pronounced mah-tay), which is steeped from the caffeine-packed yerba mate tea. Steak, herbs, and tea point to MateVeza's Organic Black Lager. It's a Schwarzbier that's brewed with yerba mate and a mix of German and American hops. The malt gives gentle roast, toffee, and chocolate to go with the char on the steak, the hops are woody and floral and bridge to the chimichurri, while the yerba mate gives a herbal, tobacco-like, smoky bitterness.

FEIJOADA

GREAT WITH: SMOKED BEER OR DARK LAGER

PERFECT PAIR: EISENBAHN RAUCHBIER
BREWED IN: BLUMENAU, BRAZIL
ABV: 6.5%

This Brazilian dish of black beans and pork, often uses bacon, belly, butt, hock, ribs, and smoked sausage. A deeply savory and meaty stew, it's served with rice, collard greens, and slices of orange. Brazil has an excellent community of craft brewers—and Eisenbahn was one of the first, specializing in German styles. The Eisenbahn brewery is in Blumenau, a town founded by Germans and still dominated by them—every year they hold one of the biggest Oktoberfests in the world. Eisenbahn's Rauchbier is chewy with toasty malt, there's smoked meat and a savory depth before a peppery bitterness, boosting the feijoda with extra meaty flavor. Eisenbahn's Dunkel or Weizenbier are both good alternatives. And have their Lust, a Champagne beer, for dessert.

ARROZ CON POLLO

GREAT WITH: AMBER ALE

PERFECT PAIR: FORT BARCELONA PALE ALE
BREWED IN: BARCELONA, SPAIN
ABV: 5.3%

This Latin American and Spanish one-pot special is reminiscent of fish-free paella, made with chicken, rice, bell (sweet) peppers, paprika, tomato, and saffron. While not much craft brewing takes place in the Caribbean, it's gradually growing in Spain. Coming out of El Vaso de Oro (The Golden Glass), a restaurant in Barcelona that serves good tapas, Fort Cerveza make a range of American-esque brews, including an American Pale Ale or IPA. Fort Barcelona Pale Ale is their gateway Pale. It has subtle honey sweetness, toasty caramel, and floral hop freshness, and a quenching, dry finish to push forward the chicken and spices. The malty middle is why this works, adding sweetness to the savory rice and bridging to the chicken skin.

EMPANADAS

GREAT WITH: IPA OR PILSNER

PERFECT PAIR: COLORADO VIXNU DIPA
BREWED IN: RIBEIRÃO PRETO, BRAZIL
ABV: 9.5%

An empanada is folded dough, stuffed with meat or cheese, which is then either fried or baked. It's popular throughout South America and is the sort of dish that many nationalities have a variation on: think pies, pasties, patties, momos (dumplings), samosas, and calzones. They are savory and salty, and so, obviously, they are great with beer. Double IPAs almost demand a snack and Colorado's Vixnu is a Brazilian DIPA brewed with lots of American hops. It's big, there's a caramel flavor from the use of rapadura (an unrefined cane sugar), and the hops are loaded with orange and lime. The pastry snack sucks up the bitterness and softens the hefty ABV. You can find IPAs throughout South America now and there's always an empanada within reach.

MEAT-FREE

VEGETABLES ARE NATURALLY SWEET: SOME
SUCH AS CARROTS AND PARSNIPS HAVE A
SLIGHTLY PHENOLIC FLAVOR, BUT THERE'S
ALSO FRUITINESS AND SOMETIMES BITTERNESS.
BOILED, VEGETABLES CAN BE A BIT BORING
BUT ROASTED, THEY TAKE ON AN EXTRA
CARAMELIZED SWEETNESS, WHILE ALSO BEING
SPONGES FOR OTHER FLAVORS. IT'S GOOD TO
INCLUDE SOME KIND OF NON-MEAT PROTEIN
BECAUSE THESE FOODS TEND TO HAVE BEER-
FRIENDLY FLAVORS AND TEXTURES—CHEESE,
BEANS, AND NUTS, FOR EXAMPLE, ARE
ESPECIALLY GOOD ADDITIONS DUE TO THEIR
SAVORY, SALTY, CREAMY FLAVORS.

ROASTED VEGETABLE QUESADILLA
GREAT WITH: PALE ALE OR IPA

PERFECT PAIR: ODELL BREWING IPA
BREWED IN: FORT COLLINS, COLORADO
ABV: 7.0%

Odell IPA is, for me, a perfect American IPA
and the epitome of balance and flavor: it's
loaded with depth of malt, giving some toast
and caramel; the hops are like a bowl of every
member of the orange family, plus some
orange blossom, mango, and herbs; the
bitterness is quenching, dry, and bold, and
yet very clean and soft. Roasted vegetables
have caramelized sweetness, alongside their
natural green flavor, and this is excellent
with the fruity bitterness in the hops. Layer
in the cheese and sandwich between tortillas,
and the hop bitterness gets balanced, the
citrus boosts the cheese, and the malt gives
veg-bridging sweetness.

STUFFED EGGPLANT (AUBERGINE)
GREAT WITH: PALE ALE OR AMBER ALE

PERFECT PAIR: BIRRA DEL BORGO REALE
BREWED IN: BORGOROSE, ITALY
ABV: 6.4%

Stuff some eggplants (aubergine) with
tomatoes, garlic, basil, toasted pine nuts, dried
chili flakes, and seasoning, top with mozzarella
and olive oil, bake in the oven, and then serve
with Birra del Borgo's ReAle. Using American
hops, this is a cracking Pale Ale, with a mix of
lemon, grapefruit, and floral and resinous hops.
It's rich in texture and the bitterness is
refreshing and herbal, with the most marvelous
depth of fruity hop flavor. The bitterness
bridges to similar flavors in the eggplant, basil,
and olives, and that gives a big boost to
everything. If you like ReAle, and you like
hoppy beers, then try ReAle Extra—it's similar
and has even more hops in it.

CAULIFLOWER CHEESE
GREAT WITH: IPA OR BROWN ALE

PERFECT PAIR: SHEPHERD NEAME INDIA
PALE ALE
BREWED IN: FAVERSHAM, ENGLAND
ABV: 6.1%

England's oldest brewery has made beer in
Faversham since at least the beginning of the
16th century. A fire in 1698 destroyed many of
the records and so the brewery gives this year
as its date of origin, but they've since managed
to trace it back to 1507. Looking into old
brewing books, they found this India Pale Ale
recipe from 1870, which they've recreated.
Amber in color, the beer is dominated by a bold
use of Kent hops with a mix of earth, berries,
and wood. With cauliflower covered in a thick
cheese sauce, you get a shared bitterness
between Brassicaceae and beer; the malt's
caramel body adds sweetness; and then the
characteristically dry, hoppy finish in a
Kentish ale cuts off the cheese's richness. If
you want meat, try adding some sausages or
roast pork on the side.

VEGETABLE BIRYANI

GREAT WITH: PORTER OR DUBBEL

PERFECT PAIR: LA TRAPPE DUBBEL
BREWED IN: TILBURG, NETHERLANDS
ABV: 7.0%

This layered rice dish is popular in South Asia—India, Pakistan, and Bangladesh—and is made with a mix of different spices, rice, and vegetables (and sometimes meat). It's a dish with enormous variety in terms of the spices and ingredients, and might contain saffron, dried fruits, and nuts, as well as all kinds of different meats and fish. It could also be served alongside a curry. I really like this with a Dubbel or Porter, something fairly soft-bodied, fruity, nutty, and smooth. La Trappe's Dubbel is a Trappist brew that's red-brown, has some similar spices to the rice (cinnamon, pepper, clove), some caramel, a tea quality, dried fruit, and nuts. The earthy hops mirror the vegetables, while a refreshing lightness comes from the carbonation.

MUSHROOM AND GORGONZOLA RISOTTO

GREAT WITH: DUBBEL

PERFECT PAIR: ALLAGASH DUBBEL
BREWED IN: PORTLAND, MAINE
ABV: 7.0%

This risotto combines the umami meatiness of mushrooms with the pungent richness of blue cheese in a bowl of belly-filling comfort food. Allagash Dubbel's dried-fruit sweetness is really good here. It has a savory nuttiness that reaches across to the rice, the peppery yeast bridges to the blue cheese, as well as the seasoning in the food, and then the caramel and fig-like fruit keeps it light and refreshing, cutting past the cheese and making the mushroom flavor more intense. Allagash's excellent Tripel is a good alternative with the risotto. Or, take the Allagash Four, a Quadrupel-style. Even their Black, a Belgian-style stout, would work well. It's a good dish for Allagash beers, it seems.

ASPARAGUS AND GRUYÈRE TART

GREAT WITH: TRIPEL OR PALE ALE

PERFECT PAIR: UNIBROUE LA FIN DU MONDE
BREWED IN: CHAMBLY, CANADA
ABV: 9.0%

Unibroue, one of Canada's top craft breweries, specializes in reverential renditions of classic Belgian beer styles, and La Fin Du Monde is a terrific Tripel. Deep gold in color, with a halo of white foam, it's elegant and yet powerful—like a graceful soprano singer. Together with peaches, apricots, pears, oranges, and banana, there are herbs and spices, while bready malt gives a fullness to the body but not a lot of sweetness, making it endlessly drinkable and interesting. With an asparagus and Gruyère tart, all of the fruitiness and depth of malt is matched with the pastry base (especially if you also include Gruyère in the dough), letting a background lemon and spiciness in the yeast pair up with the asparagus.

THE CHEESEBOARD

SOME OF THE BEST BEER PAIRINGS YOU'LL EVER HAVE ARE WITH CHEESE. THE KEY CHEESE-FRIENDLY QUALITIES ARE THE MALT SWEETNESS, WHICH MATCHES THE SWEETNESS OR CREAMINESS IN THE CHEESE, AND THE COMBINATION OF CARBONATION AND BITTERNESS, WHICH CAN FIGHT THE FAT.

BRIE AND CAMEMBERT

GREAT WITH: BELGIAN BLONDE OR SAISON

PERFECT PAIR: BRASSERIE DE LA SENNE ZINNEBIR
BREWED IN: BRUSSELS, BELGIUM
ABV: 6.0%

Brie and Camembert are soft, bloomy-rind cow's milk cheeses, which share a creamy, sweet, nutty, vegetal flavor. Brasserie de la Senne's Zinnebir is a Belgian Blonde that's floral, herbal, and citrusy, with a body that's strong but not overbearing, before an earthy, dry bitterness at the end. It highlights sweetness in the cheese and kicks out carbonation to combat the creaminess.

CAMBOZOLA

GREAT WITH: BLACK ALE OR BELGIAN DUBBEL

PERFECT PAIR: THORNBRIDGE WILD RAVEN
BREWED IN: BAKEWELL, ENGLAND
ABV: 6.6%

Cambozola is a triple-cream soft cheese with a tangy blue streak through the middle. Buttery and creamy, the blue vein isn't too intense, but you know it's there, bulking out richness and depth. With a Black Ale, such as Thornbridge Wild Raven, you get all the creamy darkness, plus a full body, and the citrusy hops bring out the blue before the bitterness balances it.

STILTON

GREAT WITH: BARLEY WINE AND IMPERIAL STOUT

PERFECT PAIR: J.W. LEES HARVEST ALE
BREWED IN: MANCHESTER, ENGLAND
ABV: 11.5%

Blue cheese's intense pungency combined with a buttery richness, caramel sweetness, and savory saltiness needs a beer with body and sweetness to give it balance. Barley Wine and Imperial Stout are unbeatable candidates for the job. J.W. Lees's Harvest Ale has brown-sugar sweetness, plus there's dried-fruit-like chutney, plenty of alcohol, and a fat-fighting fizz.

BLOOMY-RIND GOATS' CHEESE

GREAT WITH: FRUIT BEER

PERFECT PAIR: NEW GLARUS SERENDIPITY
BREWED IN: NEW GLARUS, WISCONSIN
ABV: 5.1%

Those pale logs of goats' cheese, with the edible rubbery rind on the outside, are tangy, creamy, a little acidic or lemony, and have a thick texture. The best beer to drink with them is something brewed with tart fruit. Liefmans Kriek and Founder's Rübæus are great, as is New Glarus Serendipity, which is made with cherries, apples, and cranberries. It's unbelievably fruity and juicy, and yet still refreshingly tart. They share a creamy funkiness that makes the match taste like cherry cheesecake.

GRUYÈRE AND COMTÉ

GREAT WITH: DARK LAGER OR BOCK

PERFECT PAIR: BERNARD DARK
BREWED IN: HUMPOLEC, CZECH REPUBLIC
ABV: 5.1%

These Alpine-style, cow's milk cheeses are sweet, salty, creamy, and nutty, with increasing intensity and caramel as they mature. Gruyère is Swiss and Comté is French (you could also include Dutch Gouda here). The inherently nutty, caramel flavor of these cheeses is enhanced by soft, dark malts, so a Dark Lager, such as Bernard Dark (Bernard Černý Ležák in Czech) is great—it bridges caramel and chocolate with the balance of bubbles.

BERKSWELL AND MANCHEGO

GREAT WITH: PALE ALE, CIDER, OR WILD BEER

PERFECT PAIR: CROOKED STAVE HOP SAVANT
BREWED IN: DENVER, COLORADO
ABV: 6.7%

These firm sheep's milk cheeses go together, as they share a sweet nuttiness, fruity acidity, and a lasting savory depth. Pale Ale's citrus flavor is good, while drinking Cider is like adding a slice of fruit to the cheese. Crooked Stave's Hop Savant is a Brett-fermented beer that's loaded with American hops, so you get the funkiness of yeast and then the fruitiness of hops—it's an astonishing and complex beer, which loves the saltiness, gives fresh citrus, and shares delicate acidity.

PARMIGIANO REGGIANO

GREAT WITH: PALE ALE OR IPA

PERFECT PAIR: PARTIZAN SAISON
BREWED IN: LONDON, ENGLAND
ABV: 7.4%

This is a hard cow's milk cheese aged in the form of huge, heavy wheels for around 24 months. It's very high in umami, has nuttiness, caramel, a long-lasting flavor, and hints of pineapple and tropical fruit (from similar esters to the ones that contribute to beer's aroma). Partizan's Saison is outrageously fruity, with pineapple, mango, and tangerine; it brings out so much extra flavor in the cheese without anything getting lost. Extraordinary. Batches of the beer vary, so look for those hopped with Citra, Mosaic, Galaxy, or similarly juicy hops.

LINCOLNSHIRE POACHER

GREAT WITH: ENGLISH IPA

PERFECT PAIR: MEANTIME
INDIA PALE ALE
BREWED IN: LONDON, ENGLAND
ABV: 7.4%

This is a tangy and nutty cow's milk cheese with a tropical-fruit flavor that clings to your tongue without letting go, thus demanding a hoppy beer. Made with Fuggle and Golding, Meantime's India Pale Ale is a classic British version of the style. Marmalade, orange pith, a rose bed, and roast apple, plus bread and honey, which suggest sweetness—and it all flows toward a clinging bitterness that cuts through the cheese's richness, while boosting it with extra fruit.

EXTRA MATURE CHEDDAR

GREAT WITH: AMERICAN IPA OR DOUBLE IPA

PERFECT PAIR: MAGIC ROCK
CANNONBALL
BREWED IN: HUDDERSFIELD,
ENGLAND
ABV: 7.4%

A powerful, tangy, and fruity Cheddar tastes great with a range of full-flavored beers that can handle the cheese's oomph. With strong Cheddar, I'd go for an American-style IPA or Double IPA, such as Magic Rock Cannonball or Human Cannonball (a 9.2% ABV big brother to the regular Cannonball). All the citrus and tropical fruit bring out the cheese's fruitiness, before the bitterness beats away the fat.

DESSERT AND CAKE

WITH MALT FLAVOR AND SWEETNESS ABLE TO TAKE BEER TO PLACES THAT OTHER ALCOHOLIC DRINKS CAN'T GO, GIVING BREAD, TOFFEE, CHOCOLATE, OR COFFEE, SOME OF THE MOST SPECTACULAR AND SURPRISING BEER MATCHES COME WHEN YOU POUR BEER WITH PUDDING. A FULL-BODIED BEER IS CRUCIAL, OR THE MATCH WILL TASTE THIN, OVERPOWERED, OR ASTRINGENT, SO, FOR THIS REASON, WE WANT BIG BEERS THAT ARE THE EQUIVALENT OF DESSERT.

TIRAMISÙ

GREAT WITH: IMPERIAL STOUT

PERFECT PAIR: DESCHUTES THE ABYSS
BREWED IN: BEND, OREGON
ABV: 11.0%

If you want something a bit different from the usual coffee-soaked sponges, try a strong coffee Stout and turn it into a "beeramisù" (see page 204 for the recipe). It's a great dessert to go with a beer, given the dark and bitter roast depth and sweet creamy cheese, but you need to drink something big with it. Deschutes The Abyss is bigger than most. A winter seasonal, it's darker than black, thick and velvety with bitter chocolate, and has a bourbon-barrel vanilla and toffee sweetness. It's like an espresso, only better, kicking out extra coffee flavor into dessert, and it's also got a full, creamy texture that works well with tiramisù. Any bold, intense Imperial Stout would be a good choice.

VANILLA ICE CREAM

GREAT WITH: IMPERIAL STOUT

PERFECT PAIR: EVIL TWIN IMPERIAL BISCOTTI BREAK
BREWED IN: COPENHAGEN/BROOKLYN
ABV: 11.5%

Evil Twin's Imperial Biscotti Break is a glass of chocolate, brown sugar, chocolate ice cream, coffee, vanilla, and almonds, which is slick, full-bodied, rich, chocolatey, and lusciously sweet with barely any bitterness, making it decadently dessert-like. Take inspiration from Italian affogato, and turn your drink into dessert by pouring the beer over some vanilla ice cream. Alternatively, just serve a few scoops with a glass of beer on the side—simple and a lot of fun, but still a seriously good match. (FYI: I tried making an ice-cream float with it once, but wasn't successful.) Evil Twin is a gypsy brewer that makes beers around the world. The best place to drink these is at Tørst, a world-class craft-beer bar in Brooklyn.

COCONUT CHEESECAKE

GREAT WITH: BARREL-AGED STOUT

PERFECT PAIR: GOOSE ISLAND BOURBON COUNTY STOUT
BREWED IN: CHICAGO, ILLINOIS
ABV: 13—15%

Bourbon is aged in American oak barrels, which are toasted before the spirit goes in. This process helps to remove any rougher flavors in the wood, but also generates aromatic compounds that end up getting pulled into the bourbon, where we expect vanillin (like vanilla), maltol (like malt, caramel, burnt sugar), and lactones (coconut), plus smoke, chocolate, and maple syrup. When the distillery is done with the barrels, they are frequently passed to breweries where the beer most often poured into them is Imperial Stout. Goose Island's Bourbon County Stout is probably the most outrageously bourbon-tasting beer there is, with coffee, chocolate, vanilla, coconut, soy, and an oily body with a big slug of bourbon. With coconut cheesecake, you get a brilliant bridge of flavors between dessert and drink.

BLUEBERRY MUFFINS

GREAT WITH: COFFEE STOUT

PERFECT PAIR: COLORADO
DEMOISELLE
BREWED IN: RIBEIRÃO
PRETO, BRAZIL
ABV: 6.0%

What's better for creativity: coffee or beer? Creativity takes a lot of brain activity, as busy chemicals called neurotransmitters snap through the synapses. One of those neurotransmitters is called adenosine, which measures your brainpower and, when your battery is looking low, slows things down by clinging onto adenosine receptors. To bring the creative levels back up, you need to take a break. However, the caffeine in coffee blocks the binding of the adenosine to its receptors, meaning that your brain is tricked into thinking you're fully fueled and ready to work hard. Meanwhile, alcohol reduces inhibitions and makes you more relaxed, therefore freeing up space for creativity, bearing in mind the more you drink, the less productive you become. As far as I know, no studies have looked at beers brewed with coffee to see how good they are for creativity, so maybe one day, when work gets tough, you should have a break and grab a blueberry muffin and a bottle of Coffee Stout, such as Colorado's Demoiselle, which is brewed with the best local Brazilian coffee beans, and just see what happens.

CARROT CAKE WITH ORANGE FROSTING

GREAT WITH: DOUBLE IPA OR DUBBEL

PERFECT PAIR: STONE BREWING ENJOY BY IPA
BREWED IN: SAN DIEGO, CALIFORNIA
ABV: 9.4%

You want to drink very hoppy beers as fresh as possible, since the hop flavor and aroma, and even the bitterness, dulls over time. Stone Brewing's Enjoy By IPA tells you front and center when you need to drink the beer by in order to get it at its freshest. And freshness is very good for this beer: burstingly ripe citrus, juicy stone fruit, roast pineapple, resinous pine, and all unbelievably easy-drinking for a 9.4% ABV beer with big bitterness. Have it with some carrot cake, especially if it's made with orange frosting and some pineapple in the cake mix. The hops bridge to the carrot, citrus, and spice in the cake, while the sweet frosting handles the hop bitterness. It's a brilliant pairing.

OATMEAL RAISIN COOKIES

GREAT WITH: IMPERIAL STOUT OR QUADRUPEL

PERFECT PAIR: GREAT DIVIDE OATMEAL YETI
BREWED IN: DENVER, COLORADO
ABV: 9.5%

Quadrupels, with their spicy and dried-fruit flavors, seem like a good fit with oatmeal raisin cookies (think cinnamon), but it's a little too samey. Instead, I want to hit the cookies with something bigger. And it doesn't get much bigger than a Yeti. Great Divide's Yeti Imperial Stout is a hefty brew: thick, black, and bitter with hops and dark malt. The Yeti family includes oak, espresso, chocolate, and barrel-aged variations, plus Oatmeal Yeti, which uses some raisins in the brew. Like a glass of bitter cocoa and coffee in its impact, the body is velvety, smooth, and lulling before the bitterness hits at the end like a burning pine tree falling on your head. With the sweet cookie, that bitterness is balanced and the raisins echo each other and make it playful and fun, which is exactly what a beer and cookie pairing should achieve.

FRUIT DESSERTS

Don't be tempted to go fruit-to-fruit when choosing a beer to accompany a fruit dessert because it often doesn't work. Instead, it's what you put with the fruit that makes the difference to the beer matches—pies and tarts have a buttery, savory flavor, while cream softens and balances many of the bolder beer flavors. You generally want beers with big bodies, residual sweetness, and lots of grain character, where caramel, bread, chocolate, or coffee create natural bridges to the desserts.

LEMON TART

GREAT WITH: WHEAT WINE OR TRIPEL

PERFECT PAIR: DEUS BRUT DES FLANDRES
BREWED IN: BUGGENHOUT, BELGIUM
ABV: 11.5%

Here we combine lemon tart, lemon meringue pie, and key lime pie because they are similar enough to work with similar beers. With their sweetness and acidity they are not the easiest puddings to pair, but they can be some of the most fun. Scoring a perfect 10 on the fun-factor scale is Key Lime Pie by Short's Brewing, in Bellaire, Michigan, which is made with fresh limes, milk sugar, Graham crackers (digestive biscuits), and marshmallow fluff to recreate the dessert in liquid form. That's a bit too much lime-on-lime, so try DeuS Brut des Flandres instead. This is a Bière de Champagne that is somewhere between grape and grain: lively and effervescent, rich with alcohol, some warming and savory spice, stone and tropical fruit, and a long depth of flavor. Drink it cold from Champagne glasses—it's also great with cheeses and cured meats.

BANOFFEE PIE

GREAT WITH: COFFEE STOUT

PERFECT PAIR: DIEU DU CIEL PÉCHÉ MORTEL
BREWED IN: SAINT-JÉRÔME, CANADA
ABV: 9.5%

Banoffee or banoffi pie was born in 1972 to Ian Dowding and Nigel Mackenzie of The Hungry Monk restaurant in East Sussex, England. Decades later, Dowding decided to post his original recipe online, having "come across some pretty ghastly versions of Banoffi in my career." He said, "As you can imagine, I get a bit pedantic about the correct version." For the pie's creator, it's a pastry base, a can of boiled condensed milk, bananas, and a topping of heavy (double) cream whipped with sugar and instant coffee. The only variation he condones is the "Apploffi," which hopefully needs no explanation. The coffee seems to have disappeared from most examples of the recipe, so reunite them and pour a Péché Mortel, a cracking Canadian coffee Imperial Stout: black, deeply roasty, thick, full of coffee, semi-sweet (dark) chocolate, and vanilla. It makes banoffee pie taste even better, if such a thing were possible.

STRAWBERRY PAVLOVA

GREAT WITH: IMPERIAL STOUT

PERFECT PAIR: FERAL BREWING BORIS
IMPERIAL STOUT
BREWED IN: SWAN VALLEY, AUSTRALIA
ABV: 9.1%

Anna Pavlova was a Russian ballerina who gave
her name to this celebratory dessert, which is
particularly popular in Australia and New
Zealand. Its origin is widely disputed—some
say it was made by an Aussie, while others
claim it was a Kiwi. Wherever it came from, it's
now a crowd-pleasing center-piece that begins
with a giant meringue, which is then topped
with whipped cream and fruit, typically
strawberries. Feral Brewing's Boris is a big,
dark beer loaded with rich chocolate, brown
sugar, roasted dark fruit, and a full body, where
strawberries and strong Stout combine very
well, especially with cream. In the interests of
balance, the Kiwi choice is 8 Wired's iStout, a
10.0% ABV black beauty loaded with coffee and
chocolate. They work like pouring chocolate
sauce on top of the Pavlova.

APPLE PIE

GREAT WITH: QUADRUPEL OR BARREL-AGED BEER

PERFECT PAIR: LA TRAPPE OAK AGED
BREWED IN: TILBURG, NETHERLANDS
ABV: 10.0%

This is a favorite dessert around the world,
but it's actually a tough one to find a beer for.
Belgian Quadrupel and British Barley Wine
share similar flavors and add a dried-fruit
depth that's really nice, while a strong Cider
will hit the apple with apples. However, it
takes a beer that has been barrel-aged to get
the best pairing. I also prefer the pie served
cold because hot fruit seems too aggressive for
the sweet beer. La Trappe, a Trappist brewery
from the Netherlands, makes a cracking Quad
and also releases an oak-aged version,
meaning you have a beer that's loaded with
dried fruit, brown sugar, roasted apples, and
pie spices, and then there's vanilla,
creaminess, and a wood complexity. It's a
perfect partner for pie.

FIG TART

GREAT WITH: BELGIAN QUADRUPEL

PERFECT PAIR: EXTRAOMNES QUADRUPEL
BREWED IN: MARNATE, ITALY
ABV: 9.3%

Delicately fruity, heady with a floral fragrance,
a little nutty, and great with either sweet or
salty ingredients, figs are a beer-friendly fruit.
Fig is also a common tasting note in dark
Belgian Ales. Baked into a tart, fresh figs take
on a toothsome chewiness and extra sweetness,
which is even better if you add cream and
almonds. Belgian Quadrupel is the beer to pour
with this tart. Extraomnes Quadrupel is like a
glass of liquefied bakery bread, brown sugar,
figs, plums, chocolate, and cola. It's a powerful
beer in its depth of flavor and mouth-filling
body, and yet it keeps a lightness that makes
you drink quickly. Don't fancy pastry? Wrap the
figs in prosciutto, push in some dolcelatte, and
bake. It's also excellent with Extraomnes.

PLUM CRUMBLE

GREAT WITH: BARREL-AGED BEER

PERFECT PAIR: FOUNDER'S BACKWOODS
BASTARD
BREWED IN: GRAND RAPIDS, MICHIGAN
ABV: 10.2%

Hot fruit crumble with a big scoop of vanilla ice
cream is my idea of food perfection, where the
topping is crunchy, yet chewy, and the base is
sweet, tart, and caramelized. It took a very long
time to come up with a great beer pairing and
lots of bottles came and went—Weizenbock,
Double IPA, Imperial Stout, Barley Wine,
Quadrupel—because I could never get it exactly
right. The reason Founder's Backwoods Bastard
works is that you've got a Strong Ale, which is
like a love song to malt's chewy, bready, and
toffee flavors, and then this is barrel-aged and
brings molasses, vanilla, butterscotch, dried fruit,
and woody spice, which bridges to the crumble
topping and emphasizes the fruit beneath.

CHOCOLATE

To make chocolate, the bitter cocoa seeds of the cacao tree are picked and left to ferment, which produces fruity, floral, wine-like flavors. The seeds are then dried and roasted to develop the darker flavors we expect from the treat. Next, the beans are broken apart to separate the nibs from the shells. The nibs are then pressed to produce cocoa liquor (cocoa mass)—made up of cocoa solids (cocoa powder) and cocoa butter (the fat)—which can then also be separated. If you mix the cocoa butter, cocoa solids, and sugar you create semi-sweet (dark) chocolate, in which the higher the quantity of solids, the stronger the chocolate will be. Milk chocolate adds milk or milk powder, and is lower in cocoa solids. White chocolate contains cocoa butter, sugar, and milk, but no cocoa solids.

CHOCOLATE BROWNIES

GREAT WITH: IMPERIAL STOUT

PERFECT PAIR: ALESMITH
SPEEDWAY STOUT
BREWED IN: SAN DIEGO,
CALIFORNIA
ABV: 12.0%

Chocolate, coffee, and malt share similarities in their production, with the roasting process creating the nutty, toasty, roasted flavors, and fermentation giving subtle fruitiness, so it's not surprising that they are so harmonious together. AleSmith's Speedway Stout is brewed with coffee beans, which bolsters the richness of chocolate and dark malt in the beer. With an aroma of fresh coffee, bakery bread, warm chocolate, and vanilla, the body is thick and mouth-filling. It has a wine-like 12.0% ABV and yet the refreshing carbonation makes it feel lighter. With a piece of gooey chocolate brownie, it's close to perfection.

CHOCOLATE CHIP COOKIES

GREAT WITH: SWEET STOUT

PERFECT PAIR: ODELL
BREWING LUGENE CHOCOLATE
MILK STOUT
BREWED IN: FORT
COLLINS, COLORADO
ABV: 8.5%

Is there a better accompaniment to a plate of chocolate chip cookies than a cold glass of whole milk? Yes, there is: Odell's Lugene Chocolate Milk Stout. It's brewed with milk sugar and milk chocolate, and named after the local farmer who uses the brewery's spent grain to feed his dairy cows. It's an unctuous and creamy brew, which tastes like chocolate ice cream, cocoa, rum 'n' raisin, roasted nuts, and semi-sweet (dark) chocolate, and it has the fullest, most milk-like body you'll find in a beer, making it sweetly comforting and sensational with a warm chocolate chip cookie. So simple and so good.

DARK CHOCOLATE MOUSSE

GREAT WITH: CHERRY BEER

PERFECT PAIR: LIEFMANS
CUVÉE-BRUT
BREWED IN: OUDENAARDE,
BELGIUM
ABV: 6.0%

This is a classic beer-and-food match, and the quintessential example of a boost pairing. You get the tongue-coating richness of chocolate mixed with cream and then in comes this lively, sweet-sour Cherry Beer. Suddenly, all the fruity flavors in the chocolate jump off your tongue; the tartness in the fruit and from the beer mirrors some cocoa-solid acidity; the bitter roast notes are wrapped in cherry juice; the fizz tickles and keeps the beer light—all this makes you immediately want to repeat the mouthful. Liefmans Cuvée-Brut is hazy red, a glass of cherries, vanilla, and almond; it's semi-sweet, but still tart. Fine on its own, but amazing with chocolate mousse.

WHITE CHOCOLATE PANNA COTTA AND SALTED SHORTBREAD

GREAT WITH: IMPERIAL STOUT

PERFECT PAIR: BROOKLYN BLACK
CHOCOLATE STOUT
BREWED IN: BROOKLYN, NEW YORK
ABV: 10.0%

White chocolate isn't really chocolate. It's made by mixing cocoa butter with milk solids, sugar, and often vanilla, so there are no cocoa solids in it—the cocoa solids give chocolate its color, much of its flavor, and the roasted bitterness. Regardless of semantics, white chocolate is one of the most pleasing things to eat and there's something wonderful in pairing it with a dark chocolatey Stout, as if you're reuniting the cocoa solids with the cocoa butter. Brooklyn Black Chocolate Stout, perhaps fittingly in this example, doesn't actually contain chocolate, but it definitely tastes as if it does—really roasty semi-sweet (dark) chocolate, black coffee, nuts, the same almost-tart, berry fruitiness that you find in coffee, and a bitter finish. With the sweetness in the panna cotta, the darkness in the beer creates a delicious chocolatey dichotomy that's entirely chocolate-less and yet it tastes like an adult version of a Kinder Surprise.

CHURROS AND CHOCOLATE

GREAT WITH: IMPERIAL STOUT

PERFECT PAIR: NÓMADA BREWING
ROYAL PORTER A LA TAZA
BREWED IN: BARCELONA, SPAIN
ABV: 9.5%

A churro (a type of doughnut) is a Spanish street food or breakfast, which works equally well as a dessert or late-night beer snack, and it deserves a good Spanish beer. Nómada's Royal Porter is a big, full-on, luscious Imperial Stout, loaded with sweet coffee, cocoa, berries, bourbon, caramel, and a creamy body—drinking it feels like a treat, which is a good thing for a beer. With the sugar-coated doughnuts, which are dipped in a hot chocolate sauce, the beer boosts everything like an ingredient on the side; in fact, if you're making these yourself, then use some beer in the sauce. Nómada, as the name says, is a nomadic brewery that makes beer wherever it can. Try Nómada's beers when you see them—they are excellent.

CHOCOLATE FONDANT

GREAT WITH: IMPERIAL STOUT
OR FRUIT BEER

PERFECT PAIR: NEW GLARUS
RASPBERRY TART
BREWED IN: NEW GLARUS,
WISCONSIN
ABV: 4.0%

Use this to make someone fall madly in love with you. Phenylethylamine is a chemical that's released when love hits us and is also a compound found in chocolate. It raises endorphin levels to create a rush of pleasure. Dopamine, which gives a natural high, and tryptophan, a precursor to serotonin (which influences sexual arousal), are also both released by eating chocolate. You can double the aphrodisiac qualities with a lusty chocolate fondant, a hot cake with an oozing, lava-like center. Make it even sexier by opening a New Glarus's Raspberry Tart, which is the most love-inducing beer I can think of. It's the color of a sparkling ruby and it serenades you with raspberries. A sweet kiss, a cheeky and fruity tartness, a silky smoothness— and with chocolate fondant, it's oh-my-god good.

HANGOVER FOOD

There's no point pretending otherwise: drink too much beer and you get drunk. Rather than ignore this fact of life, it's good to be prepared for the morning after and the hangover, so here are some dishes that may help you out and, of course, a beer to go with them—just in case you feel fresh enough to drink one. Having got this far through the book, now's an appropriate time to say: drink safe, drink moderately, and don't get completely wasted all the time.

PHO OR NOODLE SOUP

GREAT WITH: GINGER TEA

PERFECT PAIR: WILLIAMS BROTHERS GINGER
BREWED IN: ALLOA, SCOTLAND
ABV: 3.8%

The combination of rich broth, fresh vegetables, herbs, protein, and noodles has magic powers in dealing with a hangover. I guess it's the salt and the zingy freshness of the green ingredients, but it can ease any ailments of the "drunk-too-much" variety. Williams Brothers Ginger has malt and wheat as the base, but doesn't use any hops. Instead, it's brewed with ginger and lemons, which makes it like a glorious ginger shandy—refreshing, spicy, light, and zesty. It's like a glass of ginger tea, which works to settle your rumbling, rolling stomach and reduce feelings of nausea. Given that it's only 3.8% ABV, it won't be a hardcore hit of hair of the dog, more a gentle belly rub and headache softener. It's fantastic with pho (a type of Vietnamese noodle soup), sharing citrus in common and adding a spicy sweetness.

HUEVOS RANCHEROS

GREAT WITH: COFFEE OR COCOA

PERFECT PAIR: DOGFISH HEAD THEOBROMA
BREWED IN: MILTON, DELAWARE
ABV: 9.0%

Coffee is a go-to hangover help, but it's not the best thing to drink because, although the caffeine wakes you up, it brings an inevitable down a few hours later. It's also a diuretic, which can make you even more dehydrated. Perhaps a better drink would be champurrado, a Mexican hot chocolate that's spiced with aniseed—the full body, sweetness, and richness are the comforting equivalent of a hangover hug. Huevos rancheros is a dish of tortillas, hot tomato sauce, and fried eggs. It's spicy, filling, and healthy, and so good for perking up a tired body. Have it with Dogfish Head Theobroma, which is brewed with cocoa, honey, and chilis. It's low in bitterness, smooth, warming with alcohol and chili, sweet with cocoa and honey, and decadent with the spicy baked eggs.

BACON SANDWICH

GREAT WITH: BLOODY MARY

PERFECT PAIR: DUCHESSE DE BOURGOGNE
BREWED IN: VICHTE, BELGIUM
ABV: 6.2%

Sometimes only a bacon sandwich will help your hangover, and it's a safe bet and a guarantee that you'll feel better after eating one. With a Bloody Mary it turns into something rather more exciting and feels like a genuine pairing: umami-rich tomato loves salty bacon, Tabasco perks you up with a kick of heat, the Worcestershire sauce adds more saltiness, and you're getting a crucial hit of healthy juice. Try swapping the Bloody Mary for a Rodenbach or Duchesse de Bourgogne, which always make me think of tomato juice or ketchup: acetic, peppery with wood tannin; there's sweetness, an umami richness, iron-like, and then some vinous sour fruits. It's brilliant with bacon.

PEANUT BUTTER
AND BANANA ON TOAST
GREAT WITH: SPORTS DRINK

```
PERFECT PAIR: ERDINGER ALKOHOLFREI
BREWED IN: ERDING, GERMANY
ABV: <0.5%
```

Most alcohol-free lagers are terrible, but many of the Hefeweizens are excellent. In Germany, they are promoted as refreshing isotonic drinks because they contain protein, carbohydrates (Erdinger Alkoholfrei contains 125 calories per 17 US fl oz/500ml bottle), folic acid (one bottle gives you 50 percent of your recommended daily intake), and vitamin B12. Erdinger Alkoholfrei smells like banana, toffee, and bubble gum; the drink is light, quite sweet but refreshing, and easy-drinking. Have it with banana, which is packed with potassium and electrolytes (good for a hangover), and peanut butter on toast. It's also a good snack before going to the gym, so whether you're feeling healthy or horrible, the beer will work in either circumstance.

COLD PIZZA OR LEFTOVER KEBAB
GREAT WITH: CAFFEINE ENERGY DRINKS

```
PERFECT PAIR: HALF A SHANDY
BREWED IN: ANYWHERE AND EVERYWHERE
ABV: 2.5%
```

Perhaps the first desperate attempts at dealing with your morning-after woes, the cold pizza or leftover kebabs (see also: half-eaten burgers and cold curry) are there when you wake up, serving as reminders of last night. You know you shouldn't, you know that you'll regret it, but somehow you just can't resist. And they always taste disgustingly excellent, especially with some sweet chili sauce. You may find half a can of leftover energy drink (probably from the Jägerbombs you shot seven hours ago), but don't drink it. Instead, find half a can of leftover lager and make a shandy, an equal mix of beer and lemonade that's one of the world's greatest and most refreshing drinks, and the only "beer cocktail" worth bothering with.

BREAKFAST OMELETTE
GREAT WITH: FRUIT JUICE

```
PERFECT PAIR: LOST COAST TANGERINE
WHEAT
BREWED IN: EUREKA, CALIFORNIA
ABV: 5.0%
```

A breakfast omelette is a wise hangover choice because eggs contain cysteine, which breaks down the hangover-causing toxins in the liver. Add spinach (healthy) and cheese (tastes good, makes you feel better), and it has the ability to kick away your mournful woes. A glass of fruit juice is good. Go for the beer equivalent with Lost Coast's Tangerine Wheat, a beer that's a blast of juicy and zesty tangerines, with some residual sweetness and a dry, refreshing finish. You could even mix it into a mimosa (a champagne-based cocktail) with some orange juice, but it's fine as it is. A fruity, easy-going Pale Ale would work as well.

4 COOKING WITH BEER

As WELL AS BEING A GREAT ACCOMPANIMENT TO FOOD, BEER IS ALSO AN EXCELLENT INGREDIENT IN MANY DISHES. SOME OF THE DISHES IN THIS BOOK ARE CLASSICS, SUCH AS CARBONNADE, MEAT AND ALE PIE, AND BEER CAN CHICKEN, WHICH ARE IMPOSSIBLE TO IGNORE. OTHER DISHES ARE NEW AND SHOW THE MANY WAYS IN WHICH BEER CAN BE USED IN THE KITCHEN, WHETHER THIS IS FOR BEER-STEAMED FISH, BEER PIZZA, BEER CHOCOLATE TRUFFLES, OR EVEN BEER KETCHUP AND MUSTARD.

What you can generally expect from adding beer to a recipe is an extra richness of flavor, which is enhanced by the sweetness of malt and given complexity by the bitterness of the hops. It's possible to add beer to almost all recipes, but it's important to throw out an early warning: beer can often be brilliant in the kitchen, but it can also be really disgusting as an ingredient, so it helps to know a few things about what definitely does and does not work. For example, I once put lager in the freezer to see if it came out like a lovely, refreshing ice lolly. It didn't. It tasted like frozen perfume, and all the sweetness and grain flavor were obliterated by bitterness. I've tried to deglaze hot pans with beer, only to be left with a very bitter sauce that ruined dinner. I've made terrible, inedible ice creams and horribly hoppy bread. The good news for you is that I've already made all these mistakes so that you don't have to.

There are so many ways to use beer when cooking, whether it's in a brine, in creams or sauces, in soup, when slow-cooking, as a "raw" ingredient in a mayonnaise or salad dressing, or in desserts, cakes, and sorbets. You can even use the base ingredients of beer, such as crushed pale malt. One of the best tricks is to think about the flavors in the beer and then to use those elements in the recipe. For example, adding sugar or caramelized onions picks out the sweeter flavors in malt; chocolate highlights the roast in dark beers; orange or tropical fruits show off the citrus side of hoppy beers; and pepper and spice boost the background fragrance in many Belgian beers.

A lot of my recipes, whether great or terrible, have come from "what if" questions: What if I mix IPA and orange juice to make a frosting for that cake? What if I marinate that steak in Saison? What if raspberries are cooked in raspberry beer? What if I add dark beer to this chocolate cake? And then it's simply a question of working out how to create balance in a dish, just as you would when using any other ingredient.

The main reason that I really like cooking with beer is that it's fun. I like to experiment with recipes and ideas in the hope that I'll make something delicious for dinner. And, by adding beer, it's possible to make some incredibly delicious dishes. Beer is a great ingredient that can do wonderful things in the kitchen.

BEER IN THE KITCHEN: THE RULES

HERE ARE 14 RULES DESIGNED TO HELP YOU PRODUCE DELICIOUS RESULTS WHEN COOKING WITH BEER.

1. LEARN TO LOVE BITTERNESS

Beer is bitter, and we can't avoid that. Instead, we should embrace that bitterness and add something sweet to help create balance. For this reason, sugar and honey are important ingredients, even in savory dishes. Not only do they soften the bitterness, but they can also enhance the malt depth. Similarly, caramelized onions or meat, roasted garlic, and cooked fruit can all give sweetness to a dish. As well as adding sweetness, you can also use acidity to balance out flavors, so add a little vinegar or citrus juice to lift everything.

2. DON'T BOIL BEER

Pouring beer into a hot, dry pan, perhaps to deglaze it or create a sauce, is just going to deposit all its bitterness and boil off the aroma. It's better to add some stock first and then the beer. However, you generally still want to avoid boiling beer hard and fast.

3. USE BEER WITH CARE

You never quite know what qualities you'll amplify or lose when cooking with a beer. Just because it's got a deeply smoky flavor in the bottle doesn't necessarily mean you're adding the beer equivalent of liquid smoke to a dish. Often, the finer aromas (particularly those of the hops) and qualities in a beer are delicate and volatile, and can disappear with cooking. A good way around this is not to cook the beer: instead, add it very late in the process or use it in a dressing.

4. SLOW-COOKING WITH BEER IS GOOD

After a couple of hours, the slow-cooking process is able to break down some of the bitterness of beer (although not necessarily in high IBU brews). But you'll always need to add some stock along with the beer. Another tip is to keep some beer back—just ¼ cup (50ml), or so—and add it shortly before serving in order to boost the beer flavor.

5. USE BEER IN BRINES AND MARINADES

These can be very tasty and are an ideal method to discover what cooking with a particular beer style will bring to a dish—for example, soaking a piece of meat in a beer brine will draw the flavor of the beer into the meat. You can also tweak the brine with a selection of beer-like ingredients, such as citrus, herbs, and spices.

6. MATCH BEER AND INGREDIENT FLAVORS

You'll see that I regularly mix roasted garlic and/or orange with IPA. This is because they work so perfectly together. Embrace those ingredients that have similar flavors to the beer, whether it's citrus with IPA, Stout with roast flavors, or Belgian beers with spices.

7. COOK AND PAIR SEPARATELY

Just because a particular beer is used in the cooking process doesn't always mean that it's going to be the best one to drink with the finished dish.

8. BAKING WITH BEER IS GOOD

Who doesn't love the idea of a beer cake with beer frosting?! This is another time to find something that complements the beer and use that as an additional ingredient. Try dried fruit with Dubbel, cocoa with Stout, banana with Hefeweizen.

9. USE BEER IN SAUCES AND CONDIMENTS

Beer makes great condiments, which is a wonderful way to impress your friends— "Would you like some of my beer ketchup with that?" or "Have you tried my homemade beer mustard?"

10. GET BACK TO BEER BASICS

Think beyond the stuff in the bottle and back to the original ingredients. Malt has a range of flavors—from biscuit through caramel to bitter coffee—and can be used in lots of recipes. Just remember that you need to crush the malt first in a pestle and mortar or spice grinder before using it. Hops can be used (carefully) like a spice or you can infuse other ingredients, such as oil or salt, with hops.

11. DEAL WITH SURPLUS BEER

Many of the recipes in this book call for a small amount of beer only. The best way to deal with this is to set aside the amount you need to cook with and then drink the rest. Alternatively, just leave a little beer in the bottom of the bottle until you need it—you can cover the bottle with plastic wrap (cling film), and leave it in the refrigerator.

12. DE-FIZZ AND WARM UP BEER

You don't want the carbonation of beer when cooking (unless it's for a beer batter). To dull the fizziness, just pour the beer into a jug and stir for a minute. Also, when cooking, you'll generally want to use the beer at room temperature (again, unless it's for a batter). If the beer is cold, though, it'll still work fine.

13. TRY TO BE SUBTLE

Even though a dish is cooked with beer, it doesn't necessarily mean that it should taste overly of beer. Sometimes, you just want to use the beer as a background flavor, rather like a seasoning. Dishes can quite often be ruined because they taste too beery.

14. FINALLY, JUST HAVE FUN!

There are no real rules for cooking with beer, only a few tips to help you create the best-tasting things you can (and to avoid some terrible mistakes). If a recipe calls for a liquid, you can generally add some beer—just think about the balance of the dish and the best way to make it taste amazing.

MEASURING BEER FOR RECIPES

If a recipe says to add one bottle of beer, this means you need to add 11–12 US fl oz (330–355ml) of beer, since that's a common and consistent bottle size. An extra 1 fl oz (30ml) or so will rarely make a huge difference to most recipes. Specific quantities of beer are given for those recipes that call for amounts other than 11–12 US fl oz (330–355ml).

SNACKS

BEER CHEESE **STICKS**

A SIMPLE AND TASTY SNACK THAT IS PERFECT TO SERVE AT PARTIES, THESE STICKS ARE CHEWY ON THE INSIDE AND CRISP ON THE OUTSIDE. THE DARK ALE GIVES THE RECIPE AN EXTRA DEPTH OF FLAVOR, MAKING THE FINISHED PRODUCT TASTE EVEN BETTER.

Scant 1 cup (100g) all-purpose (plain) flour, plus extra for dusting

½ tsp cayenne pepper

½ tsp mustard powder

4 tbsp (50g) butter, plus extra for greasing

1 cup (100g) grated strong Cheddar cheese

1 egg yolk

3 tbsp Brown Ale or Stout (or even a Double IPA)

Salt and freshly ground black pepper

MAKES 20

1 Preheat the oven to 400°F/200°C/Gas 6.

2 Mix the flour with the cayenne pepper, mustard powder, and seasoning. Using your fingertips, rub the butter into the flour until the mixture resembles fine breadcrumbs.

3 Add the cheese and egg yolk, and then use the beer to bind the mixture into a thick dough.

4 Roll out the dough on a lightly floured surface until it is just under ½in (1cm) thick. Cut the dough into long rectangles and place on a greased baking tray. Bake the straws for 10–15 minutes until they are golden on the outside. Leave to cool on a wire rack—this will make the straws firmer. Delicious eaten warm or cold.

WELSH **RAREBIT**

CHEESE ON TOAST FOR THOSE WILLING TO PUT IN SOME EXTRA EFFORT FOR A LOT MORE REWARD. THIS IS A DEEPLY SATISFYING SNACK AND A FAVORITE OF MINE. IT MIGHT SEEM LIKE A HUGE AMOUNT OF CHEESE AND THAT'S BECAUSE, QUITE SIMPLY, IT IS!

2 tbsp (25g) butter

3 tbsp (25g) all-purpose (plain) flour

5 tbsp (75ml) milk

⅓ cup (100ml) dark beer (such as Porter, Brown Ale, or Bock)

1 tsp English mustard (or ½ tsp mustard powder)

Few splashes of Worcestershire sauce

1¼ cups (125g) grated strong Cheddar cheese

4 thick slices of bread

Freshly ground black pepper

MAKES 4 SLICES

1 Melt the butter in a saucepan over a medium heat. Add the flour, stirring for a few minutes to create a roux.

2 Add the milk first to get the sauce started and then pour in the beer, adding it gradually to avoid creating lumps and stirring constantly to produce a thick, smooth sauce.

3 Add the mustard and Worcestershire sauce, and season with pepper. Add the cheese, stirring continuously until it has all melted.

4 Toast one side of each slice of bread under the broiler (grill), flip the bread over, and pour over the cheese mix. Return to the broiler until the sauce bubbles and browns. This snack is great served with a beer chutney.

SIDE DISHES

STOUT MASH

UPGRADE YOUR USUAL MASHED POTATO BY ADDING SOME BEER. THIS DISH IS INSPIRED BY A RECIPE CREATED BY THE HOMEBREW CHEF—SEE WWW.HOMEBREWCHEF.COM—FOR ROAST GARLIC AND IPA MASH, WHICH IS ALSO VERY GOOD.

Around 18oz (500g) potatoes

A few sprigs of fresh rosemary

4 tbsp (50g) butter

¼ cup (50ml) milk

⅓ cup (100ml) Stout (I use an 8.0% ABV sweet stout with a full body)

Smoked sea salt (or ordinary sea salt)

Fresh lemon juice

SERVES 2

1 Prepare your potatoes in the normal way: peel, chop, place in a saucepan, cover with cold water, and bring to a boil. Add the sprigs of fresh rosemary.

2 Simmer the potatoes until they are soft, but not mushy. Drain the water and remove the sprigs of rosemary.

3 Add the butter, milk, Stout, a generous amount of smoked sea salt (ordinary sea salt is fine but the smoked version is far superior), then the juice of half a lemon. Mash the potatoes until smooth. Serve with roast or barbecued meat.

PALE ALE NAAN

TRY THESE AS AN ACCOMPANIMENT TO GUEUZE CHICKEN VINDALOO (SEE PAGE 182). WHILE NOT AS LIGHT AND CHEWY AS CURRY-HOUSE NAANS, THESE CAN BE MADE IN UNDER AN HOUR AND ARE VERY GOOD WITH THE CURRY. THIS RECIPE IS ALSO EASY TO ADJUST ACCORDING TO THE BEER AND TOPPINGS YOU'D LIKE: PERHAPS PORTER AND DRIED COCONUT, IPA AND GREEN CHILI, OR WIT AND FENNEL SEEDS.

2 cups (250g) all-purpose (plain) flour

½ tsp baking powder

2 tsp granulated sugar

1 tsp salt

4 tbsp (60ml) Pale Ale

4 tbsp (60ml) milk

2 tbsp vegetable oil

2 garlic cloves, crushed

SERVES 4

1 Mix all the dry ingredients in a bowl (apart from the garlic) and combine all the wet ingredients in a measuring jug.

2 Pour the wet ingredients into the dry ones, and form into a dough. Knead the dough for 5 minutes, place in a bowl covered with some plastic wrap (clingfilm), and leave to rest for 15–30 minutes.

3 Preheat the oven to its highest setting (around 475°F/240°C/Gas 9). Put a flat baking tray (or pizza stone) in the oven to heat up. (You may need more than one tray or stone to bake the naans.)

4 Separate the dough into four pieces and roll them out so that they are approximately ½ in (1cm) thick. Sprinkle the garlic over the top of the dough and place on the baking tray or pizza stone. Bake for 10 minutes or until golden in color.

STOUT BEANS

THIS SIMPLIFIED VERSION OF BARBECUED BEANS IS GREAT SERVED WITH GRILLED MEAT. I USE A RICH STOUT HERE, BUT RAUCHBIER OR A BELGIAN SOUR RED OR BROWN ALSO WORKS.

1 onion, finely chopped

1 tbsp olive oil

2 garlic cloves, crushed

2 rashers smoked bacon, finely chopped (leftover pork also works)

2 tbsp tomato ketchup

1 tbsp soy sauce

1 tbsp Worcestershire sauce

1 tbsp soft brown sugar

1 tbsp clear honey or maple syrup

1 tsp English mustard

½ tsp Marmite or Vegemite (optional, but it gives a good depth)

Pinch of fennel seeds

½ tsp fresh rosemary

½ tsp dried chili seeds

½ tsp smoked paprika

Pinch of ground cinnamon

18oz (500g) canned beans (cannellini, haricot, kidney, or mixed beans), drained

⅓ cup (100ml) Stout (preferably strong and rich)

Salt and freshly ground black pepper

SERVES 4
as a side dish

1 Soften the onion in the olive oil in a saucepan for a few minutes. Add the garlic and bacon, and cook for a few more minutes.

2 Add all the other ingredients, except the beer, saving the beans until last. Stir constantly until the bean mixture warms through and starts to simmer, and then remove from the heat.

3 At this point, pour in the beer and check the seasoning, adjusting it to taste—you can add more chili, more sugar, more spices, etc. (You can now either leave the beans to cool and then bake them when you are ready or bake them immediately.)

4 Preheat the oven to 400°F/200°C/Gas 6. Pour the beans into a small baking dish, cover with aluminum foil, and cook for 30 minutes. Remove the foil and then cook for a further 15 minutes, checking that the beans don't cook dry or burn.

CORIANDER FRIES

THESE FRIES, COATED WITH CORIANDER, FENNEL SEEDS, AND THYME, GO PERFECTLY WITH A WITBIER OR SAISON AND BRIDGE ACROSS TO THE BEER FLAVORS.

1 tbsp coriander seeds

Pinch of fennel seeds (about six or seven seeds)

2¼lb (1kg) potatoes (enough for four people), unpeeled

Olive oil, for roasting

A good handful of fresh thyme and/or lemon thyme

3 whole garlic cloves

Lots of salt and freshly ground black pepper

SERVES 4

1 Preheat the oven to 400°F/200°C/Gas 6.

2 Put the coriander and fennel seeds in a dry saucepan and warm on a low to medium heat for a few minutes, making sure they don't burn.

3 Grind the seeds coarsely in a pestle and mortar or use a spice grinder.

4 Cut the potatoes into large, steak-cut fries (I like to leave them unpeeled but you can peel them if you wish). Throw the fries onto a baking tray and drizzle with enough olive oil to coat, but not drown, the potatoes.

5 Sprinkle two-thirds of the coriander and fennel mix over the potatoes, season well with salt and pepper, and add the thyme. Press the heel of your hand down on the garlic cloves to open them up, and add them to the tray.

6 Mix together the potatoes and seasonings—I find it's easier to use my hands for this. Bake the fries for around 40 minutes or until they are crisp and golden, turning them over after 30 minutes. Add the remaining ground spice mix to season before serving. The fries taste great with a dollop of lemon mayo on the side.

MAIN COURSES

SPICY **SCOTCH ALE PORK**

THIS DISH IS INSPIRED BY A MASH-UP OF CARBONNADE AND JERK PORK, AND COMBINES THE BELLY-WARMING DEPTH OF SLOW-COOKED MEAT WITH THE HEAT AND SPICES OF THE CARIBBEAN. I USE SCOTCH ALE FOR ITS SWEET MALTY DEPTH, BUT DOPPELBOCKS AND BELGIAN QUADS ALSO WORK WELL.

1 tbsp all-purpose (plain) flour

1 tsp each paprika, dried thyme, cayenne pepper, ground allspice, dried ginger, and salt and freshly ground black pepper

2–3 tbsp olive oil

Approximately 1½lb (700g) skinless and boneless belly pork, chopped into big chunks

2 onions, cut into large chunks

4 garlic cloves, crushed

2 red chili peppers, deseeded and chopped

2 green bell (sweet) peppers, deseeded and chopped

1 tbsp tomato paste (purée)

6 sprigs fresh thyme

2 bay leaves

2 cups (500ml) hot beef stock

1 bottle of Scotch Ale (reserve ¼ cup/50ml)

¼ cup (50ml) malt vinegar

1 tbsp clear honey

1 Scotch bonnet chili pepper

SERVES 4

1 Preheat the oven to 325°F/160°C/Gas 3.

2 Mix together the flour and ½ teaspoon each of the dried spices, and rub the mixture into the pork. Heat the oil in a large ovenproof casserole dish and brown the pork on all sides.

3 Remove the pork from the pan and set aside. Sauté the onion in the pan, stirring until it begins to soften. Add the garlic, chili pepper, bell (sweet) pepper, tomato paste (purée), and the remainder of the spices. Stir for a minute or two before adding the thyme and bay leaves.

4 Add the stock, beer, vinegar, and honey, and then return the pork to the pot. Add the Scotch bonnet chili pepper—just add it whole and not chopped up. Put the lid on the casserole dish and cook in the oven for 2 hours.

5 Just before serving remove the thyme sprigs and bay leaves, then mix in the remaining ¼ cup (50ml) of beer. Serve with some rice, roasted sweet potatoes, and green vegetables—or whatever you fancy. Don't eat the Scotch bonnet unless you are a maniac! Have this one with a Scotch Ale or Sweet Stout.

MAC 'N' CHEESE

Beer added to a cheese sauce gives it the kind of depth for which you usually rely on mustard—it provides a rich, peppery warmth. I like to use dark and moderately sweet beers to try to capture their toasty, caramelized flavors. I also add mustard powder and cayenne pepper because I love the mix of comforting cheese with that spike of heat. This serves two, but is easily multiplied up.

7oz (200g) macaroni

3 tbsp (40g) butter

¼ cup (30g) all-purpose (plain) flour

1¼ cups (300ml) whole milk

⅔ cup (150ml) Sweet Stout, Bock, or malty Brown Ale

½ tsp English mustard powder

½ tsp cayenne pepper

1 cup (100g) grated mature Cheddar cheese

Salt and freshly ground black pepper

Some bonus ingredients: why not try smoked ham and/or softened leeks in the cheese sauce or breadcrumbs and freshly grated Parmesan cheese on top? You could also use an alternative mix of cheeses, including Parmesan, Gruyère, Double Gloucester, or even a little blue cheese.

SERVES 2

1 Cook the macaroni in salted boiling water until soft.

2 Meanwhile, melt the butter in a saucepan over a medium heat and add the flour, stirring for a few minutes to create a roux.

3 Gradually whisk in the milk and then the beer until you have a smooth sauce. Continue to heat and stir as the sauce thickens and add the mustard powder, cayenne pepper, and cheese (reserving a little). Stir the sauce until the cheese melts. Season to taste.

4 Drain the macaroni and mix with the cheese sauce. Pour the cheesy macaroni into a large baking dish and top with the remaining cheese. Place under a broiler (grill) until the top is golden. Let the molten heat cool a little before serving.

5 Tastes great with Brown Ale, IPA, cider, or a fruity Farmhouse Ale.

PUNK ASS CHICKEN

OFTEN KNOWN AS BEER CAN CHICKEN, THIS RECIPE IS ALWAYS GOING TO BE IN A BEER AND FOOD BOOK FOR A FEW SIMPLE REASONS: IT'S AWESOME, IT'S OUTRAGEOUS, AND IT'S A LOT OF FUN. ALTHOUGH CLASSICALLY A BBQ RECIPE, I DON'T KNOW ANYONE WITH A BBQ BIG ENOUGH TO COOK A WHOLE CHICKEN LIKE THIS, PLUS THIS WORKS FINE IN MOST REGULAR OVENS.

I HAVE IDENTIFIED FOUR ISSUES TO OVERCOME IN ORDER TO MAKE THIS RECIPE. THE FIRST IS CHOOSING THE BEER. YOU CAN USE ANY YOU WISH— I LIKE BREWDOG PUNK IPA BECAUSE PUNK ASS CHICKEN IS A COOL NAME— BUT MAKE IT A GOOD ONE BECAUSE SOME OF THE BEER'S CHARACTER WILL PERMEATE THE CHICKEN. IPA, STOUT, SAISON, AND FRUIT BEER ARE ALL GOOD CHOICES. THE SECOND ISSUE IS ACTUALLY PUTTING THE CAN INSIDE THE CHICKEN. THIS IS NOT A GLAMOROUS JOB, ESPECIALLY IF YOU'VE ALREADY SEASONED AND OILED THE BIRD, BUT THE GOOD NEWS IS THAT, LIKE A FOREFINGER AND A NOSTRIL, A BEER CAN IS THE EXACT SAME SIZE AS A CHICKEN'S BUTT. THE THIRD PROBLEM IS MAKING SURE IT DOESN'T FALL OVER. I HAVE NO USEFUL TIPS FOR THIS EXCEPT THAT IF YOU SEE IT LEANING TO ONE SIDE, THEN YOU'D BETTER CATCH IT BEFORE IT FALLS (BECAUSE IT WILL FALL). THE FOURTH PROBLEM IS GETTING THE CAN OUT AT THE OTHER END OF THE COOKING BECAUSE THE CHICKEN AND THE CAN, PLUS THE BEER STILL IN THE CAN, ARE VERY HOT, SO BE CAREFUL.

1 roasting (whole) chicken

1 can of beer

Olive oil

Selection of seasoning, herbs, and spices (salt and freshly ground black pepper are essential, the rest are down to you—I like to use garlic, fresh thyme, and paprika, but you can also go with chili powder, curry powder, or other spices)

SERVES 4-6

1 Remove all the shelves from the oven apart from the lowest one. Preheat the oven to 400°F/200°C/Gas 6. Place a baking tray in the oven for the chicken to sit on.

2 Now open the can of beer and approach the bird… Rub the oil, seasoning, herbs, and spices over the bird, plus some of the beer if you wish. I also like to add some garlic cloves and thyme inside and under the skin of the chicken and to the baking tray.

3 Pour half of the can of beer into a glass. (You can also use this "spare" half can of beer as a brine if you want to start your recipe preparation earlier.) Now, try to push the can inside the chicken—you may need some help with this. Once the can is secure, stand the chicken up and balance it on the baking tray (at this point it may look very sorry for itself, but it'll soon look incredible). Close the oven door and cook for around 1½ hours, depending on the size of the bird.

4 I love this dish served with a plate of fries and some coleslaw or salad. Have a cold beer on the side. It really doesn't matter which one.

BEEF **CARBONNADE**

THIS IS THE CLASSIC BELGIAN BEEF AND BEER STEW, A BROTHER OF STEAK
AND ALE, AND A COUSIN OF BOEUF BOURGUIGNON.

THERE ARE DIFFERENT THOUGHTS ABOUT WHICH BEER TO USE IN THIS
RECIPE: SOME SAY THAT A DARK BELGIAN ALE IS BEST, OTHERS OPT FOR A
SOUR RED OR BROWN, OR A GUEUZE, WHICH ARE PROBABLY MORE
TRADITIONAL. MANY RECIPES INCLUDE VINEGAR, WHICH ALSO HINTS AT
REPLICATING THE SHARPNESS IN THOSE SOUR BEERS. I ONCE SIMULTANEOUSLY
COOKED TWO BATCHES OF THIS DISH, USING EXACTLY THE SAME INGREDIENTS
AND PROCESSES IN BOTH. HOWEVER, I USED A TRAPPIST DUBBEL IN ONE AND
A GUEUZE IN THE OTHER. WHILE THE DISHES DIDN'T TASTE EXACTLY THE
SAME—THE DUBBEL WAS SWEETER AND FRUITIER, WHEREAS THE GUEUZE
HAD MORE DEPTH—THEY WERE CLOSE ENOUGH NOT TO FRET TOO HARD
ABOUT THE BEER USED, ALTHOUGH I PREFERRED THE GUEUZE IN THE DISH
AND THE DUBBEL WITH THE DISH. IF YOU HAVE RODENBACH, OR A SIMILAR
SOUR RED OR BRUIN, THESE ARE GREAT BEERS TO USE.

1¼ –1¾lb (600–800g)
beef stew meat (stewing steak),
cut into chunks

2 tbsp all-purpose (plain)
flour, seasoned with salt and
freshly ground black pepper

1–2 tbsp each butter
and olive oil

4 large onions, thickly sliced

3 garlic cloves, crushed

1 tsp fresh thyme

2 bay leaves

2 cups (500ml) hot beef stock

2 cups (500ml) beer (such as
Belgian Red/Bruin, Dubbel,
or Gueuze)

2 tbsp brown sugar

1 tbsp wholegrain mustard

SERVES 4

1 Preheat the oven to 325°F/160°C/Gas 3.

2 Toss the chunks of beef in seasoned flour before browning
in the butter and olive oil in an ovenproof casserole dish on
the stove-top. Remove the beef from the pan and set aside.

3 Soften the onions in the pan before adding the garlic,
thyme, and bay leaves. Add the stock, beer, sugar, and
mustard, and return the beef to the pan.

4 Once the carbonnade starts to bubble, put the lid on the
casserole dish and place in the oven for 2½ hours, giving it
a stir after 60 minutes. Check the carbonnade again after
another hour—the sauce should be really thick, so you may
wish to remove the casserole lid for the final 30 minutes (if
you do this, then remember to check the carbonnade regularly
to make sure it doesn't dry out completely).

5 I like to eat this dish with oven-baked fries: simply cut
some potatoes into thick fries, season with salt and freshly
ground black pepper, and some fresh thyme, lay on an oiled
baking tray, and throw on a couple of whole garlic cloves.
Cook at 400°F/200°C/Gas 6 for around 45 minutes or until
golden brown, turning halfway through the cooking time.
(If your oven is set at 325°F/160°C/Gas 3 for the Beef
Carbonnade, then cook the fries for around 60 minutes.)

ROAST GARLIC **AND DUVEL SOUP**

I'VE DISCOVERED THAT GARLIC SOUP HAS MAGICAL HEALING POWERS WHEN I'VE HAD TOO MANY BEERS THE NIGHT BEFORE, SO THIS IS A SLIGHTLY ODD RECIPE IN THAT IT USES SOMETHING I USUALLY EAT TO GET RID OF A HANGOVER AND TWEAKS IT TO BECOME SOMETHING THAT COULD CREATE A HANGOVER... DUVEL, THE CLASSIC BELGIAN GOLDEN ALE, GIVES A GLORIOUS DEPTH OF FLAVOR TO THIS SOUP AND, IN ORDER TO KEEP MUCH OF ITS AROMA—IT LENDS A FRUITINESS LIKE APPLE AND BANANA—THE BEER IS ADDED RIGHT AT THE END, AS YOU WOULD BLEND CREAM INTO A SOUP BEFORE SERVING.

2 garlic bulbs

Olive oil, for roasting

2 white onions, finely sliced

1 leek, washed and finely sliced

1 tbsp (15g) butter

1 tbsp granulated sugar

2 garlic cloves, finely chopped

2 floury potatoes (such as Maris Piper or King Edward), diced

1 tsp fresh thyme

1 rosemary sprig

2 fresh sage leaves

2 bay leaves

4 cups (1 liter) hot chicken (or vegetable) stock

2 tbsp crème fraîche

⅓ cup (100ml) Duvel

Salt and freshly ground black pepper

Snipped chives, to serve (optional)

SERVES 2
as a starter

1 Preheat the oven to 400°F/200°C/Gas 6.

2 Remove the pointed tops of the garlic bulbs so that the cloves are slightly exposed. Place the bulbs on enough aluminum foil so that you can wrap them in a ball. Drizzle some olive oil over the bulbs and season with salt and pepper. Wrap up the bulbs and roast them in the oven for 45 minutes. Remove from the oven, allow to cool slightly, and then squeeze the bulbs so that the cloves come out and you're left with a thick purée.

3 Gently soften the onion and leek in a saucepan with the butter, a little olive oil, and the sugar—don't let the onions caramelize or burn; you want them to go soft and translucent, which should take around 15 minutes.

4 Add the finely chopped garlic, stirring for a minute, and then add the roasted garlic purée and potatoes. Add all the herbs and some seasoning, and pour in the stock. Place a lid on the pan and allow to simmer gently for 30 minutes.

5 Remove from the heat, stir in the crème fraîche, and add the beer. Blitz to a smooth, creamy soup in a blender. To finish, sprinkle some snipped chives on top.

RECIPE VARIATIONS:

There are two possible additions that work very well in this recipe. Firstly, you can add 1 level tablespoon of curry powder to the leek and onion, and then follow the recipe as before. Or simply add 1 teaspoon of Dijon mustard and ½ cup (50g) of freshly grated Parmesan cheese just before blending.

BEER **PIZZA**

BEER BREAD IS A CLASSIC USE OF BEER AS AN INGREDIENT, BUT I'VE NEVER REALLY ENJOYED IT—I FIND THAT THE BEER CAN MAKE THE BREAD TASTE ODDLY BITTER. I MUCH PREFER BEER PIZZA DOUGH IN WHICH THE MALT SWEETNESS WORKS BETTER TO GIVE CARAMEL-LIKE FLAVORS THAT ENHANCE WHATEVER'S ON TOP OF THE PIZZA. THE BEST BEERS TO USE ARE AMBER LAGER, OKTOBERFEST, VIENNA, OR HEFEWEIZEN—THAT IS, BEERS WITH MALT FLAVOR BUT LOW BITTERNESS. IF YOU WANT MORE BEER FLAVOR IN YOUR PIZZA, THEN TRY MAKING THE TOMATO BASE SAUCE WITH RAUCHBIER OR SWEET STOUT, OR SOFTEN ONIONS FOR THE TOPPING IN GARLIC, ROSEMARY, SUGAR, AND PALE ALE.

1 x ¼oz (7g) sachet fast-action dried yeast

1 tbsp granulated sugar

1 fl oz (25ml) olive oil

⅔ cup (150ml) beer, at room temperature

¾ cup (180ml) warm water

4 cups (500g) "00" or bread (strong white) flour

1 tsp salt

MAKES 4-6 PIZZAS

1 Mix the yeast, sugar, olive oil, beer, and water in a jug, and leave for a few minutes.

2 On a clean work surface, sift the flour and salt into a mound and create a well in the middle. Gradually pour the liquid ingredients into the well, and bring the flour and liquid together using a fork. Keep mixing the wet and dry ingredients together until you are able to work the dough with your hands.

3 Knead until the dough is soft and springy. Place in a large, flour-dusted bowl and cover with a damp towel. Leave in a warm place for an hour for the dough to double in size.

4 Preheat the oven to its highest setting (around 475°F/240°C/Gas 9), preferably with a pizza stone in it.

5 Knead the dough on a floured work surface, pulling, pushing, and knocking the air out of it. Divide the dough into smaller balls and roll out the pizzas until they are about ¼in (½cm) thick.

6 Cover with your favorite pizza toppings and place in the oven—the pizzas will cook in 8–10 minutes.

MILK STOUT **MOLE**

MOLE IS A MEXICAN DISH MADE USING SEMI-SWEET (DARK)
CHOCOLATE, SO I COOK IT WITH A MILK OR CHOCOLATE STOUT TO
EMPHASIZE THE CHOCOLATE FLAVOR. I PREFER MAKING THE SAUCE
IN ADVANCE AND LEAVING IT IN THE REFRIGERATOR OVERNIGHT.
PURISTS, PLEASE BE WARNED: THIS ISN'T AN AUTHENTIC MOLE
RECIPE; IT'S MY OWN INTERPRETATION.

5 fresh chili peppers

5 plum tomatoes, quartered

½ tsp smoked paprika

3 tbsp olive oil

1 large onion, cut into
chunks

4 garlic cloves, crushed

5 dried chili peppers

2oz (55g) semi-sweet (dark)
chocolate, minimum 70%
cocoa solids

¼ cup (50g) raisins

3¼ cups (750ml) hot beef,
chicken, or vegetable stock

1 bottle of Stout (you can
use Milk Stout,
Chocolate Stout, or even
Imperial Stout)

2 tsp peanut butter

1 tbsp granulated sugar

1 cinnamon stick

2 bay leaves

½ tsp dried chili flakes
(optional)

1lb 12oz (800g) chicken
thighs or 18oz (500g)
pork loin, diced

Salt and freshly ground
black pepper

SERVES 6

1 Authentic mole uses lots of smoky, dried chili peppers.
I use some of these and also roast a few whole fresh chili
peppers with quartered tomatoes and smoked paprika to
give a great additional depth of flavor. Simply roast the
vegetables drizzled with a few tablespoons of olive oil
and sprinkled with the smoked paprika in the oven for
30 minutes at 400°F/200°C/Gas 6.

2 While the vegetables are roasting, heat some more olive
oil in a saucepan and sauté the onion and garlic. Add the
roasted tomato and chili pepper mix. Stir in the dried chili
peppers, chocolate, raisins, stock, beer, peanut butter, sugar,
cinnamon stick, bay leaves, and dried chili flakes (if using).
Season with salt and pepper. Simmer for 30 minutes.

3 Allow to cool before removing the cinnamon stick
and bay leaves. Put the sauce in a food-blender and blitz
until smooth (this will take a few minutes). Store in the
refrigerator for 24–48 hours until you're ready to cook
the meat.

4 To cook the meat, brown the chicken thighs or pork
loin in a little oil in a large frying pan and then lower the
heat to cook through (you can use pre-cooked meat if
you prefer).

5 Pour the prepared sauce over the meat and let the mole
warm through until everything is thoroughly cooked.

6 Serve with some rice (I like to pop a cinnamon stick and
a whole garlic clove in the pan when cooking the rice) and a
glass of Chocolate Stout or Oatmeal Stout on the side—you
then get a double hit of cocoa, which works wonderfully.
The soothing sweetness and body of the beer also cools the
chili heat.

IMPERIAL CHILI

THIS IS THE BEST CHILI RECIPE IN THE WORLD. AS DECADENT AS EATING GOLD-LEAF SANDWICHES, IT UNAPOLOGETICALLY USES A WHOLE BOTTLE OF BARREL-AGED IMPERIAL STOUT TO GIVE AN UNBEATABLE DEPTH OF FLAVOR. DON'T TRY TO MAKE THIS QUICKLY; IDEALLY, YOU SHOULD START MAKING IT 24 HOURS BEFORE YOU WANT TO EAT IT. THE BEER SHOULD BE AS STRONG AND RICH AS YOU CAN FIND.

18oz (500g) ground (minced) pork or beef

2–3 tbsp olive oil

2 large onions, finely chopped

1 green bell pepper, finely chopped

4 garlic cloves, finely chopped

Red chili peppers, deseeded and chopped, to taste

½ Scotch bonnet chili pepper, deseeded and chopped

1 chipotle chili pepper (optional), deseeded and chopped

½ tsp dried chili flakes

1 tsp smoked paprika

1 tsp ground cumin

1 tsp ground coriander

1 cinnamon stick

2 tbsp tomato paste (purée)

1⅔ cup (400ml) hot beef stock

1 tbsp clear honey

4 anchovy fillets

2 bay leaves

14oz (400g) can kidney beans, drained

1 bottle of Imperial Stout

Salt and lots of freshly ground black pepper

SERVES 4

1 Preheat the oven to 300°F/150°C/Gas 2.

2 In a large casserole dish, brown the ground (minced) pork or beef in the olive oil.

3 Add the onion and green pepper, and cook for a couple of minutes before adding the garlic, selection of chili peppers, and spices.

4 Add the tomato paste (purée) and cook through for about 3 minutes, continuing to stir and making sure that nothing burns.

5 Add the remaining ingredients, starting with the hot stock and finishing with the beer. Season to taste.

6 Bring to a gentle simmer, put the lid on the casserole dish, and place in the oven for 2 hours, checking regularly to make sure the chili isn't cooking dry—it should be thick, but neither too wet nor too dry.

7 After 2 hours—and after removing the cinnamon stick and bay leaves—you can serve up and eat straight away. Alternatively, allow the chili to cool and leave it in the refrigerator overnight, reheating it in the oven when needed.

8 Serve with rice and a glass of Milk Stout or Hefeweizen.

STEAMED FISH WITH
IPA AND PINEAPPLE SALSA

THIS DISH USES IPA AND A MIX OF FRUITY, SPICY INGREDIENTS
TO STEAM A PIECE OF WHITE FISH. IT THEN SERVES A PINEAPPLE
SALSA ON THE SIDE, WHICH IS MADE WITH THE SAME IPA—
IT'S BEST SERVED IN SOFT TACOS OR TORTILLAS WITH SOME
CHOPPED AVOCADO ON TOP. THE FISH RECIPE IS PER PERSON
WITH THE FILLET BEING WRAPPED IN INDIVIDUAL FOIL PARCELS.

FOR THE IPA AND PINEAPPLE SALSA

¼ of a fresh pineapple, chopped into small pieces

1 green chili pepper, deseeded and finely chopped

Juice of 1 lime

1 tsp granulated sugar

1 tsp salt

A handful of cilantro (coriander) leaves, finely chopped

2 tbsp (30ml) IPA

FOR THE STEAMED FISH

1 fillet white fish (such as cod or haddock)

Juice of ½ an orange, plus 1 thick slice of orange

2 garlic cloves

½ fresh chili pepper, deseeded and finely chopped

1in (2cm) piece of fresh ginger, chopped into matchsticks

1 star anise

A few cilantro (coriander) leaves

1 tsp clear honey

1 tsp soy sauce

2 tbsp (30ml) IPA

SERVES 1

1 The salsa is best made an hour or two before you eat. To make the salsa, mix all the ingredients together apart from the beer and then leave in the refrigerator until you are ready to serve. Add the beer to the salsa just before serving—this ensures that you get the maximum amount of beer flavor and fragrance.

2 To steam the fish, preheat the oven to 400°F/200°C/Gas 6. Put all the steamed-fish ingredients on top of a piece of aluminum foil and wrap them up until you have a neat parcel. (I recommend double-wrapping for this: simply take two sheets of foil and fold up the edges to create a parcel.) Place the parcel on a baking tray and cook for 25–30 minutes. Remove the fish from the parcel when you're ready to serve.

3 To serve, I like to put the fish in some soft tacos, spoon over the salsa, and then add some chopped avocado. It's great with a glass of IPA.

BELGIAN BEER **BARBECUE RIBS**

IMAGINE A BELGIAN MONK DISCOVERED BARBECUE FOOD WHILE ON HOLIDAY IN TEXAS AND TOOK IT BACK HOME TO HIS MONASTIC BROTHERS. THESE ARE BIG BEEF RIBS BAKED IN A BELGIAN-BEER-INSPIRED BARBECUE SAUCE, IN WHICH A BOTTLE OF QUADRUPEL IS JOINED BY CINNAMON, CHINESE FIVE SPICE POWDER, FENNEL, AND BLACK PEPPER; THE SAME FLAVORS THAT YOU TASTE IN THE BEER. WHAT YOU'RE LEFT WITH IS THE JUICIEST, MOST TENDER, AND WONDERFUL RIBS. THIS MARINADE IS ENOUGH TO COVER UP TO EIGHT BEEF RIBS.

FOR THE MARINADE
1 bottle of Belgian Quadrupel or Dubbel

3 tbsp soy sauce

2 tbsp tomato ketchup

1 tbsp Worcestershire sauce

2 tbsp malt vinegar

2 tbsp soft brown sugar

Juice of 1 orange

3 garlic cloves, crushed

1 tsp English mustard

1 tsp Chinese five spice powder

1 tsp onion powder

½ tsp fennel seeds

½ tsp dried chili seeds

A pinch of ground cinnamon

1 tsp fresh rosemary

1 tsp fresh thyme

2 bay leaves

Salt and freshly ground black pepper

SERVES 2-4
*2–3 beef ribs
or 6–8 pork ribs,
per person*

1 Mix together all the marinade ingredients in a bowl. Place the ribs in a large, flat dish and pour the marinade over the ribs. Cover with plastic wrap (clingfilm), place in the refrigerator, and leave to marinate for 6–24 hours (ideally, for over 12 hours).

2 Preheat the oven to 300°F/150°C/Gas 2. Cook the ribs in a large roasting tin, covered with aluminum foil, for 3 hours, basting them every 45 minutes. You may wish to uncover the ribs for the last 30 minutes so that the sauce turns thick and sticky; check to see if you need to do this, however, and make sure that the ribs don't burn or cook dry.

3 These ribs are great served with Stout Beans and Stout Mashed Potato (see pages 167 and 166). And a bottle of Dubbel works really well on the side—try Chimay Red, Westmalle Dubbel, or Ommegang Abbey Ale.

GUEUZE CHICKEN VINDALOO

In the United Kingdom, vindaloo comes with a fire-hazard warning: eat one of these curries and part of your body will burst into flames. Vindaloo's reputation for being fearsomely spicy is a British development on a dish that has Portuguese roots. It was originally meat cooked with wine and garlic, which then evolved (when the Portuguese took it to India) into meat cooked with vinegar and the addition of chili and other spices. The beer-evolution is to take out the vinegar and use Gueuze for the acidity instead (this also adds some peppery depth). I serve mine with Pale Ale and Garlic Naan Bread on the side (see page 166 for the recipe for this).

FOR THE MARINADE

1 tsp each cumin seeds, coriander seeds, mustard seeds, and cardamom pods

1 tsp ground turmeric

1 tsp granulated sugar

A thumb-sized piece of fresh ginger, finely chopped

½ tsp ground cinnamon

6 garlic cloves

3 fresh green chili peppers

¼ cup (50ml) Gueuze

Salt and freshly ground black pepper

FOR THE CURRY

4 skinless and boneless chicken thighs, chopped into large chunks

2–3 tbsp olive oil

1 large white onion, finely sliced

3 plum tomatoes

⅔ cup (150ml) chicken stock

⅓ cup (100ml) Gueuze

A few cilantro (coriander) leaves, to serve

SERVES 4

1 Dry-fry the cumin, coriander, and mustard seeds, and the cardamom pods in a saucepan for a few minutes. If you are using ground versions of the spices, then just use ½ teaspoon of each and mix them straight into the marinade.

2 Add the dry-fried spices to a food-blender with all the other marinade ingredients and blitz into a paste—this might take a couple of minutes.

3 Cover the chicken with the marinade and leave in the refrigerator for 4–8 hours, reserving any excess marinade.

4 Heat the oil over a medium heat in a large saucepan and fry the chicken. When the chicken has colored, add the onion and tomatoes, and then fry for a couple of minutes until they soften.

5 Add the remainder of the marinade liquid, the stock, and about half of the beer. Bring to a simmer, cover, and cook for 30 minutes. Add the other half of the beer just before serving and decorate with a few cilantro (coriander) leaves.

6 Don't drink this one with Gueuze—it may be cooked in it, but the beer doesn't taste great with it. Instead, you want a Dark Lager or Witbier.

BREWMASTER'S PIE

BREWERS ARE NOT USUALLY REGARDED AS THE GREATEST OF
GOURMETS, ALTHOUGH THEY CERTAINLY TEND TO EAT A LOT!
SO, THIS IS MEAT COOKED IN BEER AND THEN TOPPED WITH
"FRIES." SIMPLE AS PIE.

TO MAKE THE PIE FILLING

1½lb (700g) chuck steak
(braising steak), cut into
large chunks

2½ tbsp (20g) all-purpose
(plain) flour, seasoned with salt
and pepper

1–2 tbsp olive oil

2 onions, thickly sliced

4 large flat mushrooms,
roughly chopped

1⅔ cups (400ml) hot beef stock

1⅔ cups (400ml) dark beer
(try a Stout, Porter, Bock,
Dunkel, or Brown Ale)

1 tbsp granulated sugar

1 tbsp Worcestershire sauce

2 tbsp tomato ketchup

1 tsp fresh thyme

TO MAKE THE PIE TOPPING

6 large potatoes

2–3 tbsp (25–40g) butter

Salt and freshly ground black
pepper

SERVES 6
(or 4 if they are all brewers)

1 Preheat the oven to 325°F/160°C/Gas 3.

2 Coat the chunks of steak in the seasoned flour and
then brown in a frying pan in a little of the olive oil.
Remove the steak and set aside.

3 Sauté the onion in the same frying pan and then add
the mushrooms, stock, beer, sugar, Worcestershire sauce,
tomato ketchup, and thyme. Return the meat to the pan
and bring to a simmer.

4 Pour the meat mix into a pie or baking dish with a lid
or cover with aluminum foil instead. Cook for 1½ hours
in the oven.

5 Meanwhile, cut the potatoes into the shape of
French fries and parboil for about 10–15 minutes in a
saucepan. Drain and season the "fries" before placing
them on top of the meat mix with a few pieces of butter.
Turn the oven up to 400°F/200°C/Gas 6 and bake the pie
for 35–45 minutes or until the fries are golden.

RECIPE VARIATIONS:

*Add some parsnips to the potatoes on top of the pie
and omit the tomato ketchup from the recipe. Instead,
serve with some horseradish sauce on the side.*

*Use the Beef Carbonnade for the meat mix
(see page 173) and then top with the fries.*

*Use ground (minced) beef instead of steak, add some
finely diced carrots, and then top with mashed potato.
You now have a classic Shepherd's Pie.*

CHICKEN AND WIT PIE

CHICKEN PIE WITH SWEET LEEKS AND A WIT AND CRÈME FRAÎCHE SAUCE, GIVING A SPICY, LEMONY SHARPNESS. YUM. USE WHATEVER TOPPING YOU PREFER, ALTHOUGH I LIKE TO USE PUFF PASTRY.

3 tbsp (40g) butter

2 leeks, washed and diced

1 tsp fresh thyme

Scant ½ cup (50g) all-purpose (plain) flour

⅓ cup (100ml) hot chicken stock

⅓ cup (100ml) Wit beer

¾ cup (200ml) crème fraîche

6 cooked chicken breasts or thighs, skinless and diced

Small bunch of tarragon, leaves picked

Ready-rolled pie-crust (shortcrust) or puff pastry (you could also top with some mashed potato)

Salt and freshly ground black pepper

SERVES 6

1 Melt the butter in a large saucepan and sauté the leeks until softened. Add the thyme and some seasoning, stir in the flour, and cook for a minute or two.

2 Start off the sauce with the stock and then add the beer, followed by the crème fraîche. Add the cooked chicken (you could also add some smoked bacon at this stage if you wish) and the tarragon.

3 Check the seasoning before pouring the filling into a pie or baking dish. Top the filling with the pastry (or some mashed potato if you prefer) and bake in the oven according to the directions on the pastry packet.

4 This pie is really good with a Belgo-American beer, a hoppy Belgian Blonde, or a Brown Ale.

YAKIMA CHICKEN

THIS USES AMERICAN HOPS AS ONE OF THE SPICES TO COAT CHICKEN THIGHS, WINGS, OR LEGS. OF ALL THE RECIPES IN THIS BOOK, IT'S THE ONE I COOK THE MOST OFTEN, AS IT COMBINES MY OBSESSION WITH HOPS AND CHICKEN IN THE BEST POSSIBLE WAY. I DON'T FRY THE PIECES OF CHICKEN, AS I PREFER TO BAKE THEM. THE KEY IS TO GET A REALLY CITRUSY HOP LIKE CASCADE, CITRA, OR AMARILLO, WHICH GIVES A BACKGROUND HIT OF PEPPERY BITTERNESS AND GRAPEFRUIT PITH—USE A DRIED HOP FLOWER, IF YOU CAN, AS THIS WORKS MUCH BETTER THAN HOP PELLETS. THE MIX COVERS ENOUGH CHICKEN FOR TWO PEOPLE.

1 dried hop flower, crushed in a pestle and mortar

1 tbsp all-purpose (plain) flour

1 tsp salt

1 tsp freshly ground black pepper

1 tsp cayenne pepper

1 tsp fresh thyme

1 tsp paprika

1 tsp garlic salt

1 tsp brown sugar

½ tsp ground cinnamon

½ tsp ground ginger

½ tsp ground coriander

½ tsp fennel seeds

4–6 chicken pieces (such as wings, thighs, or legs), per person

SERVES 2

1 Preheat the oven to 400°F/200°C/Gas 6.

2 Create a rub with all the dry ingredients and use your fingertips to rub this into the pieces of chicken. Leave for 10 minutes.

3 Place the pieces of chicken on an oiled baking tray and cook for 30–50 minutes, depending on the cut of chicken. As a guide: cook wings for 30 minutes, thighs for 40 minutes, and legs for 50 minutes.

4 Serve with some coleslaw and corn on the cob, plus a glass of juicy, floral IPA.

BEER **MUSSELS**

WHITE WINE IS THE TRADITIONAL LIQUID FOR
COOKING MUSSELS, BUT THIS DISH ALSO
WORKS REALLY WELL WITH CIDER OR BEER.
WITBIER, GUEUZE, HELLES, OR BLONDE ARE
ALL GOOD BEER CHOICES BECAUSE THEY ARE
SUBTLE AND LOW IN BITTERNESS. YOU CAN
USE OTHER BEERS, THOUGH, PLUS OTHER
INGREDIENTS, TO CREATE VARIATIONS, SUCH
AS STOUT AND SMOKED BACON; PILSNER,
CHILI, AND LIME; AND PALE ALE, CURRY
POWDER, AND COCONUT MILK. THIS VERSION
MIXES WITBIER WITH LEMON, THYME,
AND FENNEL SEEDS.

2 shallots, finely chopped	2¼lb (1kg) mussels, cleaned, de-bearded, and any with broken or open shells discarded
1 tbsp each butter and olive oil	
1 garlic clove	1 bottle of Witbier
1 tsp granulated sugar	Juice of ½ a lemon
1 tsp fennel seeds	Salt and freshly ground black pepper
1 bay leaf	

SERVES 2

1 Fry the shallots in the butter and olive oil
in a large saucepan until soft.

2 Add the garlic, sugar, and fennel seeds, and
fry for a minute before adding the bay leaf.

3 Add the mussels to the pan, stirring them
around for a minute before pouring in the
beer. Put the lid on the saucepan and cook,
shaking the pan occasionally, for around
5 minutes, or until all the mussel shells
have opened. Squeeze with lemon juice and
season to taste.

4 Serve in large bowls with French bread
and fries on the side. Great with Witbier.

SPICED **FISH PIE**

THIS FALLS SOMEWHERE BETWEEN
KEDGEREE AND A CLASSIC FISH PIE, AND
INCLUDES A CURRIED FISH, LAGER,
AND CREAM SAUCE WITH A SPICED
MASHED POTATO TOPPING. IT'S ALSO
A NOD OF LOVE TOWARD ONE OF MY
FAVORITE PIES IN THE WHOLE WORLD:
THE CHICKEN BALTI PIES THAT I CAN'T
RESIST EVERY YEAR AT THE GREAT
BRITISH BEER FESTIVAL IN LONDON.
AMAZING THINGS.

FOR THE PIE TOPPING	FOR THE PIE FILLING
2¼lb (1kg) potatoes (floury potatoes such as Maris Piper and King Edwards are best), cut into large cubes	14oz (400g) white fish fillets and/or salmon (I like to use a mix of both)
2 garlic cloves, crushed	14oz (400g) smoked white fish (such as haddock)
1 tsp turmeric powder	4 tbsp (50g) butter
1 tsp curry powder	Scant ½ cup (50g) all-purpose (plain) flour
2 bay leaves	2 tsp curry paste or curry powder (or use a mix of spices, such as turmeric powder, ground coriander, and ground cumin)
2 tsp chicken or vegetable bouillon powder (or ½ bouillon/stock cube)	
4 tbsp (50g) butter	1⅔ cups (400ml) stock (fish, chicken, or vegetable)
¼ cup (50ml) milk	⅓ cup (100ml) Lager or Pale Ale
	1 stick lemongrass
	A few curry leaves and lime leaves
	⅔ cup (150ml) heavy (double) cream
	7oz (200g) peeled and cooked shrimp (prawns)
	4 hard-boiled eggs, shelled and quartered
	Salt and freshly ground black pepper

SERVES 4

1 Preheat the oven to 350°/180°C/Gas 4.

2 To make the potato topping, put the potatoes in a saucepan of cold water and add the garlic, turmeric powder, curry powder, bay leaves, and the bouillon powder or cubes. Bring to a boil and simmer until the potatoes are soft in the middle. Drain the potatoes and remove the bay leaves. Add the butter and milk, and beat into a smooth mash.

3 While the potatoes are cooking, you can cook the fish. Either poach the fish in some water, stock, or milk, or place in an ovenproof dish and bake for 15 minutes.

4 Meanwhile, melt the butter in another saucepan and stir in the flour and spices. Continue stirring for a couple of minutes. Add the stock, followed by the beer, lemongrass, and curry and lime leaves. Simmer for 10 minutes. Season to taste. Remove from the heat and add the cream.

5 Arrange the cooked fish, shrimp (prawns), and eggs on the base of a baking dish. Cover with the curried white sauce and then top with the mashed potato. Bake in the oven for 30 minutes or until golden.

6 Serve this pie with a Pale Lager or Dark Lager.

COQ À LA **DUVEL DOO**

THE NAME CAME BEFORE THE RECIPE ON THIS ONE. I WAS LOOKING
INTO COQ À LA BIÈRE RECIPES WHILE DRINKING A BOTTLE OF DUVEL,
AND THE NAME HIT ME SQUARE IN THE FUNNY BONE AND LEFT ME
CHUCKLING TO MYSELF FOR FAR TOO LONG. THIS DEVELOPS THE
CLASSIC DISH WITH FLAVORS THAT REALLY COMPLEMENT DUVEL.

8–10 skinless chicken
thighs

2–3 tbsp olive oil

1 large white onion,
finely chopped

1 large leek,
chopped into rings

2 sticks celery,
finely chopped

4 garlic cloves,
finely chopped

1 tbsp curry powder

1 tsp ground coriander

½ tsp fennel seeds

1½ cups (350ml)
hot chicken stock

1 bottle of Duvel

2 bay leaves

4 sprigs lemon thyme

1 tbsp clear honey

7oz (200g) crème
fraîche

Salt and freshly
ground black pepper,
to taste

SERVES 4

1 First, preheat the oven to
350°F/180°C/Gas 4.

2 Brown the chicken thighs in a
tablespoon or so of olive oil in a large
casserole dish on top of the stove, and
then remove and set aside.

3 In the same casserole dish, soften
the onion, leeks, and celery in the
remainder of the olive oil for 5 minutes
over a medium-low heat, stirring
regularly. Add the garlic, curry powder,
coriander, and fennel seeds, and stir
for a further minute.

4 Return the chicken to the dish and
add the stock and beer, followed by the
bay leaves, lemon thyme, honey, and
seasoning.

5 Bring to a gentle simmer, put a lid
on the casserole dish, and place in the
oven for 60 minutes, stirring halfway
through the cooking time. You may
wish to cook the dish uncovered for
the final 10–15 minutes to create a
thicker sauce. Add the crème fraîche
just before serving.

6 Serve this dish with some rice or
Coriander Fries (see page 167). It's
great with a Belgian Blonde or Witbier.

CONDIMENTS

BEER MUSTARD

I NEVER REALIZED JUST HOW EASY IT IS TO MAKE MUSTARD UNTIL I TRIED IT MYSELF. THIS MAKES MUSTARD SOMETHING CHEAP, SIMPLE, AND EASY TO CUSTOMIZE.

HERE IS THE RECIPE FOR A BASIC MUSTARD:

3oz (70g) mustard seeds (yellow, brown, or a mix of both)

⅔ cup (150ml) beer (see below for suggestions)

¼ cup (50ml) malt vinegar

Salt and freshly ground black pepper

MAKES APPROXIMATELY 14OZ (400G)

Mix the seeds, beer, and vinegar in a bowl. Cover with some plastic wrap (clingfilm) and leave in the refrigerator for 24–48 hours. After that time, add seasoning to taste, and blitz in a food-blender to the consistency you want (you may wish to add a little extra liquid—either beer or water—to get the texture you desire).

NOW, CHOOSE YOUR MUSTARD FLAVOR:

IPA, ROASTED GARLIC, AND HONEY MUSTARD

Use a super-fruity IPA. Roast 1 garlic clove in aluminum foil for 15 minutes and add to the food-blender. Add 2 tablespoons of clear honey.

LAGER AND CHILI MUSTARD

Inspired by hot dogs. Use any lager you have, but not a bitter one, and only yellow mustard seeds. When blending, add 1 teaspoon each of dried chili flakes, brown sugar, turmeric powder, onion granules, and garlic powder.

RAUCHBIER MUSTARD

Use a Rauchbier, preferably Schlenkerla. Add 1 teaspoon of maple syrup when you're blending and use smoked sea salt, if you have it. Great with roast meat.

CIDER MUSTARD

Use cider, 1 teaspoon each of granulated sugar, salt, and finely chopped rosemary. Brilliant in a roast pork sandwich.

BEER MAYO

JUST A SMALL AMOUNT OF BEER FLAVOR TENDS TO COME THROUGH THIS RECIPE, MEANING THE BEST MAYOS ARE MADE WITH REALLY INTENSE BEERS

TO MAKE A BASIC BEER MAYONNAISE:

2 egg yolks

1 tsp Dijon mustard

Pinch of salt

¾ cup (200ml) oil (preferably something neutral, such as groundnut or sunflower oil)

2 tbsp beer

1 tbsp citrus juice or vinegar

Put the egg yolks, mustard, and salt in a bowl and whisk together. Very gradually add the oil, stirring constantly and vigorously so that it emulsifies. Continue to add all—or most of—the oil. When the oil is safely mixed in, you can add the beer, a few drops at a time, continuing to whisk. Finish with your choice of flavorings and the citrus juice or vinegar.

IMPERIAL STOUT AND CHILI MAYO

Follow the basic beer mayonnaise recipe, but use 2 tablespoons of Imperial Stout. Then, add either hot sauce or some dried chili flakes. Finish with lemon juice. This is made for a burger.

IPA AÏOLI

Follow the basic mayonnaise beer recipe, but then transform it into aïoli by including garlic. I like the softer, sweeter flavor of roasted garlic. To roast garlic, just put whole garlic cloves in some aluminum foil and roast for 15 minutes at 350°F/180°C/Gas 4. Mash the garlic into a paste and add to the mayonnaise with the IPA at the end, using grapefruit or orange juice as the citrus. This is really great with seafood or mixed into a potato salad, or just with a big plate of fries and a glass of IPA.

Mayo-making tip: *If your mayo splits... freak out, swear, etc., and then transfer everything you have into a clean bowl and whisk like mad until it comes back together. Either that or get some beer in there a little earlier, but only a drop or two.*

BLACK IPA **KETCHUP**

THIS MIXES ROASTED TOMATOES WITH THE ROASTY BITTERNESS OF BLACK IPA, WHICH ADDS A DISTINCTIVE AND DELICIOUS DEPTH.

1 large red onion, finely sliced

1¼lb (600g) tomatoes (I use a mix of cherry and plum tomatoes), quartered

3 whole garlic cloves

1 thyme sprig

1 level tsp each of ground cinnamon, fennel seeds, cloves, and onion powder

Olive oil, for roasting

14oz (400g) can plum tomatoes

A handful of basil leaves, torn

⅓ cup (60g) brown sugar

⅓ cup (100ml) malt vinegar

1 tsp Marmite or four anchovies

¾ cup (200ml) Black IPA)

Salt and freshly ground black pepper

MAKES FOUR 1LB (450G) JARS

1 Preheat the oven to 325°F/160°C/Gas 3.

2 Place the onion and tomatoes in a large roasting tin and add the garlic cloves, thyme, all the spices, and plenty of salt and pepper, and then drizzle with olive oil.

3 Cover the tray with aluminum foil and slow-roast for 30 minutes, and then uncover and cook for a further 30 minutes.

4 Remove the thyme before pouring everything into a large saucepan on the stove-top. Add the canned tomatoes, basil, sugar, vinegar, Marmite (or anchovies), and half of the beer. Season to taste. Simmer for 20 minutes.

5 Allow to cool slightly and then add the remainder of the beer. Transfer to a food-blender and whizz until thick and smooth.

6 Pour into sterilized jars. (To sterilize jars: clean the jars and lids in hot, soapy water and place upside-down in an oven at 250°F/120°C/Gas ½ to dry for 30 minutes.)

BAMBERG **BBQ SAUCE**

WHAT IF I MADE A BBQ SAUCE USING SMOKED BEER? THAT WAS THE QUESTION I HAD TO ANSWER... THE BEST BEER FLAVOR COMES IF YOU ADD HALF THE BEER TOWARD THE END OF COOKING AND THE OTHER HALF WHILE YOU'RE BLENDING THE SAUCE—THAT PRESERVES THE DELICATE SMOKY AROMA THAT WORKS SO WELL WITH BARBECUED MEAT.

1–2 tbsp olive oil

1 large onion

5 garlic cloves, crushed

½ chili pepper (optional), deseeded

1 tsp each fennel seeds, fresh thyme, paprika, mustard powder, and ground coriander

¼ cup (50g) brown sugar

⅓ cup (100ml) apple juice

¼ cup (50ml) soy sauce

2 tbsp Worcestershire sauce

2 tbsp malt vinegar

⅔ cup (150ml) ketchup (beer ketchup is good!)

1 tsp Marmite

1 cup (250ml) Rauchbier

Salt and freshly ground black pepper

MAKES FOUR 1LB (450G) JARS

1 Soften the onion in the olive oil in a saucepan. Add the garlic, chili pepper, herbs and spices, and sugar.

2 Add all the liquid ingredients, including the ketchup and marmite, but not the beer. Allow to simmer for 10 minutes and then add half the beer and simmer for a further 5 minutes. Remove from the heat and allow to cool.

3 Pour into a food-blender and add the remainder of the beer. Blitz for a few minutes until the sauce is thick. Check the seasoning.

4 This makes a great condiment on the side of the plate or you can use it to cook ribs.

DESSERTS

SWEET, BISCUITY PALE MALT IS GREAT TO NIBBLE ON AS A BAR SNACK. BUT THIS GOT ME THINKING: WHAT ELSE COULD I DO WITH MALT? THEN IT HIT ME: WHAT IF I RECREATED THE BREWING PROCESS, BUT MIXED THE MALT WITH MILK AND CREAM INSTEAD OF WATER? WHAT I ENDED UP WITH WAS A RICH, TEXTURED, MALTY CREAM THAT HAD A CARAMEL DEPTH—IT WAS EVEN BETTER THAN I IMAGINED IT WOULD BE.

IF YOU DON'T KNOW WHERE TO GET MALT, THEN TRY A HOMEBREW STORE (BUT DON'T GET MALT EXTRACT—IT WILL WORK, BUT THIS IS TASTIER) OR VISIT A LOCAL BREWERY. EVEN THE TIGHTEST BREWER IN THE WORLD CAN SPARE 5½OZ (150G) OF GRAIN.

3¾ cup (900ml) heavy (double) cream

1 cup (250ml) whole milk

1 vanilla bean (pod), cut in half and seeds removed

5½oz (150g) pale malt, crushed

8 egg yolks

¼ cup (50g) superfine (caster) sugar

6 tsp Demerara sugar, to decorate

MAKES 6

1 Heat the heavy (double) cream and milk to around 21°F (70°C)—a cooking thermometer helps with this, although it's not essential. Simply heat the cream and milk over a low to medium heat, and don't allow the liquid to simmer or bubble.

2 Add the vanilla bean (pod) and pale malt, and allow to simmer gently for around 20 minutes (or until you are happy with the malt flavor), stirring almost constantly to avoid clumps forming. Strain the cream into a clean saucepan and bring to a boil.

3 Preheat the oven to 300°F/150°C/Gas 2. Place six ramekins in a deep roasting tin. Pour cold water into the tin until it reaches about two-thirds of the way up the outside of the ramekins.

4 In a bowl, whisk together the egg yolks and superfine (caster) sugar. Continue to whisk while gradually pouring in the hot cream and milk. Pour the mixture into the ramekins. Bake the brewlées for 30–40 minutes—after 30 minutes, check them every 5 minutes until they are set on top but still wobble slightly. Chill in the refrigerator for at least 6 hours.

5 Before serving, top each ramekin with a sprinkling of Demerara sugar and then heat under a broiler (grill) to caramelize. You could also blast the ramekins with a kitchen blowtorch if you have one.

6 Have these with a Bourbon-Barrel-Aged Stout, a Kriek, or a Framboise.

RECIPE VARIATION:
You might also like to put some finely sliced banana on top of the set cream before adding the Demerara sugar and caramelizing—this works really well with the malt flavor.

cooking tip: You can use the spent grain from this recipe in a cake or cookie recipe, such as for the Pale Malt Cookies on page 201. If you decide to throw it away, be warned that, inside, it'll start to get stinky very quickly on a hot day!

RHUBARB AND RASPBERRY **FRAMBOISE FOOL**

A SUPER SUMMER DESSERT,
THIS MIXES THE TARTNESS OF
RHUBARB WITH THE SWEET AND
SOURNESS OF RASPBERRY BEER.

14oz (400g) rhubarb, cut into
thumb-sized pieces

4 tbsp vanilla sugar (if you are using
ordinary sugar, just add 1 tsp vanilla
extract/essence)

6 tbsp raspberry beer

7oz (200g) raspberries

1¼ cups (300ml) whipping cream

SERVES 4-6

1 Put the rhubarb in a large
saucepan along with the sugar
and beer. Cook until the fruit is
soft but still holds its shape.

2 Once the rhubarb is nearly
cooked, add the raspberries to
the pan and cook for a further
minute. Drain off the liquid—
drink it, if you like, as it tastes
good! Allow the fruit to cool.

3 Whip the cream until it
thickens and then fold into
the fruit.

4 You can serve this fruit fool
on its own or perhaps with a
shortbread biscuit or pale malt
cookie (see page 201 for the
recipe) on the side. This is
really amazing with a glass
of raspberry beer—I like to
use Liefman's.

BEER JELLY

THESE RECIPES ARE INSPIRED BY EATING JELLY AND ICE CREAM AS A
KID, AS WELL AS BY AN ADULT DESIRE TO GIVE THEM A PLAYFUL UPDATE
BY INCLUDING BEER, PLUS I LIKE TO SERVE THE JELLY AND ICE CREAM
IN SMALL GLASSES SO THAT THEY LOOK LIKE TINY PINTS OF BEER.
THERE ARE A LOT OF POSSIBLE VARIATIONS WITH THESE RECIPES,
WHETHER YOU HAVE THEM TOGETHER OR APART, SO I'LL GIVE YOU THE
BASIC RECIPES AND THEN SHOW YOU HOW TO VEER IN THE DIRECTION
YOU WANT TO TAKE THEM. IF YOU PUT THE JELLY AND ICE CREAM
TOGETHER, THEN CHOOSE COMPLEMENTARY FLAVORS.

¾ cup (200ml) beer (see
below for suggestions)

4 gelatine sheets (leaves)
or ½oz (11g) sachet
powdered gelatine

¾ cup (200ml) water

½ cup (100g) superfine
(caster) sugar

1 Pour your choice of beer into a bowl and whisk
to dull the carbonation. Add the gelatine to the
beer and leave until it softens or dissolves.

2 Meanwhile, heat the water and sugar in a
saucepan to create a sugar syrup. Boil for a couple
of minutes and then remove from the heat. Mix in
the beer and gelatine mixture.

3 Allow the jelly liquid to cool a little before
pouring it into small serving glasses. Leave to set
overnight or for at least 8 hours.

NOW, CHOOSE YOUR JELLY FLAVOR:

IPA JELLY

Use ¾ cup (200ml) of orange or tropical
fruit juice instead of water. Choose a
fruity IPA without a huge amount of
bitterness.

FRUIT BEER JELLY

Use 1¼ cups (300ml) of Fruit Beer (such
as raspberry, cherry, or whatever else
you feel like) and ⅓ cup (100ml) of water
or an appropriate fruit juice. Please note
that if you use fruit juice, you won't
need to add any sugar. If you wish, you
can also add some whole fruits, such
as raspberries or blueberries,
to the glasses.

STOUT JELLY

Use ⅔ cup (150ml) of water, ¼ cup (50ml)
of strong black coffee (you could also
add some cocoa), and ¾ cup (200ml) of
rich Stout (try to avoid anything too
acidic and dry). Depending on your taste,
you may wish to increase the quantity
of sugar a little.

CIDER JELLY

Use apple juice instead of water,
sweet cider instead of beer, and use
only ¼ cup (50g) sugar.

BEER ICE CREAM

AS WITH THE JELLY, I'VE STARTED WITH A BASIC ICE-CREAM RECIPE, WHICH CAN BE EASILY ADJUSTED WITH WHATEVER BEER YOU WANT TO USE. IT'S BEST TO AVOID BITTER BEERS, BUT, IF YOU REALLY WANT TO TRY THEM, JUST INCREASE THE AMOUNT OF SUGAR TO 1 CUP (200G). THIS IS BEST MADE IN AN ICE-CREAM MACHINE.

⅔ cup (150ml) beer (see below for suggestions)

1¾ cup (450ml) heavy (double) cream

1 vanilla bean (pod) (optional)

⅔ cup (150g) granulated sugar

4 egg yolks

1 Open the beer and whisk it in a mixing bowl to flatten out the carbonation.

2 Heat the cream (and vanilla, if you're using it) in a saucepan and mix in the beer. Warm to a simmer.

3 In another bowl, whisk together the sugar and egg yolks. Take the warm cream and beer mixture (removing the vanilla pod first), and gradually pour it into the egg and sugar mix, whisking constantly.

4 Pour the ice-cream mixture into a clean saucepan and heat, stirring constantly with a wooden spoon, until it thickens—this takes a few minutes (if you start to get scrambled eggs, then remove the pan from the heat and whisk like crazy). Once the mixture has thickened, remove from the heat and chill in the refrigerator for a few hours before churning in an ice-cream machine.

NOW, CHOOSE YOUR ICE-CREAM FLAVOR:

The type of beer you use will obviously affect the final flavor. I like rich, strong, and sweet beers, such as Imperial Stout, Scotch Ale, Doppelbock, Oatmeal Stout, and Weizenbock. Using these beers ensures that the beer flavor comes through. If you want more than just a simple beer ice cream, then here are some more delicious ideas:

DOPPELBOCK AND BANANA

Mash or blend 2 very ripe bananas and fold into an ice-cream mix made with Weizenbock or Doppelbock (or even Imperial Stout). Add a cinnamon stick to the custard mix.

CHOCOLATE STOUT

Add 3½oz (100g) of good-quality semi-sweet (dark) chocolate to the cream. Use a rich Stout.

IMPERIAL BOURBON BARREL-AGED STOUT AND SOUR CHERRY

Like rum and raisin but better. Use the Stout in the ice-cream mix. Then soak dried sour cherries in enough Imperial Bourbon Barrel-Aged Stout to cover (do this for a couple of hours as you wait for the cream mix to cool). When you churn the ice-cream machine, simply add the cherries (but not the beer that they have been soaked in).

STRAWBERRY BEER

Use strawberry beer in the custard mix—the sweet ones, such as Fruli, are the best. Blend 14oz (400g) of fresh, ripe strawberries with ¼ cup (50g) of vanilla sugar and 1 tablespoon of fresh lemon juice. Strain. Add the fruit mix to the ice-cream machine while you churn.

IMPERIAL STOUT
ICE CREAM FLOAT

RASPBERRY BEER
SORBET

I like to keep things simple and this one nails it. Take a strong, sweet Stout (the strongest and sweetest you can find), and either pour it over some vanilla ice cream or pour into a glass and then top with a scoop of ice cream.

You can also make an ice-cream sauce with the Stout. Make a thick sugar syrup (using ¼ cup/50g of granulated sugar and ¼ cup/50ml of water) and then allow to boil and reduce a little. Add the beer—either a Stout or Fruit Beer—and remove from the heat.

¾ cup (200ml) water
⅓ cup (75g) superfine (caster) or vanilla sugar
18oz (500g) raspberries

¾ cup (200ml) raspberry beer
Juice of half a lemon

SERVES 4

1 Put the water and sugar in a saucepan and heat, allowing the liquid to boil for a minute or two and turn into a syrup.

2 Blitz the raspberries together with the beer in a food-blender and then strain through a sieve to remove the pips.

3 Mix the syrup with the fruit, beer, and lemon juice, and either churn in an ice-cream machine or place in a container in the freezer right away. Stir the sorbet every hour or so to break up the ice crystals—this will result in a better texture.

QUADRAPPLES
(OR APPLES BAKED IN QUAD)

This is apple poached in Belgian Quadrupel and spiked with the same spices that the beer evokes—cinnamon, clove, pepper, and aniseed. You can serve this hot or let the apples cool and serve them with some blue cheese and more of the Quad (it's worth making extra just so that you can do this). Alternatively, you could also use a strong cider (and drink the "mulled" poaching liquid afterward).

⅔ cup (150ml) water

¾ cup (200ml) fresh apple juice (not from concentrate)

3½oz (100g) superfine (caster) sugar

1 cinnamon stick

3 cloves

1 star anise

6 pink or black peppercorns

6 coriander seeds (this is optional, but don't add ground coriander instead)

1 vanilla bean (pod)

Zest of 1 orange

2 tbsp clear honey

4 crisp eating apples (Pink Lady work well), peeled, cored, and quartered

1 bottle of Belgian-style Quadrupel or Dubbel

SERVES 4

1 Bring the water, apple juice, and sugar to a boil in a saucepan to dissolve the sugar, then turn down the heat and allow to simmer gently.

2 Add the spices, vanilla bean (pod), orange zest, and honey to the pan, followed by the quartered apples, and, finally, the beer.

3 Put the lid on the pan and cook for 10–20 minutes or until the apples are soft, but not falling apart. You can check the apples by piercing them with the point of a knife—note that different apple varieties will cook at different rates.

4 Don't be tempted to reduce the sauce—as you would with pears poached in wine, for example—because it will end up bitter. Instead, just serve with a little sauce poured over the apples and lots of vanilla ice cream.

5 If you want to serve the apples cold, then set them aside in a bowl or plastic container with some extra sauce. Keep them cool until needed, but you absolutely must eat them with blue cheese.

BEER ETON MESS

THIS DESSERT OF CRUSHED MERINGUE, WHIPPED CREAM, AND STRAWBERRIES GETS A "BEER SPIN" WITH THE ADDITION OF IMPERIAL STOUT TO THE MERINGUE MIX AND THE CREAM. THE RECIPE IS DELIBERATELY GENERAL AND CAN BE TWEAKED BY USING DIFFERENT BEERS AND FRUIT, ALTHOUGH THE VOLUMES SHOULD REMAIN THE SAME. FOR EXAMPLE, A CHERRY BEER WITH CHERRIES IS EXCELLENT; IMPERIAL STOUT WITH BANANA IN THE CREAM IS SUPERB; AND BELGIAN QUADRUPEL (WITH A PINCH OF GROUND CINNAMON IN THE MERINGUE) WITH DRIED FIGS IS VERY NICE, TOO (I'D ALSO ADD MASCARPONE TO THE CREAM FOR THIS ONE).

IF YOU ARE MAKING SOME BEER ICE CREAM (SEE PAGE 195), FOR WHICH YOU NEED JUST THE EGG YOLKS, THIS IS A GOOD WAY TO USE UP THE WHITES (OR VICE-VERSA, OF COURSE). THIS MAKES ENOUGH FOR FOUR PEOPLE, PROBABLY WITH SOME LEFTOVER MERINGUE.

FOR THE MERINGUE

3 egg whites

5½oz (150g) superfine (caster) sugar

Pinch of salt

3 tbsp beer

FOR THE BEER CREAM

2 cups (500ml) heavy (double) cream

1 tbsp confectioners' (icing) sugar

A few drops of vanilla extract (essence)

3 tbsp (45ml) beer

3½–5½oz (100–150g) fruit

SERVES 4

1 Preheat the oven to 250°F/120°C/Gas ½.

2 Whisk the egg whites, sugar, and salt until the mixture forms stiff peaks. Add the beer at the last minute, stirring it in gently.

3 Spread the meringue out in large dollops on a baking sheet then place on a baking tray, and cook for around 75 minutes. Once the meringue has cooked, remove from the oven and allow to cool completely.

4 To make the beer cream, whisk together the cream, sugar, and vanilla extract (essence), adding the beer when the mixture is almost ready—you want the cream to be thick. Fold in the fruit.

5 To serve, break the meringue into the cream and mix together. This Eton Mess is excellent served with whatever beer you used to cook with or just go for an Imperial Stout.

BEER DOUGHNUTS

DOUGHNUTS MADE WITH BEER ARE THEN ICED WITH A BEER GLAZE.
I USE A WHEAT ALE WITH LOTS OF FRUITINESS AND LOW BITTERNESS—
IT WORKS VERY WELL AND I RECOMMEND YOU USE STONE & WOOD
PACIFIC ALE OR BOULEVARD 80 ACRE. A FRUITY PALE ALE, BELGIAN
QUADRUPEL, OR IMPERIAL STOUT ARE ALL GOOD ALTERNATIVES. YOU
CAN LET THEM COOL AND SMOTHER THEM IN A BEER GLAZE OR,
ALTERNATIVELY, YOU CAN DUST THEM IN SUGAR AND EAT THEM WARM.

7oz (200g) bread (strong white) flour, plus extra for dusting

2 tbsp (25g) superfine (caster) sugar

1 x ¼oz (7g) sachet fast-action dried yeast

¼ cup (50ml) milk

2 tbsp (25g) butter, softened

1 tsp salt

5 tbsp (75ml) beer

1 egg, beaten

About 8 cups (2 liters) sunflower or vegetable oil

FOR THE BEER GLAZE:

4 tbsp (28g) confectioners' (icing) sugar

2 tbsp (30ml) beer

MAKES 6–8

1 Combine the flour, sugar, and yeast in a mixing bowl.

2 Warm the milk by letting it simmer in a saucepan and then remove from the heat. Add the butter, salt, and beer into the milk.

3 Pour the combined liquid ingredients into the flour and sugar, and then add the egg. Mix together until you have a thick dough.

4 Tip out the dough onto a clean working surface lightly dusted with flour. Knead the dough until it is smooth and elastic, which should take around 10 minutes.

5 Place the dough in a greased bowl, cover with a dish towel, and leave in a warm place for an hour or so—it should double in size.

6 Knead the dough again, knocking it back a few times, and then divide into 6–8 doughnuts. Place the doughnuts on a greased baking tray, cover with a dish towel, and leave to rise for another hour.

7 Now it's time to bring out the deep fat fryer. (You can also use a large pan, but try to use a thermometer as well to help you reach the correct temperature.)

8 Pour the oil into the fryer or pan—remembering always to leave some space free at the top of the pan—and heat to 325°F/160°C/Gas 3.

9 Carefully lower the doughnuts into the oil in batches and cook for 3–4 minutes on each side, or until golden. Remove from the fryer and place on a wire rack to cool.

10 Once the doughnuts have cooled, you can add the glaze. Simply mix together the confectioners' (icing) sugar and beer, and dip in the doughnuts. Leave to harden. (If you want just to coat the doughnuts in the sugar and beer, transfer them straight from the fryer to the sugar, and then allow to cool—I would do this if you want to eat the doughnuts fresh.)

BREAKFAST FLAPJACKS

I'VE ALWAYS WANTED SOMEONE TO BREW A COFFEE OATMEAL STOUT WITH MAPLE SYRUP AND SOME BACON-LIKE SMOKED MALT. IN MY HEAD, IT'S THE BREAKFAST BEER OF MY DREAMS, ESPECIALLY IF SOME OF IT ENDED UP IN BOURBON BARRELS WITH BLUEBERRIES... I'VE STILL NEVER DRUNK THAT BEER, SO I DECIDED TO TURN THE IDEA INTO FLAPJACKS.

10½oz (300g) rolled oats

⅓ cup (100ml) Stout

1¾ sticks (200g) butter, plus extra for greasing

2 rashers smoked bacon or pancetta (optional but great!)

¼ cup (50g) brown sugar

2 tbsp maple syrup

2 tbsp golden syrup

Pinch of dried cinnamon

1 tsp of salt

4½oz (125g) fresh blueberries

MAKES 12 SQUARES

1 Take 3½oz (100g) of the oats and put them in a bowl. Pour over the Stout and mix together. Cover with plastic wrap (clingfilm) and set aside for 30 minutes. Preheat the oven to 350°F/180°C/Gas 4.

2 Melt the butter in a large saucepan on the stove-top and add the bacon to infuse the butter with its smoky flavor. Cook slowly for a couple of minutes, being careful not to let the butter bubble too much.

3 Remove the bacon—just eat it!—and add the sugar, syrups, cinnamon, and salt to the butter, stirring everything together.

4 Add the remaining 7oz (200g) of oats to the pan, plus the 3½oz (100g) that have been soaking in the Stout.

5 Mix in the blueberries and then pour the mixture into a greased baking tin. Cook for 25 minutes. Remove from the oven and allow to cool slightly before cutting into squares.

PALE MALT COOKIES

THESE ARE COOKIES MADE WITH CRUSHED PALE MALT. THE RECIPE MAKES 10 FAT COOKIES, CRISP ON THE OUTSIDE AND CHEWY IN THE MIDDLE. ASK YOUR LOCAL BREWER FOR THE MALT, THEY SHOULD BE HAPPY TO GIVE YOU SUCH A SMALL AMOUNT.

1¼ sticks (150g) unsalted butter, plus extra for greasing

⅓ cup (75g) superfine (caster) sugar

Scant ½ cup (85g) soft brown sugar

1 egg

2 drops of vanilla extract (essence)

1⅔ cups (200g) all-purpose (plain) flour

Large pinch of salt

½ tsp baking soda (bicarbonate of soda)

3oz (75g) lightly crushed pale malt

¼ cup (25g) rolled oats

MAKES 10

1 Preheat the oven to 325°F/160°C/Gas 3 and grease a baking tray.

2 Cream the butter and sugar together in a food-mixer. Add the egg and mix together. Add the vanilla extract (essence) and then mix in all the remaining ingredients. If the mixture becomes too sticky, then add a few drops of water or beer (Oatmeal Stout rocks in this).

3 Form the dough into individual cookies, sprinkle them with some more malt or oats on top if you have any left, and bake for about 15 minutes.

CITRUS UPSIDE-DOWN **IPA CAKES**

This is inspired by one of my favorite treats: pineapple upside-down cake. It involves lining a large cake tin with golden syrup and pineapple chunks, and then topping with a classic sponge. My version takes that old recipe and shakes it about, adding one of my favorite styles of beer and different citrus fruits. I also add orange peel to the cake mix to give more citrus flavor. This is great served hot or cold.

6 tbsp golden syrup or maple syrup

1 small can mandarin segments in fruit juice

1 small can grapefruit segments in fruit juice

5 tbsp (75ml) IPA

FOR THE SPONGE TOPPING:

4oz (125g) softened butter

4oz (125g) superfine (caster) sugar

2 extra large (large) eggs

4oz (125g) self-rising (self-raising) flour

1 tsp baking powder

Grated peel of 1 large orange

MAKES 10-12 SMALL CAKES
(or 1 large one)

1 Preheat the oven to 375°F/190°C/Gas 5. Grease a muffin tray and put ½ teaspoon of corn (golden) syrup in each hole. Save the remainder of the syrup. If you're baking a whole cake, then grease and line a 7-inch (8-cm) diameter cake tin with some waxed paper, then add the syrup.

2 Drain the cans of pineapple, mandarin, and grapefruit, reserving about 5 tablespoons (75ml) of the fruit juices. Boil the juices in a saucepan until they reduce by half.

3 Once the fruit juices have reduced, add the remainder of the syrup and then the beer. Allow the liquid to simmer for 1 minute and turn off the heat.

4 Add the canned fruit to the pan and leave to infuse for 15–20 minutes.

5 To make the sponge topping, cream together the butter and sugar. Add the eggs one at a time, beating them in thoroughly. Sift the flour and baking powder into the mixture. Add the orange peel and mix in well, then add 3 tablespoons (45ml) of the liquid infusing the fruit.

6 Place some pieces of fruit at the bottom of each muffin hole. Top with the sponge mixture and bake in the oven for 20 minutes. (A whole cake should be baked for around 45 minutes.)

7 The best beer to drink with this cake is a Black IPA or Black Ale that's loaded with orangey citrusy hops—the combination is like the best chocolate orange you've ever tasted.

CRUSHED MALT AND
FRUIT BEER CHEESECAKE

USE YOUR FAVORITE FRUIT BEER, BUT MAKE SURE IT'S A SWEET ONE—YOU
DON'T WANT ANY SOURNESS IN THIS CHEESECAKE. I USE SAMUEL SMITH
BEERS, WHICH ARE AVAILABLE IN CHERRY, RASPBERRY, STRAWBERRY, AND
APRICOT; THEY ALL WORK WELL HERE. THE BASE OF THE CHEESECAKE USES
SOME CRUSHED PALE MALT OR MUNICH MALT, WHICH ADDS A BISCUITY,
NUTTY, MALTY SWEETNESS AND EXTRA CRUNCH—TRY NOT TO SKIP THIS
PART (GET THE GRAIN FROM YOUR LOCAL BREWERY).

FOR THE CHEESECAKE BASE

1 stick/8 tbsp (125g) butter

9oz (250g) Graham crackers
(digestive biscuits)

2oz (55g) pale or Munich malt,
crushed

FOR THE CHEESECAKE TOPPING

1¼lb (600g)
mascarpone cheese

4 tbsp confectioners'
(icing) sugar

4–6 tbsp Fruit Beer

1 drop of vanilla extract
(essence) (almond extract
is nice if you're using
Cherry Beer)

**FOR THE FRUIT BEER
SAUCE** (optional)

10½oz (300g) fresh fruit
(whatever matches your beer)

2 tbsp vanilla sugar
(ordinary sugar is fine)

4 tbsp (60ml) Fruit Beer

MAKES 10

1 If you are making the Fruit Beer sauce, make
it in advance so that it's cool when you need it.
Simply cook the fruit with the sugar until soft.
Remove from the heat, add the beer, and mix
through. Blitz into a smooth sauce in a food-
blender, and strain to remove any pips.

2 To make the cheesecake base, melt the butter
in a saucepan over a low heat.

3 Crush the Graham crackers (digestive biscuits)
into a fine gravel. Grind the malt in a coffee
grinder or use a pestle and mortar—don't grind
too much or it'll turn into dusty flour.

4 Mix the crushed crackers (biscuits) and malt
into the butter and then pour into a large pie dish
(or smaller individual ones, if you prefer). Put in
the refrigerator for a few hours to set.

5 To make the cheesecake topping, mix all the
ingredients together in a bowl. Taste the mixture
in case you want to add a little more beer, but make
sure that this doesn't make the topping too thin.

6 Pour the topping mixture over the cheesecake
base and either serve straight away, preferably
with the Fruit Beer sauce, or return to the
refrigerator until you serve.

7 This cheesecake is great with a Fruit Beer on
the side, but even better with an Imperial Stout.
(If you make an apricot cheesecake, then try it
with a Tripel.)

BANANA BEERAMISÙ

THIS INCREDIBLE DESSERT IS A BEER-FILLED MASH-UP OF BANANA PUDDING, BANOFFEE PIE, AND TIRAMISÙ, WHICH BRINGS TOGETHER SOME OF THE BEST COMBINATIONS IN THE FOOD WORLD. USE A STOUT, COFFEE STOUT, OR BARREL-AGED STOUT, THE ONE WITH THE STRONGEST FLAVOR YOU CAN FIND AND PROBABLY AROUND 10.0% IN ALCOHOL CONTENT. AVOID A BEER THAT'S HIGH IN HOP BITTERNESS—BARLEY'S ROASTED BITTERNESS IS OKAY.

1 Whip the cream and sugar together until thick, and then mix in the mascarpone. Set to one side.

2 Pour the Stout and espresso into a bowl. Dip half the ladyfingers (sponge fingers), one at a time, into the beer/coffee mix, and then line the base of a deep, wide dish with the fingers—ideally, the dish should be able to hold a few layers of the dessert. Cover the base of the dish completely and don't let the sponge get soggy—a quick dip is fine.

3 Cover the fingers with a layer of banana rings, using all the banana you have, and then add a layer of cream. Add another layer of beer-dipped fingers, followed by a final layer of cream.

4 Dust the top with the cocoa powder and then grate the chocolate on top. Place in the refrigerator for 4–24 hours (it improves after time in the refrigerator).

5 Serve with a strong Stout, preferably the one that you cooked with.

1 cup (250ml) heavy (double) cream

¼ cup (50g) golden superfine (caster) sugar

18oz (500g) mascarpone

⅔ cup (150ml) Stout

1 shot of espresso, at room temperature

7oz (200g) ladyfingers (sponge fingers)

4 ripe bananas, sliced into rings

3 tbsp cocoa powder

1oz (25g) semi-sweet (dark) chocolate, minimum 70% cocoa solids

SERVES 6

BEER TRUFFLES

THESE ARE SO EASY AND CAN BE PERSONALIZED WITH ANY BEER YOU LIKE. THE MAIN THING TO KNOW IS THAT THE TYPE OF CHOCOLATE USED WILL AFFECT THE RECIPE: SEMI-SWEET (DARK) CHOCOLATE WORKS ON A ONE-TO-ONE BASIS WITH THE LIQUIDS: 7OZ (200G) OF CHOCOLATE AND ¾ CUP (200ML) OF LIQUID (A MIX OF CREAM AND BEER); MILK AND WHITE CHOCOLATE BOTH REQUIRE AT LEAST DOUBLE THE AMOUNT OF CHOCOLATE TO LIQUID TO ENSURE THAT THE TRUFFLES SET—SO YOU'LL NEED 7OZ (200G) OF CHOCOLATE TO ⅓ CUP (100ML) OF LIQUID.

DOUBLE IPA AND WHITE CHOCOLATE TRUFFLES

¼ cup (50ml) heavy (double) cream
¼ cup (50ml) Double IPA
1½ tbsp (20g) butter
1 tbsp blossom honey
7oz (200g) white chocolate
Desiccated coconut, for coating

MAKES 10-20 TRUFFLES
(depending on how big you roll them)

1 Gently warm the cream, beer, and butter in a saucepan, but don't allow the mixture to boil—this should take a minute or two only.

2 Remove from the heat and add the chocolate and honey to the pan, stirring with a wooden spoon until all the chocolate has melted. Pour the mixture into a bowl, allow to cool, and refrigerate for 4 hours until the mixture has set.

3 Take the set mixture and use a melon-baller or two spoons to shape it into truffle-sized balls.

4 Roll the balls in a coating your choice: coconut, cocoa powder, or roasted barley, are all good. (Please note that if you are using roasted barley, you'll need to blitz it to a powder first in a coffee grinder or use a pestle and mortar.)

5 Keep the truffles in the refrigerator until you want to eat them.

ACKNOWLEDGMENTS

I spent half of 2013 eating and drinking more than any normal person would, so first I'd like to thank my Nike Free trainers for keeping me in a decent physical state on a lot of long runs.

I used a lot of resources when researching this book and the following are those that I think every beer and food lover should own: Garrett Oliver's *The Brewmaster's Table*; Niki Segnit's *The Flavour Thesaurus*; Harold McGee's *Food and Cooking*; *The Oxford Companion to Beer*, edited by Garrett Oliver; Randy Mosher's *Tasting Beer*; François Chartier's *Taste Buds and Molecules*. And, thanks also to Adam Dulye and Rich Higgins who took the time to talk to me in San Francisco.

My mates got the tough jobs of eating and drinking a lot of stuff with me, plus trying out recipes and giving their matching suggestions. There was the night with 10 curries and 15 beers, and the one with 15 cheeses and 25 beers. Thanks to Matt Stokes, Mark Charlwood, Lee Bacon, Chris Perrin, Nathan Nolan, and Jonny Garrett.

Thanks to Pete Jorgensen for suggesting I write this book and making it happen. Big high-fives to Nicholas Frith for his amazing illustrations. Thanks to editor Caroline West for tidying up my words and Mark Latter for the design. And thanks to the team who cooked and took photos of the dishes—they definitely didn't look that good when I cooked them.

My Dad deserves a lot of thanks: he has been the one I've shared most of these beers with; he's the one who's had many dinners interrupted with one beer, then another, then another. I couldn't have done it without you being willing to share a beer. And thanks to my Mum as well: you had to do a lot of washing up when I cooked in your kitchen and had to eat a lot of recipes cooked with beer, even the ones which didn't work out right. Thanks to you both for always being there and supporting me.

The publishers would like to thank all the brewers who took the time to send us bottle and label images. We're sorry we couldn't fit all of them in, blame Mark for writing too much!

A